# DOWNFALL

How the Labor Party
ripped itself apart

AARON PATRICK

ABC
Books

The ABC 'Wave' device is a trademark of the Australian Broadcasting Corporation and is used under licence by HarperCollins*Publishers* Australia.

First published in Australia in 2013
by HarperCollins*Publishers* Australia Pty Limited
ABN 36 009 913 517
harpercollins.com.au

Copyright © Aaron Patrick 2013

The right of Aaron Patrick to be identified as the author of this work has been asserted by him in accordance with the *Copyright Amendment (Moral Rights) Act 2000*.

This work is copyright. Apart from any use as permitted under the *Copyright Act 1968*, no part may be reproduced, copied, scanned, stored in a retrieval system, recorded, or transmitted, in any form or by any means, without the prior written permission of the publisher.

**HarperCollins***Publishers*
Level 13, 201 Elizabeth Street, Sydney NSW 2000, Australia
31 View Road, Glenfield, Auckland 0627, New Zealand
A 53, Sector 57, Noida, UP, India
77–85 Fulham Palace Road, London W6 8JB, United Kingdom
2 Bloor Street East, 20th floor, Toronto, Ontario M4W 1A8, Canada
10 East 53rd Street, New York NY 10022, USA

National Library of Australia Cataloguing-in-Publication entry:

Patrick, Aaron.
 Downfall: how the Labor Party ripped itself apart / Aaron Patrick.
 978 0 7333 3175 6 (paperback)
 Includes bibliographical references and index.
 Australian Labor Party.
 Political leadership – Australia.
 Political entrepreneurship – Australia.
 Political planning – Australia.
 Political development.
 Australia – Politics and government – 2001–
324.294

Cover design: Design by Committee
Cover images: Heads: Julia Gillard by Andrew Meares/Fairfax Syndication; Kevin Rudd by Bay Ismoyo/AFP/Getty Images; Craig Thomson by Robert Cianflone/Getty Images; Eddie Obeid by Joseph Barrak/AFP/Getty Images; Bill Shorten by William West/AFP/Getty Images; all other images by bigstockphoto.com
Typeset in Bembo Std by Kirby Jones
Printed and bound in Australia by Griffin Press
The papers used by HarperCollins in the manufacture of this book are a natural, recyclable product made from wood grown in sustainable plantation forests. The fibre source and manufacturing processes meet recognised international environmental standards, and carry certification.

5 4 3 2 1    13 14 15 16

Formerly a business reporter for the *Wall Street Journal* in London, Aaron Patrick is now a senior editor with the *Australian Financial Review*. He is a former member of Young Labor.

*To my mother, Frances Maria O'Sullivan-Smith,
who loved the party and could see its faults.*

# Picture section credits

**Newspix**

p.1 (top) Rob Baird, (below) Bill McAuley; p.7 (top L) Brad Hunter, (top R) David Crosling; p.8 (top) Jeff Camden, (below) John Feder.

**Fairfax Syndication**

p.2 (L-R; top to bottom) Lisa Wiltse, Ken Irwin, Colleen Petch, Andrew Meares, Michael Clayton-Jones, Phil Hearne, Glen McCurtayne, Penny Bradfield; p.3 (below) Steven Siewert; p.4 (top) Peter Rae, (centre) Edwina Pickles, (bottom) Dean Sewell; p.5 (top) Kate Geraghty, (below) Louise Kennerley; p.6 (top) Jon Reid, (below) Mick Tsikas; p.7 (bottom) Andrew Meares.

# Contents

| | | |
|---|---|---|
| Prologue | | 1 |
| 1 | Meet the future – Bill Shorten and Julia Gillard – How the Labor Party really works – The battle for a trade union – A secret slush fund – Taking control of the AWU | 7 |
| 2 | Peddling influence in the NSW Labor Party – A lucrative 'training' mine – The Minister for Mining has lunch – Cheap cars and cheap land | 37 |
| 3 | Kevin 07 – Hard times at the Health Services Union – Craig Thomson and his credit card problem – The Minister for Defence loses his job | 93 |
| 4 | The plot to remove Kevin – In the corridors and in the newsrooms – Mining tax, what mining tax? | 121 |
| 5 | Julia Gillard's first election – Campaign leaks – Power outages in Victoria and NSW | 149 |
| 6 | Craig's little problem gets bigger – Kathy Jackson steps in – Bill Shorten, Minister for Industrial Relations | 171 |
| 7 | The return of the king – a Queensland campaign goes wrong – Blackout in the Sunshine State | 193 |
| 8 | Smears, scandals, sexual harassment and a Speaker called Slipper – Who controls the HSU? – Julia, files and union slush funds | 213 |
| 9 | The biggest show in town – ICAC – Eddie Obeid's amazing networks – Craig Thomson's challenge – Follow the leader – What went wrong and what Labor can do about it | 291 |
| Acknowledgements | | 315 |
| Author's note | | 317 |
| Endnotes | | 318 |
| Index | | 320 |

# Prologue

It was 10.02 a.m. on a warm summer's day in February. Clouds hung ominously over the Sydney skyline, threatening to drench the city with rain at any moment. In converted offices on the seventh floor of a beige thirty-one-storey office building in the centre of the city, Edward Moses Obeid, an Order of Australia medal pinned to the lapel of his navy blue suit, placed his right hand on a King James Bible. Overlooking him, on a high bench, sat David Ipp, head of the New South Wales Independent Commission Against Corruption. Opposite Ipp stood one of the veterans of the state's bar, Geoffrey Watson, a barrister who served as the commission's prosecutor and was formally known as counsel assisting the commission. To Obeid's left sat dozens of lawyers, including his own, former *Media Watch* presenter Stuart Littlemore. Behind them, a public gallery, which could seat forty-two people, was full. Some of the spectators had queued for two hours for the prized positions, waiting on canvas camp stools, fortified with newspapers, novels and cups of coffee. They were there for the biggest political melodrama in town, a story too elaborate – too improbable – for fiction.

In the confident voice of one of the most powerful politicians in New South Wales for two decades, a man who made and broke premiers, Obeid recited the oath to tell the truth. With barely a pause for Obeid to replace the Bible on the bench in front of him, Watson began his examination with a simple but loaded question. 'Mr Obeid, tell me, would you think it appropriate for a minister knowingly to create a mining tenement over his friend's property?' he asked.

'Could you repeat that?' Obeid replied.

'Would you think it appropriate for a minister knowingly to create a mining tenement over his friend's property?' Watson asked again.

'No,' Obeid replied.

'Why not?'

'Well, I don't know, I'm not aware of the details and my immediate answer is no.'

Watson tried again to get Obeid to explain what he thought was wrong about a minister helping out a mate. Obeid refused to be drawn. He, like every lawyer in the crowded room, understood the point.

The minister in Watson's hypothetical question existed in real life. It was Ian Macdonald, Obeid's protégé, who for five years had overseen the state's resources. Now Watson was telling the room that Obeid, his family and Macdonald had participated in one of the greatest abuses of political power in the state's history: a secret deal to make millions – perhaps as much as $200 million – through a ministerial-issued coal licence that covered land the Obeids owned.

Watson put a different version of the scenario to Obeid. 'If a minister created a mining tenement over a friend's property, would you think it appropriate for the friend to accept that?'

Obeid stonewalled. 'I'm not in a position to–to–to either accept or deny,' he stammered.

Watson tried another tack: should someone in Obeid's position disclose when he or she receives a favour from a minister who is also a friend? Again, Obeid dodged and weaved. Question after question Watson tried to pin him down. When Obeid sensed Watson was becoming frustrated and grinned, the lawyer lost his cool. 'Mr Obeid, don't smile,' Watson snapped. 'If you do not answer my questions, at the end of the day I'll be submitting to the commissioner that that was deliberate.'

Obeid didn't back down. 'Mr Watson,' he almost shouted, 'I will not be intimidated by you or anyone else.'

Ipp stepped in to calm the situation. Watson apologised and ploughed on. Twenty-six times he tried to draw an answer from Obeid that could be used against the former politician. Twenty-six times Obeid evaded him. Eventually, Watson got to his point. 'I'm going to submit that you – you, Mr Obeid – you engaged in a criminal conspiracy,' he said. 'You engaged in that with Ian Macdonald and with members of your family and the design was to effect a fraud on the people of New South Wales.'

'That's incorrect,' Obeid calmly replied.

Eddie Obeid isn't the only Labor Party figure accused of being a criminal. Ian Macdonald, the former New South Wales resources minister, Eric Roozendaal, the former New South Wales treasurer, Craig Thomson, a federal MP, and Michael Williamson, a former party president, have all been charged by police or accused of dishonest or illegal conduct in hearings at the Independent Commission Against Corruption (ICAC). Peter Slipper, who Labor appointed speaker of the House of Representatives, has been charged with fraud by the Australian Federal Police over abuse of his travel entitlements as an MP.

The fate of these men is likely to be decided by their fellow citizens sitting on juries. The fate of the party they represented or answered to, the Australian Labor Party, has and will be decided by all Australians who vote.

At the end of 2007 Labor held power federally and in every state and territory. It was one of the world's most successful centre-left political parties. Now, Prime Minister Julia Gillard's government is heading for a landslide defeat in the 14 September 2013 election at the hands of an electorate weary of scandal, infighting and the sheer bitterness of the political debate. In New South Wales in 2011 and in Queensland in 2012, previously the party's two strongest states, Coalition victories decimated Labor governments. Voters kicked out an overconfident Labor government in Victoria in 2010. Indigenous voters in the Northern Territory abandoned Labor and helped elect a Country Liberal Party government in 2012. The Australian Capital Territory, whose large public service population should reliably vote Labor, avoided falling to the Liberal Party in a 2012 election by the vote of a single Greens MP. A minority Labor government clings to power in Tasmania. West Australians re-elected a Coalition government in March 2013 and increased its majority. South Australians are likely to vote Labor out of government at their March 2014 election, polls show.

How could a party run by some of the most talented Australians of the day, governing over the greatest period of wealth generation in the nation's history, lose voters' trust? Many events, actions and personalities are responsible. Underlying them is a fundamental problem: ethics.

Labor has many competent, honest leaders. They were sidelined, or chose to remain silent, while the party's reputation was trashed by the behaviour of ministers, backbenchers, party apparatchiks and union officials who cared more about themselves than the people they were paid to serve.

The win-at-any-cost culture of Labor's factions allowed dubious characters like Obeid, Macdonald, Williamson and Thomson to remain in privileged positions far too long. Instead of working to reform the party from within, factional leaders were focused on grabbing power for themselves. Their disastrous decision to overthrow Prime Minister Kevin Rudd in 2010, an event described in detail in these pages, compounded the immense damage caused to the party by the allegations of corruption against Obeid and other Labor figures.

Labor's problems matter for all Australians. A strong and vibrant Labor Party is good for the nation. When Labor leads by example it lifts the quality of political debate, the conduct of government and contributes to a better society.

Effective Labor oppositions keep Coalition governments honest. Labor governments, often supported by the Liberal-Nationals Coalition, have been responsible for enlightened policies that have helped create a society more harmonious, just and wealthy than almost anywhere.

This book isn't a comprehensive history of modern Labor or the Rudd and Gillard governments. Rather, it focuses on the people and events that saw a once great progressive party go so wrong. It also takes the first close look at the politician who epitomises modern Labor, Bill Shorten, the minister for employment and workplace relations, financial services and superannuation.

Shorten, who is widely tipped to take over as federal Labor leader after the 2013 election, is at the centre of a clique of industrial relations lawyers and union officials who have become Australia's political elite. His early political experiences provide an insight into the inner workings of Labor and the factions that control the party apparatus. As this book will show, the factional system has been used to place the interests of a few over the interests of the many, with disastrous consequences.

As an effective public communicator, Shorten has already cleared the first hurdle towards becoming a potent political leader. If he fulfils his lifelong ambition to lead Labor and eventually become prime minister, he will have to decide if he is prepared to clean out the sleaze that has crippled his party or overlook it. The party's very future is at stake.

# 1

Meet the future – Bill Shorten and Julia Gillard – How the Labor Party really works – The battle for a trade union – A secret slush fund – Taking control of the AWU

## Class conscience

Bill Shorten's decision to help bring down Prime Minister Kevin Rudd wasn't an aberration. Shorten had spent his entire political career mastering the art of Labor politics: fighting party and union elections, striking alliances with rivals, discarding former allies, expertly managing the press and generally getting himself ahead.

His upbringing, education, career and family history encapsulated many of the contradictions of the modern Labor Party. He had a privileged schooling, yet his grandfather was an official in the Printing & Kindred Industries Union. He became a trade union leader and a champion of the disadvantaged, yet he sought the patronage of the very wealthy. He espoused politics as a noble cause and practised it like a street fighter. He was a leader of the Right faction and owed his power to an alliance with the Left.

Shorten's mother, Ann McGrath, was a descendent of Irish Catholic convicts deported to Australia for minor indiscretions. Her printer father was the PKIU's head shop steward at Melbourne's *Argus* and *Herald* newspapers. Ann won a scholarship to train as a high school teacher and later taught university-level history in Townsville. She then took the daring step of enrolling in a law degree at Monash University as a middle-aged mother. Achieving top marks in her year, she became an academic, an achievement that her son was immensely proud of. In 1965 she met William Robert Shorten on a cruise to Yokohama from Brisbane. He was the ship's second engineer. They fell in love and married. From Newcastle in England and the son and grandson of elected union officials, Bill senior left school at fifteen to become a marine fitter and turner. He retired from the sea in 1967 when Bill junior and his twin brother Robert were born, and was hired as a manager on Melbourne's dry docks. The workplace was a hotbed of union activity – the notorious Painters and Dockers Union was at its peak.

Bill and Ann sent their sons to Xavier College, where for generations Jesuit priests had educated Melbourne's Catholic elite in the importance of social justice. The all-male school's high-testosterone and athletic atmosphere wasn't a perfect fit for Bill junior, an overweight teenager who preferred military board games to sport. But his quick tongue and sharp mind made him one of the school's star debaters and his confidence grew. He soon learnt to deploy theatrics to help win arguments. Part way through one debate, Shorten, then fifteen, ripped up his notes and threw them on the floor. His opponent's argument was 'so hopeless' he could demolish it ad lib, he said.[1] Shorten's debating prowess became one of his strongest suits and he used it relentlessly and instinctively in political and social settings throughout his early adulthood. Even his closest friends ended up exhausted by the continual barrage of argument.

Shorten could hardly claim to be working class. Yet his parents' union backgrounds had leached into his identity. He saw himself as an opponent of privilege surrounded by the wealthy sons of Melbourne's establishment, who were represented, politically, by the Liberal Party. Labor and the union movement were for everyone else: the hard-working middle and working classes forced to bind together through unions to protect themselves from exploitation.

In 1984, Shorten scored among the top students at Xavier College in his year 12 exams. Rather than enrol at the more prestigious and 'establishment' University of Melbourne, he took arts and law degrees at Monash University, the hub of student political radicalism in the 1970s. He joined the Army Reserve and Young Labor. Not a great soldier, he quickly gave up on the army. The Labor Party became his life.

Shorten's parents divorced while he and Robert were still at school. Bill senior, who remarried, died in 2000. As Shorten rose through the Labor Party he would sometimes reference his father's waterfront roots to enhance his working-class credentials. Yet the two Bills weren't close and had little contact for the last seven years of Bill senior's life, according to someone who knew them both. Shorten has never publicly discussed the breakdown of the relationship, although a friend who once saw the pair together said there appeared to be a deep fissure between father and son. 'Bill seemed very uncomfortable with, and bristly towards, his father and stepmother,' said Christina Cridland, a Young Labor supporter of Shorten's. 'Afterwards, he was apologetic about his father and stepmother's working-class ways. He told me I was the only person from Young Labor who had ever met his father.'

The Australian Labor Party is Australia's oldest political party. The party contested elections as early as 1891, four years before Britain's first Labour Party. Chris Watson, who became Australia's third prime minister in 1904, is regarded as the world's first national leader from the labour movement. Labor has held power at a federal level for fifty of the 112 years since Federation and has reigned for long periods in all states.

The Labor Party works one way on paper and another in reality. The party's constitution establishes that the supreme decision-making body is its national conference, which is held every two years. Elected by members and trade unions affiliated with the party, delegates to the conference set policies and rules that are binding on all members, including the leader. If a diagram were used to show the party structure, power would flow from union members and individual members through party officials, committees, elected representatives and conferences down to the federal leader. At the bottom of the chart, the leader would appear as the recipient of authority granted to him or her by the party's internal democratic processes and he or she would be answerable to the party membership.

In reality, though, individual Labor members have about as much control over their leadership as ordinary members of the Chinese Community Party have in choosing the Politburo. A cabal of mostly former and current union officials, who use a system of factions and patronage to preserve their power, runs the Labor Party. The factions choose official Labor Party candidates and, ultimately, the party's parliamentary leaders.

The two main factions – the Left and the Right – operate as parties within a party. Only ALP members can join. The factions have their own membership fees, websites, meetings, newsletters, internal elections, sub-factions and Christmas parties. Of the 102 current federal Labor MPs, only two don't belong to a faction: Peter Garrett, the minister for school education, early childhood and youth, and Andrew Leigh, a lower house MP from Canberra.

The Left's formal name is the Socialist Left, which reflects its ideological origins as an opponent of capitalism, American global hegemony and state funding of private schools. In more recent political debates the faction, known in party shorthand as 'the SL', has opposed the state of Israel and pushed for more sympathetic treatment of refugees. The Right faction has different names in different states: in New South Wales it's called Centre Unity; in Victoria, Labor Unity. It believes in free enterprise, a limited role for the state, and the military alliance with the United States (one fad among some of the faction's leaders in the 1990s was an interest in the American Civil War). The faction is more socially conservative than the Left, a reflection of the influence of the Catholic Church.

To get ahead in the ALP you must join a faction. Almost every internal vote above branch level – whether for policies, seats or party positions – is a contest between the factions. To earn the support of the Right or the Left, party members spend years voting for their faction in internal elections. Loyal followers are rewarded with jobs and seats.

Within the factional system, unions occupy a position akin to corporate members. In return for large annual contributions, known as affiliation fees, they get a say in internal Labor Party elections based on their membership figures, regardless of whether the members are ALP supporters. Therefore, the bigger the membership unions declare, the more votes they get.

Most unions sign up. Often their members don't even realise that some of their membership dues are being funnelled to a political party. Affiliated unions almost always align themselves to a faction, sometimes on ideological grounds. The leadership of the Shop, Distributive and Allied Employees' Association, also known as the shop assistants' union, is closely aligned with the Catholic Church and opposes abortion and gay marriage. It is an important player in the Right faction.

In some states unions are required to register membership numbers with the government. In 1990 there was a big disparity between many unions' official membership figures and the number used to determine representation in the Labor Party. The gap suggested some unions understated their memberships to reduce their financial contributions to the party, a decision that saved money, while others inflated numbers to increase their influence, at a higher financial cost. The system places mass unions like the shop assistants' union, which has about 300,000 members, and the Australian Workers' Union, with roughly 100,000 members, at the centre of party power. Through their influence over the party's finances and internal votes, the unions can get their candidates elected to parliament. These union-sponsored MPs, who are often although not always former union employees or officials, invariably remain loyal to their union. Through their proxies in parliament, unions can exercise power via Labor governments.

In the 1990s under Prime Minister Bob Hawke, the Right controlled federal Labor. Many of the influential figures of the

Hawke government, including Hawke himself, defence minister Robert Ray and foreign minister Gareth Evans, came from the Right. Embarrassingly for the faction, the ALP at a state level was in the grip of the Left. Peter Batchelor, a Socialist Left leader who later became the Victorian minister for energy and resources, ran his state's party organisation. The Right was not in a position to change the party rules, influence how it was run or set policy. Most importantly, the Left had more control over who was selected for seats in parliament and who became leader. When John Cain, a member of the Independents faction, resigned as premier in 1990, the Left replaced him with one of its own, Joan Kirner.

At university Shorten joined the Right and helped set up a Young Labor group called Network. He knew that while the Left controlled the Victorian Labor Party his political prospects would be limited. Network had one primary objective: to crush the Left. The corollary plan, which Shorten didn't spell out because he didn't really need to, was to launch his political career.

As leader of Young Labor, Shorten was too young to challenge the Left's dominance at the state level. But he and a close friend, Michael Borowick, controlled the youth wing. A former electrician from a middle-class Jewish family, Borowick was Shorten's mentor. His blue-collar background and maturity tempered his ally's sometimes reckless energy. The Right encouraged Shorten and Borowick's enthusiastic band of Labor activists. Shorten was hired as an adviser to the Victorian minister for labour, Neil Pope, a member of the faction. The ministerial suites at Nauru House, in Melbourne's Collins Street, became Network's well-equipped headquarters. Network used the offices – complete with computers, phones, fax machines, photocopiers and a beautiful view of the

CBD – so much that a separate entrance was installed to save the Young Labor members having to walk through the minister's foyer.

Borowick, who was on the electorate staff of foreign minister Gareth Evans, worked in grand offices reserved for federal ministers in Treasury Place, not far from the Victorian parliament. They functioned as Network's second headquarters.

For a treat, Borowick would sometimes take members into Bob Hawke's office and let them sit in his chair, where they would gaze in awe at the prime ministerial speed dial. Evans once described the pack of activists who camped in his office at night as Borowick's and Shorten's 'storm troopers'.

Bill Shorten was immensely driven, juggling a part-time job advising Pope on youth issues with his law degree studies and his leadership of Network, which had more than 100 members eligible to vote in Labor elections. The only way he could retain control of Young Labor was by convincing people to join party branches and vote for the faction in internal elections. Shorten urged his followers to do whatever it took to win, pressuring everyone to recruit members and once trying to sign up a sales clerk at a supermarket checkout himself. Sometimes recruits were friends or family members whose only involvement in politics was voting when asked. Others became deeply committed and went on to political careers, including Martin Pakula, who became Victorian minister for transport, and Tim Holding, who became the Victorian minister for police.

As Shorten's political influence grew, tensions emerged with other members of the faction. The Right's day-to-day organiser, Stephen Conroy, was a few years older than Shorten and worked for Senator Robert Ray, who controlled the Right in Victoria. Conroy was quick to practise his oily charm on Network members, but Shorten and Borowick saw him as a rival.

At Melbourne University, the Young Labor Right faction was split into two camps. Shorten controlled one. David Feeney and Andrew Landeryou – the son of a famed Victorian union leader, Bill Landeryou – led the other. In 1990, a few Network members from the university tried to oust the left-wing secretary of the local Labor Party branch, a tough young lawyer named Julia Gillard. She easily saw off the challenge.

At a national level, the Left, mainly due to the faction's dominance in NSW, controlled Young Labor. In 1990, Shorten was a delegate to the National Young Labor conference in Brisbane, which was to appoint a delegate to the national conference, the party's top rule-making body. Wresting a spot from the Left in this forum would be a coup.

Manipulation of procedure can be a powerful tool in politics, a lesson Shorten learnt at the conference. The Left had the most delegates. Shorten and the other leaders of the Right decided to hold their own conference, in the same room at the same time, and their own election. With both sides refusing to recognise the other, two conferences were held, simultaneously. The Left's chairman asked for someone to speak to one of the policy proposals up for a vote. Left delegates raised their hands and began speaking. Sitting a few metres away, the Right did the same thing. The Left had a volume advantage: they had taken control of the speaker system. It was chaos.

Thanks to the duelling meetings, it was unclear who controlled Young Labor at the end of the conference. The party's national executive – on which the prime minister sat – had to sort it out.

Instead of ruling who were legitimate delegates and who were not, the national executive split the office-holding positions – the spoils of the conference – equally between the Left and Right factions. That was a great result for the Right, which didn't otherwise have the numbers to get elected. 'They [the national executive] were completely pragmatic about it,' Shorten said.

## Getting theatrical

There was a buzz about the young Bill Shorten. His success in Young Labor, charming self-confidence, political maturity and rampant ambition marked him. At the age of 21 he was already being talked about as a future member of federal parliament. Perhaps even a senior minister. He had seemed to walk onto campus a fully formed political operative. He was charming, scheming, worldly. He made wry comments about international affairs. Women liked him. He was adept at befriending younger followers who would come to idolise him. He would never accept losing an argument, and didn't try very hard to hide his belief in his own talent. He never stopped working or thinking about how to climb the political ladder.

In 1990 Shorten, Michael Borowick and other Network leaders came up with an audacious plan to propel their influence into the senior party: capture a trade union from the Left. They chose the Victorian division of the Australian Theatrical & Amusements Employees' Association, a union that since 1910 had represented theatre workers and sports ground staff, many of them casual workers. The ATAEA wasn't a powerful force in the union movement. It had a few thousand members in Victoria. Most worked low-paid, simple jobs; they were gate attendants at greyhound races, car park supervisors at football matches and theatre ushers. Taking control of the union would give Shorten and his allies a small block of votes in Labor Party elections. More importantly, defeating the Left would send a powerful signal to party leadership that the group that had captured Young Labor deserved to be taken seriously. The union would provide Network with a logistical and political base to eventually try to take control of the entire Right.

Under the plan, Network members would sign up for jobs covered by the union, get familiar with the industrial relations environment and identify other employees who might support the campaign. When an election was due, Network would catch the existing union leadership off guard and kick them out of office. The strategy was loosely based on a 1980s approach, when activists from the Left undermined right-wing union leaders who had grown complacent after years in power. Lindsay Tanner led one of the most high-profile upsets, seizing the Victorian arm of the Federated Clerks' Union in 1988. As an electorate officer for a Labor MP he had been considered a clerk.

A problem occurred almost as soon as the campaign to take over the ATAEA kicked off. Candidates for elected positions had to have been union members for at least a year. The election was twelve months away and most Network members hadn't yet obtained jobs in the industry. Network leadership decided to press ahead. Steve Moore, a Monash University law student and Network leader, was already a member of the union and a credible candidate for secretary. The rest of Network agreed to support him on the unspoken understanding he would give them jobs in the union after the election.

A committee of all the Network members who had joined the union ran the campaign. Most didn't realise the key decisions were being made by another, smaller committee, run by Moore, Borowick, Shorten and the other Network leaders.

Shorten's and Borowick's political jobs gave them latitude to work on the campaign. Shorten took a weekend job as an usher at Flemington Racecourse, the home of the Melbourne Cup, and Victoria Park, Collingwood Football Club's home ground. Other members of the group found work at the Victorian Arts Centre, the Melbourne Cricket Ground, Festival Hall, major racecourses and other entertainment venues. They planned to keep a low profile, identify the main complaints of the workforce and launch a slick election campaign, run mainly from Gareth Evans' offices in Treasury Place. Pamphlets and letters to all members were professionally produced. Right-wing unions provided financial backing.

At night and on weekends, the group hit sporting and entertainment venues drumming up support. They spent a couple of days in eastern Victoria at a training camp working on strategies. Law and economics students from Melbourne's top private schools role-played speaking to poor, older men.

The group thought carefully about which issues would resonate and recruited candidates who had worked in the industry a long time – because almost everyone in Network was ineligible to stand. At the last possible moment, Network's candidates registered for the election. The union's officials were stunned. They had expected to be returned unopposed. They quickly worked out that a Young Labor group was backing the challengers. They responded with their own messages to members: an outside group is trying to take control for political purposes; we've worked hard for you; stick with us.

Flushed with their success in Young Labor, Shorten and the other Network members were confident their youth, energy and brains would deliver them control of the union. The union's suite of offices on the second floor of Trades Hall in Lygon Street, Carlton, would become Network's new headquarters so they wouldn't need to rely on political patrons like Gareth Evans or Neil Pope for a physical base.

When the postal vote began, the Electoral Commission issued daily updates on the number of ballot papers being sent in. For a union with a little-educated casual workforce, the returns were staggering. More than 60 per cent of the membership had decided to vote. Clearly Network's campaign had had a huge impact on the workforce. As the last day of voting drew near, the young challengers were so excited they could barely sleep.

The day after voting closed, both sides gathered at the Electoral Commission's offices in Melbourne to watch the ballot count. Within an hour the result was clear: Network had been crushed.

Shorten and the other Network leaders had been too naive to understand that the union leadership was doing a good job. It was committed to helping its members, didn't make cosy arrangements with employers and wasn't badly run. It simply didn't deserve to be kicked out.

Another force worked against Network. The power of incumbency is so strong that even well-resourced union challengers find it incredibly difficult to win votes. That's why many of Australia's biggest unions haven't faced credible challenges in decades.

No-one involved in Network participated in a hostile bid for a union again. And Bill Shorten learnt a valuable lesson: the next time he tried to take over a union it had to be from the inside.

A year after Network's defeat, the factional balance of power flipped in Victoria. Several far-left unions in the Socialist Left were unhappy with their leader, Kim Carr, and quit to form an alliance with the Right. The breakaway group called themselves the 'Pledge group' after vowing to oppose Liberal premier Jeff Kennett's plans to privatise Victoria's state-owned electricity companies. One of the unions in the group was the Theatrical and Amusements Employees' Association.

With the Theatricals' help, the Right finally took control of the party. Not through the democratic process of convincing union members to vote for their candidates, but because of schism among their opponents. The realignment made it clear that ideological divides meant to define the differences between the factions no longer had any meaning. It was only about power.

## Young lawyers in trouble

Bill Shorten wasn't perfect. His flagrant confidence grated with other ambitious Young Labor members and turned potential allies into rivals. After the failed attempt to take over the ATAEA, he fell out with the other Network leaders and left the group, which was taken over by Martin Pakula and Tim Holding. He ended close relationships with followers whom he no longer needed. His law grades were lacklustre. Too busy politicking to attend lectures, he relied on notes from political and work contacts.

Despite his shortcomings, no-one who knew Shorten doubted he had a bright political future. The question was: how would he make it happen? His plan, it emerged, was to get a job at a law firm, become a solicitor and find a safe seat in the Victorian or federal parliament. Though Shorten rarely discussed his ambitions with other Young Labor members, once, as he left a dinner honouring then prime minister Bob Hawke, he told a colleague: 'Everyone in there wants to be prime minister, but they're all behind me [in the queue].'

Shorten's first and only job in the law was at Maurice Blackburn, a Melbourne firm steeped in Labor tradition. The managing partner, John Cain junior, was the son and grandson of Labor premiers. The firm generated a lot of revenue working for right-wing unions, which made it the perfect launch pad for Shorten's political career. People who worked with him said Shorten was a disorganised lawyer. He did, however, embrace the firm's social scene. One night during work drinks, Shorten scooped a fish out of the office fish tank and put it in his mouth as a prank. He then spat the fish onto the carpet, according to a person who was there.

Shorten didn't last long in the law. In 1994, after less than two years in the workers' compensation department at Maurice Blackburn, he decided to enter the union movement. He had two offers: he could become national legal officer of the Transport Workers' Union or join Organising Works, an innovative program established by Bill Kelty, the secretary of the Australian Council of Trade Unions. The scheme placed young organisers in unions and gave them time off to attend training seminars on the fundamentals of industrial relations, including negotiating, recruiting and safety rules. Shorten chose to become an organiser, knowing it would allow him to build his support in the union from the shop floor up. He joined the Australian Workers' Union, which represented more than 100,000 men and women in heavy and light industry, including steel and paper mills, aluminium smelters, mines, oil platforms and construction sites. The right-wing union, Australia's oldest, had a reputation for being badly run in Victoria and was trying to recover from scandal after its Victorian secretary was accused of extorting hundreds of thousands of dollars from big companies. When confronted by other union officials he skipped town. The police were called in and the allegations had been reported in the press. The union was demoralised and desperate for decent leadership.

As Shorten networked his way around Melbourne he occasionally ran into another young lawyer who had a connection to the scandal, Julia Gillard. A student politician who moved from her hometown of Adelaide to Melbourne to attend university, Gillard worked at Slater & Gordon, Maurice Blackburn's main rival in the niche labour law market.

Gillard, the AWU's lawyer, had joined the Labor Party at sixteen and was determined to win a seat in federal parliament. In the meantime, she was building her support in the Socialist Left while pursuing her law career.

Around 1991 Gillard started dating Bruce Wilson, her client and the head of the West Australian and later Victorian divisions of the union. Wilson was a charismatic union guy on the way up. In 1992, at his request, Gillard helped him register an incorporated association in Western Australia with the stated purpose of improving safety on construction sites. Wilson and his friend, Ralph Blewitt, another West Australian union official, personally controlled the entity, which was named the Australian Workers' Union Workplace Reform Association Inc. The union's other officials weren't told about it, which made sense – Wilson and Blewitt intended to use the association as a fund to raise cash for their own use. They convinced several large construction and engineering companies, including Thiess Contracting, John Holland, Fluor Daniel and Woodside Petroleum, to hand over roughly $385,000 in total. The companies were apparently told the money would be spent training AWU members.

Normally when lawyers receive new business they open a file so billable work hours can be recorded. In a break with protocol, Gillard didn't create a file for Wilson's fund. She didn't charge for the work either. Gillard would later say it was common practice at Slater & Gordon not to open files on small jobs for unions. But the omission would raise damaging questions within three years and far into the future as to whether Gillard knew, or should have known, about her boyfriend's scam.

Wilson used some of the money from the fund for a deposit on a modest house in Fitzroy, an edgy suburb slowly gentrifying in Melbourne's inner suburbs. Gillard, who went to the auction with Wilson on 13 February 1993, handled some of the paperwork and waived Slater & Gordon's $1600 conveyancing fee. For reasons never clearly explained, the $230,000 house was put in Blewitt's name. 'Mr Blewitt will be registered owner of the unit you are purchasing,' a letter from Gillard's office to Wilson on 22 February 1993 said. Wilson lived in the house, which became something of a headquarters for his union mates. (Blewitt sold the house three years later for $233,000. Part of the money not spent on the house had been buried in his backyard, where it deteriorated in the moist earth.)

Roughly two years later, in mid-1995, the union's new Victorian secretary, Bob Smith, and a joint national secretary, Ian Cambridge, discovered financial irregularities while trying to sort out the mess of bank accounts left from a merger in 1993 with another union, the Federation of Industrial, Manufacturing and Engineering Employees.

Confronted by his fellow officials about the discrepancies, Wilson quit and took a redundancy payment, which he was later ordered to return. He and Blewitt disappeared from the union movement.

Cambridge repeatedly asked the fraud squads in Victoria and Western Australia to investigate. In January 1996 he was so concerned about the internal handling of allegations against Wilson that he called publicly for a royal commission to investigate his own union. Five months later Victoria Police said it wouldn't press charges due to lack of evidence. Another police investigation in Western Australia went nowhere.

Even though there was no definitive evidence that Gillard knew Wilson was involved in a financial scam, the scandal essentially ended her legal career. Slater & Gordon's senior partner, Peter Gordon, and the general manager, Geoff Shaw, formally interviewed Gillard on 11 September 1995 to discuss what had happened. The conversation was recorded and transcribed, a sign of how seriously the matter was taken.

Gillard said the association she helped set up for Wilson was a 'slush fund' to help get AWU officials re-elected. It's a common and perfectly legal practice for union officials to open savings accounts for this purpose. But this one was different. None of the members or other officials knew of its existence, making it impossible for them to make legitimate contributions.

Gordon quizzed Gillard about her own two-bedroom house, in Abbotsford, which she had bought in July 1991. There were rumours flying around Labor circles that her builder had asked the AWU to pay for renovations on Gillard's house. Was there any connection between the slush fund and the renovations, Gordon asked? Did Gillard pay for the grout in her new bathroom? Could she provide receipts from her floorer? Was she still dating Wilson?

Gillard acknowledged that one of her builders had gone to the AWU's offices seeking payment for some of the work. He was in a dispute with Gillard, who was refusing to pay because he had replaced the front wooden windows of her Victorian terrace with ugly aluminium frames. The union didn't pay him and the request was an innocent mistake, she said.

Gillard, who had recently broken off the relationship with Wilson, gave lengthy, detailed answers to the questions. However, she was equivocal on the pivotal question: could she be certain the union or Wilson's slush fund didn't pay for her home renovations? 'I can't categorically rule out that something at my house didn't get paid for by the association [the slush fund] or something at my house didn't get paid for by the union or whatever,' she told Gordon. '[But] it doesn't seem to me looking at the house and working through it mentally that there is sort of thousands of dollars of free unexplained work lying around in the house.'

Gillard's career was on the line. The head of Slater & Gordon's commercial department, Nick Styant-Browne, was doubtful about her explanations and thought there was a case for dismissal. Gordon didn't agree. Nonetheless, the firm's involvement with Wilson had poisoned the atmosphere between Gillard and some of the partners. She was angry they hadn't stood by her; they thought she had kept them in the dark.

Her relationships with her colleagues ruptured, Gillard, who was thirty-four, took a leave of absence to stand as a Senate candidate for the Labor Party. She did no further work for the firm after the September interview with Gordon. After failing to get elected to the Senate in the 1996 election, which Paul Keating lost to John Howard, she formally left Slater & Gordon in May 1996 and was hired by the Victorian opposition leader, John Brumby, as his chief of staff. Her mentor at Slater & Gordon, Bernard Murphy, also resigned and switched to Maurice Blackburn, Shorten's old firm. Years later Murphy would credit Gillard with teaching him a lot – in a speech to mark his appointment as a Federal Court judge by her government.

## Peacemaker

While Julia Gillard's legal career was being snuffed out by her work for the AWU, Bill Shorten was building a power base within the union. When he joined as a young trainee organiser, power in the AWU was split between two forceful personalities. Bill Ludwig, a former shearer, headed the union's biggest division, Queensland. Steve Harrison had become the dominant figure in New South Wales when his union, the Federation of Industrial, Manufacturing and Engineering Employees, merged with the AWU in 1993. The two determined men were fierce rivals. When Harrison retired in 1997, Ludwig was left as the union's top dog.

Since his university days Shorten had lived in Carlton and other suburbs just north of the city near Melbourne University. After joining the union he rented a flat in the state electorate Melton, about 45 kilometres west of the CBD. One of his friends who visited said the flat was barely furnished and there was no food in the refrigerator. Shorten was selected as the Labor candidate for the safe seat, which all but guaranteed he would be elected to parliament at the 1999 election. He didn't realise his boss, AWU state secretary Bob Smith, had a similar plan. Through the AWU's influence on the state Labor party, Smith was offered his own seat in Melbourne's south-eastern suburbs.

Smith decided to step down and move into the state upper house. The move left the 31-year-old Shorten with a choice:

became a state MP or gun for Smith's old job. Shorten knew union leaders, especially those of big unions like the AWU, were far more influential than all but the most powerful backbenchers. Leadership of the union would give him the autonomy to push his profile in a way being an MP wouldn't, because in parliament he would be subject to the discipline of the party leader. He would also control the AWU's numbers in the party, which would allow him to put his own supporters into parliament, thus shoring up his future support base. On the flip side, safe seats don't come around very often and Shorten didn't know when he'd get another chance to get into parliament. Still, he decided to shoot for Smith's job.

Smith resigned midway through his term, which made the union's state executive responsible for his replacement. Shorten's rival to lead the AWU in Victoria was another, more experienced union official, Mick Eagles. Terry Muscat, the union's national secretary, and two Victorian officials, David Cragg and Frank Leo, were convinced Shorten had the leadership qualities to rally the union's members. The union wasn't in great shape. Members were leaving and its finances were in a mess. The bad taste of the Bruce Wilson scandal lingered. There were about forty employees in the Victorian office and they wanted a leader who could give the organisation back its dignity. Eagles was gently told over lunch with one of the organisers, Cesar Melhem, that he was too confrontational to become state secretary and Shorten was going to get the job. Eagles didn't run. Shorten was elected unopposed.

Three months later a federal election was held. Julia Gillard had recovered from her acrimonious departure from Slater & Gordon and had been selected as the Labor candidate for Lalor in western Melbourne. She easily won the blue-collar seat as the country swung back towards the ALP after its 1996 thrashing. In his first election as leader, Kim Beazley won almost 51 per cent of the vote. He fell only eight seats short of winning government. Beazley would never come as close again to becoming prime minister.

As leader of the AWU, Shorten was a paradox. A university academic's son, a private-school debater and a lawyer, he came from a world inaccessible to the union's members.

A slight speech impediment meant he sometimes mispronounced the 'th' sound, making him sound a little posh. When he spoke at union rallies, there was often a brief hesitation from the crowd as they sensed he wasn't one of them. But Shorten had honed his public speaking skills as a trainee organiser and a Young Labor activist. He was an astute judge of moods: of an individual, a room or a group of men at a worksite. It normally took him less than a minute to win over a crowd. His skill was explaining complexity clearly without talking down to people, according to Ben Davis, an AWU organiser who worked closely with him. He had learnt to control his natural tendency to turn every discussion into a debate.

In private, though, he was rarely, if ever, modest. 'This would be so much easier to explain if they [the members] were as intelligent as me,' he once told AWU staffers as he was trying to work out how to rally support for one of his plans. Staff have also said he would become wildly enthusiastic about an idea and ring them at 1 a.m. to discuss it. A few months later, after they did a lot of work trying to turn his idea into reality, he would lose interest.

Among the union's membership, though, Shorten was developing a god-like status. At union functions he'd be surrounded by members lapping up his tales of out-negotiating employers and other union leaders. He stabilised the union's finances, established good relationships with employers and attracted new members. Morale was improving. 'We wanted him to be our saviour,' a union official later said. 'And he was. He brought everyone together.'

In his private life, Shorten churned through a series of short-term relationships. Then, while studying for a master's of business administration at Melbourne University, he met Deborah Beale, the daughter of a wealthy Liberal federal MP, Julian Beale. Their quick marriage, in 1999, propelled Shorten into the ranks of Melbourne high society. Julian Beale was close friends with Richard Pratt, whose private cardboard-manufacturing group, Visy Industries, had made him the fourth-richest man in Australia with a wealth of $5 billion, according to the *BRW* Rich List. The Beales and Pratts were like an extended family. They holidayed together. The Beales sometimes stayed at the Pratts' Manhattan apartment, which took up a floor of the Sherry-Netherland Hotel on Fifth Avenue. As a wedding present, Pratt and his wife, Jeanne, held a lavish engagement party for the couple at their grand mansion in Kew, Raheen, which had once been the residence of Catholic Archbishop Daniel Mannix, himself a powerful figure in Australian politics. 'Debbie has joined the union,' her father said in his wedding speech. 'A union of two.' Beale and Shorten became a glamorous couple on the Labor Party social circuit. Despite her Liberal background, Beale, who was intelligent, funny and friendly, was genuinely popular among Shorten's political circle. She struck up a friendship with Kathy Jackson, a leader in the Health Services Union, and Liberty Sanger, a lawyer dating David Feeney, Shorten's best man and key factional ally.

Pratt was proud of Shorten and encouraged his political career. One year he took the couple on a family holiday to Easter Island,

Cuba and Argentina, where they spent New Year's Eve in Buenos Aires, according to one of Beale's friends. Covering the long distances wasn't difficult. They flew in the Pratts' private jet.

Soon after he took over the AWU, Shorten was advised by senior figures in the union movement that he needed help to patch up his union's tattered public image. Shorten convinced Andrea Carson, an industrial relations writer for *The Age*, to become his publicist. 'You should stop watching from the sidelines,' he said. 'It's time to strap your footy boots on and get involved.'

Carson's job was to promote the union by promoting Shorten. She quickly got a lesson in his distinction between work and play – there wasn't one. Not long after she started work at the union, Carson and her husband went to Hamilton Island for their honeymoon. Shorten was holidaying with Beale on nearby Hayman Island and invited the newlyweds to stay at his resort. (He didn't pay.) Each night Shorten insisted on a hand of 500, a game similar to bridge and usually played in pairs. He recorded statistics obsessively and won a lot. It was a different story on the tennis court. Each day the two couples played mixed doubles. Beale tried her best but couldn't overcome her husband's lack of coordination. Shorten, endlessly competitive, would go quiet after losing.

Back in Melbourne Carson and Shorten set about schmoozing industrial relations and political journalists across the country. Over dinners, lunches and coffee, Shorten created a network of media contacts and a personal narrative. He knew he was rare talent: young, articulate and educated. He could fulfil the media's insatiable need for someone credible to talk about almost anything.

Three years after becoming state secretary, Shorten stood for the position of national secretary. His successes in Victoria gave him credibility. Along with Bill Ludwig and others he had worked hard to seal a peace deal to end the rivalry between different divisions – a hangover from the 1993 merger. Once again, Shorten was elected unopposed. It was the first uncontested AWU election at the national level in many years. His transformation into a national political figure had begun.

## Loyalty is nothing

Taking over the Australian Workers' Union thrust Bill Shorten into the front line of Labor Party factional power plays. Not only was the union a significant donor to the party, he now controlled a chunk of the Victorian biennial Labor conference. He had the power to give loyal followers jobs in the union and influence the selection of Labor Party candidates for seats at state and federal levels.

Shorten soon got a lesson in the brutality of factional politics. After Young Labor Network broke up, he aligned himself with two former rivals: Stephen Conroy, who was chosen by the Right to fill a Senate vacancy in 1996, and David Feeney, who became the state secretary – administrative head – of the party in 1999. The partnership later became known as the 'Short-Con' alliance, after its two founders. Rival Network leaders, including Martin Pakula and Tim Holding, decided to become part of a sub-faction run by the party's national president, Greg Sword, who headed the National Union of Workers. The Right was still united in its never-ending struggle against the Left, but Shorten's ambitions were creating fissures in the faction that were getting out of hand.

Sword was tired of Shorten's aggressive tactics. The veteran union leader had proposed several candidates for safe seats but, each time, Shorten, Conroy and Feeney intervened to get their own candidates chosen. Finally, in 2002, after twenty-five years in the Right, Sword withdrew the National Union of Workers from the faction and joined with the Socialist Left to create what he dubbed the 'Modernisation Alliance'. Sword controlled about 10 per cent of the votes at the Labor state conference. The Left had 44 per cent. Combined, they controlled the party.

The split had two immediate effects. Shorten, who was running to become state president of the party, lost the vote to a candidate from the Left, Jim Claven. Feeney, who was in charge of the administrative functions of the party, was removed as state secretary and replaced by another left-winger. Premier Steve Bracks, grateful for Feeney's help winning the 1999 state election, hired him on his personal staff. The Left was back in charge.

One thing became clear to Shorten: factional loyalty was worth nothing when power was at stake. Four years later he had his revenge. The Short-Cons offered the National Union of Workers and several Socialist Left unions, including the far-left Electrical Trades Union, three federal seats for their support. They agreed. Greg Sword was frozen out and retired from active involvement in the leadership of the party.

It was time for Shorten to make his next move. He had moved into the electorate of Maribyrnong, a safe Labor seat in Melbourne's working-class western suburbs wedged between Essendon Airport and Flemington Racecourse. The sitting member was Bob Sercombe, a veteran MP who was shadow minister for overseas aid and Pacific Island affairs. Shorten, who already had a high public profile, started attending branch meetings and functions to become known personally. Sercombe quickly realised the younger man planned to take his seat and end his political career. Sercombe was fifty-six. Shorten was thirty-eight.

Under party rules, Labor candidates are chosen through two equally weighted ballots: one of local branch members and another of a head-office panel chosen by the unions and factions. The system makes ordinary members feel like they get a say over their local MP, while preserving the power of the factional leaders, in most cases, to allocate safe seats.

Sercombe didn't want to give up Maribyrnong. He had been an MP for nineteen years, including almost a decade in state politics, where he had risen to be deputy leader. He'd never been a minister and the upcoming 2007 election was his best chance of finally running a government department. To lift his media profile Sercombe was churning out policy papers proposing ways to improve the operation of Australia's aid budget. In 2005 he had scheduled a press conference in Canberra with Kevin Rudd, the shadow minister for foreign affairs, to discuss a new plan to promote economic development in the South Pacific. Shorten heard about the event in advance, rang Rudd and asked him not to participate. Shorten didn't want his opponent attracting sympathetic media attention. Rudd, who didn't seem to take Shorten seriously, went ahead with the press conference and told Sercombe of Shorten's request.

Shorten would later tell journalist Sally Neighbour he was chosen as the Labor candidate for Maribyrnong after wooing the 642 regular members who lived in the seat. 'I won the preselection by knocking on more doors,' he said. But while Shorten did distribute glossy leaflets to Labor branches promoting his achievements, his victory, in reality, was delivered through the Short-Con alliance with the Left that gave him almost 70 per cent of the central selection panel. That meant Sercombe needed seventy per cent of branch members to keep the seat, an almost impossible task in an area heavily factionalised by years of recruitment of Labor members by state and federal Labor candidates.

Sercombe knew he had no chance of winning. But he stayed in the contest until one week before the vote was due in March 2006, forcing Shorten and his allies to concentrate their energy on removing him. Sercombe hoped his persistence would distract them from their grander plan.

The arrangement to secure a safe seat for Shorten was one part of a complex deal. To fulfil their promises on the Right and Left, the Short-Cons were trying to replace six sitting federal members. They succeeded in three seats: Maribyrnong, which Shorten won; Corio, a Geelong-based seat, where Gavan O'Connor was replaced with Shorten's ally Richard Marles; and Isaacs, in Melbourne's south-east, where another Shorten loyalist, lawyer Mark Dreyfus, dislodged Ann Corcoran.

Shorten's candidates failed in the other three seats, Scullin, Hotham and Bruce. Each had been promised to the forces in the Right and the Left that had supported the Short-Cons. Hotham, which was held by Simon Crean and covered Moorabbin Airport in Melbourne's south-east, was allocated to the National Union of Workers. At least 100 members of the Cambodian community who lived in the electorate were signed up to support the challenger, Martin Pakula. Amid much bitterness about a challenge to a previous party leader, Crean fought back and kept his seat. Pakula would later be given the consolation prize of a spot in the Victorian upper house.

The factional deals over seats were so blatantly cynical and lacking any underlying principled motivation they became an embarrassment to the party in Victoria. They prompted former Labor president Barry Jones to remark that many of the party's factional chiefs had merely become political traders dealing in blocs of votes.

Shorten shrugged off the criticism. 'It's not a case of Left or Right in the Labor party,' he said. 'It is a case of two groups in the Labor party: one that is prepared to make the hard decisions in order to win elections and those that are perhaps satisfied with opposition.' Shorten was now all but guaranteed a safe seat for as long as he pleased. His political career was working out perfectly.

# 2

**Peddling influence in the NSW Labor Party – A lucrative 'training' mine – The Minister for Mining has lunch – Cheap cars and cheap land**

## Politics NSW style

Ian Macdonald's path into politics was common among the Labor left: childhood hardship, protest and public service. Macdonald's mother raised five children alone. A history student at Melbourne's La Trobe University during the Vietnam War, Macdonald became a firebrand student activist and joined the Labor Party. After graduating with honours, he was hired as a research officer at the Australian Council of Overseas Aid.

Macdonald's political activities at university caught the eye of the party's left wing. The reforming New South Wales attorney-general Frank Walker offered him a job on his personal staff in Sydney. Macdonald became the political operative in the minister's office, building support for Walker in the Left, including lining up candidates for public elections and jockeying for positions inside the government. He also got involved in some policy work. Macdonald concentrated on organised crime and the illicit drug industry, and became something of an expert on the Nugan Hand Bank, an Australian investment bank which collapsed in sensational circumstances in 1980 and was accused of being used for drug running, money laundering and large-scale tax avoidance.

The 1988 election, which ended the Labor government of Premier Barrie Unsworth, was a big step up for Macdonald. With the support of the Amalgamated Metal Workers' Union and its leader, George Campbell, the obscure ministerial adviser was elected to the NSW upper house. The state's Legislative Council, as the upper house is called, doesn't have electorates, which means MPs don't have to worry about constituents. While lower house MPs often spend their weekends attending local fetes, sporting contests and community meetings, upper house members only need to worry, once every eight years, about the support of the party officials who select the official list of candidates for the public to vote on.

Macdonald's first speech in parliament on 8 June 1988, three months after he was elected, is one of the great ironies of his life. Liberal premier Nick Greiner planned to create an independent commission to clean out the government and police corruption that had become endemic under Unsworth and his Labor predecessor, Neville Wran. One of the worst scandals involved the minister for corrective services, Rex Jackson, who was jailed in 1987 for taking bribes to release prisoners early. (Jackson himself left prison early – for good behaviour – and bought a hot-dog van.) The commission would operate separate to the police and conduct its own investigations and public inquiries. The Director of Public Prosecutions would then use its evidence to prosecute corrupt officials.

Many Labor MPs were worried the commission's powers would be too great. They felt the definition of corruption was too broad, the commission lacked democratic accountability and it would be able to destroy reputations based on evidence that wouldn't be allowed in a regular courtroom. In parliament, Macdonald argued the Independent Commission Against Corruption law was potentially the most dangerous ever considered by the NSW parliament. 'I fear that a great many citizens will be found guilty of corrupt conduct although they have committed no crime,' he told parliament.

Macdonald's prophecy proved eerily accurate. In 1992 Greiner's reputation was tarnished by an ICAC investigation into whether he tried to induce an independent MP, Terry Metherell, to side with the Coalition by offering him a cushy government job. The commission found Greiner behaved 'contrary to known and recognised standards of honesty and integrity'. His credibility shot, Greiner stepped down. The courts cleared him a week later.

Greiner was succeeded by John Fahey, who struggled to lead the scandal-prone government. The police minister, Terry Griffiths, was forced to resign over sexual harassment allegations. Another Coalition MP, Barry Morris, made bomb threats against a local newspaper in a bad Italian accent and was sent to jail.

After seven years in opposition, Labor leader Bob Carr won power in 1995 by one seat. Carr promised a cleaner, less wasteful approach to office. Carr had learnt lessons from his predecessors on both sides of politics. He successfully presented a unified, considered and responsible front to voters. His ten years in power became the longest continuous reign by a New South Wales premier. But Labor's success hid a darker drama that would have terrible consequences for the party's reputation in New South Wales and beyond.

Under the party's rules, Carr's government was answerable to the 'caucus', the collective noun for the state's seventy-one Labor MPs. Caucus was, like in other states and federally, run along factional lines. The Right, known as Centre Unity, had roughly two-thirds of the state MPs, which allowed the faction to choose the leader and most of the ministers.

In theory, caucus was the ultimate authority over the government. It signed off on the main decisions and legislation. It selected the leader and the ministry. (The leader allocated portfolios.) In reality, the factional leaders told caucus what to do and it mostly obliged. Carr, and his successor in 2005, Morris Iemma, enforced tight discipline over their MPs through an alliance with the party's head office, which was run out of a dingy office building bordering Sydney's Chinatown. Head office, using the party's rules for the selection of candidates, could threaten to remove MPs from their seats if they said or did things embarrassing to the government. MPs who bucked the system risked their careers.

In the early 1990s four men decided to challenge the established order: Graham Richardson, who was then a federal Labor minister; Morris Iemma, one of his advisers; Carl Scully, a lawyer who had joined the party when he was nineteen; and Eddie Obeid, a wealthy businessman who owned an Arabic-language newspaper, *El Telegraph*. With the support of John Della Bosca, the party state secretary, they set about challenging the dominant grouping in the Right, which was known as the 'Trogs' because someone had once referred to them as 'troglodytes sitting in a cave'. The new group was named after the NSW Central Coast town of Terrigal, where the Obeid family had a holiday home and where the group first met. The Terrigals worked to replace retiring Labor MPs with their own candidates. They recruited many of the most ambitious activists from Young Labor, including Joe Tripodi, Reba Meagher, Michael Costa and Eric Roozendaal, and helped them win seats.

With Richardson's help Obeid was appointed to the upper house. Through his ingratiating personality and sheer workload – he spent day after day on the phone networking – Obeid emerged as the Terrigals' coordinator and leader. His office on the eleventh floor of the parliamentary annex overlooking Sydney's Domain became a kind of barber's shop for MPs from the Right. Anyone was welcome to drop by. Often five or six MPs were there at a time, gossiping, plotting and complaining. Political contacts were allowed to use the family ski lodge at Perisher Valley. Day after day Obeid patiently listened to gripes, soothed conflicts and doled out advice. He racked up favours. A short man with a warm smile and friendly manner, Obeid rarely raised his voice, was careful never to cause offence and liked to sum up situations with an apt homily. In politics you have to 'walk between the raindrops', he once said.

Obeid used his growing power in caucus to get himself elected to cabinet in 1999. Carr gave him the natural resources portfolio, which included oversight of the state's mining industry. He continued to help the party raise money for election campaigns, mainly to get more Terrigals into parliament. In 2002 the *Sydney Morning Herald* reported that Obeid had sought a $1 million bribe for the Labor Party to help the Canterbury-Bankstown Rugby League Club get approval for a $900 million residential and commercial development at Liverpool in western Sydney.

When Obeid later sued the newspaper for defamation in the Supreme Court, Bob Carr, who was suffering from a severe case of the flu, appeared in 2006 as one of Obeid's witnesses. Carr told the court he believed that Obeid hadn't asked for the bribe. The *Herald* was so determined to damage Obeid's reputation, Carr said, he decided, six months later, to ask him to resign from cabinet. 'While I believed he was innocent – and ICAC said he was free of these imputations – the *Herald* would continue to go against him,' Carr explained to the court. The judge ordered the *Herald*'s parent company, Fairfax, to pay Obeid $150,000 compensation with interest.

From the backbench, Obeid's power grew. When Carr decided to step down in 2005, Obeid and the other Terrigals decided to replace him with one of their own, Iemma. Carr's seventeen years as leader and three election victories had given him unquestionable authority over the party. Iemma was far more reliant on Obeid and the other Terrigals. Once a week Iemma had Obeid to his house for a private breakfast.

Among the Right, everyone knew the best way to get a better job, and a higher salary, was to stay onside with Obeid and his cronies. When Sydney's high-profile lord mayor Frank Sartor was about to enter parliament in 2003, Obeid asked to meet for a coffee. Sartor, who was about fifty and wasn't paid for a time as mayor, admitted he was worried about his lack of retirement savings. According to Sartor, Obeid asked him: 'Well, what do you want to retire on?' Sartor told him it would be nice to retire on a million dollars. 'Well, I could help you with that,' Obeid allegedly replied. Sartor didn't take up the offer, which he thought improper, even though Obeid didn't ask for anything specific in return.

When Obeid left cabinet, he was determined that Macdonald should go in. Macdonald's bald, square head, powerful shoulders and expensive suits made him look like a nightclub bouncer who had aged into a prosperous property developer. A member of the Left, he was one of the sharper operators in caucus. He knew how to tell people what they wanted to hear. Often, later, they would wonder if what he said was true. Macdonald and Obeid, both members of the small upper house, were assigned to manage negotiations with the minor parties who held the balance of power in the late 1990s. They quickly realised they were kindred spirits.

Obeid wanted Macdonald put in the planning portfolio, an important job that required its minister to strike a balance between the property industry and heritage and environmental interests. Deciding the job was too sensitive for a political wheeler-dealer like Macdonald, Carr gave him agriculture and fisheries. A year later Macdonald got the primary industries portfolio as well, and minerals the following year.

By 2007 about half the members of the Right – roughly twenty-five MPs – were Terrigals. Because they voted as a disciplined bloc, and the rest of the Right didn't, the Terrigals were able to control the whole faction, which in turn allowed them to determine which way caucus voted. A system of factional patronage had developed to reward loyal MPs. More than three-quarters of all Labor MPs had been given a position that meant they earned more than the backbencher's $126,560 base salary. The nineteen ministers, deputy premier and premier got an extra $105,000 to $165,000 depending on their seniority. There were loadings of up to $105,000 for the speaker, deputy speaker, assistant speaker and government whip. Ten parliamentary secretaries got an extra $25,000, except for the 'leader of the house', who got an extra $63,000. Thirteen chairs of parliamentary committees, including the children and young people committee, got an extra $18,000. Ordinary members of the public accounts committee each got $3910. MPs who weren't compliant could be stripped of their extra responsibilities.

Macdonald's departments, which didn't get a lot of public attention, played an important role in the state's economy. When equine influenza spread through the state in 2007, it was regarded as one of the most serious threats to animal welfare in Australian history. To limit the spread of the disease, Macdonald approved strict rules regarding the movement of horses. A special area was established in the Hunter Valley that allowed horses to be transferred from stud to stud. The decision allowed the horse-breeding industry, which had a lot of money invested in the area, to continue operating.

Another of Macdonald's responsibilities was important to the economy: approving and regulating mines. Booming coal prices were creating huge fortunes almost overnight. Nathan Tinkler, an electrician from Newcastle, borrowed $500,000 and took on debt to buy an unwanted coal deposit in Queensland. Eighteen months later he sold out to Macarthur Coal for cash and shares. When Macarthur became a takeover target the following year, the 32-year-old sold his stake for $440 million. Much of the money flowing into the industry was going to New South Wales, which has about 40 per cent of Australia's black coal. Black coal is cleaner than brown coal, is used to produce steel and run power stations, and is in heavy demand in China. Rail links to Newcastle helped get the coal relatively quickly to ships for transport to Asia.

Few people knew the coal industry as well as John Maitland, the national secretary of the Construction, Forestry, Mining and Energy Union. After retiring from the union in 2006, Maitland started working on an audacious plan: to make himself millions of dollars from coal. He just needed Macdonald's help.

As Maitland and Macdonald began working on this get-rich scheme, the rest of the government was distracted by attempts to sell the state's power assets. The move, which was designed to avoid future power blackouts, was bitterly opposed by head office and elements of the union movement, including the head of the Electrical Trades Union, Bernie Riordan, who was also the party's state president. Exhausted by the fight, Iemma quit as leader on 5 September 2008. The Terrigals replaced him with Nathan Rees, a minister from the Left who they thought would buoy the party's public support and be easy to control. They were wrong.

## Calling in favours

With a powerfully built chest, deep voice and walrus moustache, John Maitland looked like he'd walked out of a casting studio for old-school union leaders. He had spent decades fighting mining companies across Australia and loved to rally his members with the rhetoric of class struggle. In 1997 he told the managing director of Rio Tinto's coal operations in New South Wales his job was at risk if he didn't give in to the union. When the manager complained publicly about the threat, Maitland accused him of being a liar. There was no question in Maitland's union that the 'bosses' – the executives who ran big mining companies like BHP Billiton – were the enemy.

On 22 January 2007, when many Australians were winding up their Christmas holidays, the now retired Maitland sent an unusual proposal to Ian Macdonald, minister for natural resources. Maitland wanted a licence to build an underground educational facility to teach people how to mine coal. He described the project as a 'training mine' that would help alleviate the shortage of experienced personnel that had driven up costs across the industry. The location he chose was Doyles Creek, a coal deposit 105 kilometres west of Newcastle. What better place to teach miners than above an actual mineral deposit in the heart of the New South Wales coal belt?

Maitland's request may have been unique in the history of the New South Wales public service. There was no such thing as a 'training mine' licence in the state. What Maitland was actually seeking was an exploration licence, which he planned to use to set up the training facility. Exploration licences are normally sold to mineral exploration companies to allow them to measure how much coal there is underground, how deep it is and how much it will cost to extract. They are a step towards full-blown mining leases and are valuable assets. Granted the licence, Maitland would be free to search for coal in the area irrespective of whether he was training miners. In the proposal, Maitland insisted training was his primary objective, not searching for coal seams.

A month after Maitland's unusual request arrived at the state ministerial offices in central Sydney, the Department of Primary Industries raised a warning flag. Brad Mullard, a senior public servant in charge of coal and petroleum development, told Macdonald other companies had expressed interest in the Doyles Creek deposit and were waved off by the government because of the environmental sensitivity of the area. The deposit sits on the edge of Wollemi National Park, a rough and spectacular reserve that is part of the Greater Blue Mountains World Heritage area. On the other side of the deposit is Jerrys Plains, a small town surrounded by vineyards with buildings dating to the 1870s. Mullard essentially posed a question to Macdonald: do you really want to encourage the construction of a coalmine next to a national park and a quaint town?

The rules were clear too. The estimated 62-million-tonne coal deposit was big enough that a competitive tender was required to select which company would get the right to exploit it, Mullard told Macdonald, although in special circumstances the rule didn't have to be followed. He offered Macdonald three options: reject Maitland's plan, sell the licence to the highest bidder, or seek advice from the Mine Safety Advisory Council, an independent government body that tries to reduce accidents in the industry. Mullard favoured going to the safety council, which had rejected a similar proposal in 1999.

Macdonald didn't grant Maitland's request. The public servant's advice appeared to have killed the plan. Then, in March 2008, Maitland tried a different approach. Instead of going through Macdonald, Maitland wrote to the Department of Primary Industries requesting it issue him an exploration licence. Once again, the department baulked. A response prepared for a deputy head of the department, Alan Coutts, recommended some kind of competitive auction for the licence.

On 17 June Macdonald and two of his advisers treated Maitland to lunch at Parliament House in Sydney. Not long after, Maitland started calling in favours accumulated over decades in union, political and community circles to back his plan. Letters poured into Macdonald's office expressing the urgent need for a training mine in the Hunter Valley. Two contained identical wording. They all argued the training mine would be good for the industry and the workforce. The advocates included Sharan Burrow, who was president of the Australian Council of Trade Unions; Greg Combet, the minister for climate change; Brian Flannery, the managing director of coal miner Felix Resources; Mick Buffier, the chief operating officer of Xstrata Coal in NSW; Cliff Marsh, the chairman of the Westpac Rescue Helicopter Service; Stuart Barnett, a lawyer at Slater & Gordon's Newcastle office; Gary Kennedy, the secretary of the Newcastle Trades Hall Council; and local MPs Kerry Hickey and Robert Coombs. Even the vice-chancellor of the University of Newcastle, Nicholas Saunders, an eminent medical academic, offered his support. Under Maitland's plan the university would receive an annual $250,000 research grant from the mine.

The correspondence seemed to work. Macdonald suddenly got keen on a training facility for a new generation of miners. He sent Maitland a letter on 21 August inviting him to apply for an exploration licence over the Doyles Creek deposit. Macdonald cited the wave of community support, including the letters from the Westpac Rescue Helicopter Service and the University of Newcastle. A subsequent search of the department's records found the rescue service's and university's letters to Macdonald were dated after Macdonald formally invited Maitland to apply for the coal licence. Many of the other letters of support didn't arrive until the following month.

Macdonald's department, which had successfully fought off the training mine plan for a year, was out of the loop. It didn't know about the offer to Maitland until two weeks later, when it got an email from a journalist who covered the coal industry for the *Newcastle Herald*. The reporter wanted to know if it was true that the big-name unionist had finally got his hands on the long dormant Doyles Creek deposit. (Macdonald later claimed his department advised him to offer Maitland the coal licence, an assertion contradicted by documents from his office and the department.)

The deal was sealed on 5 December, when Macdonald and Maitland met at Macdonald's ministerial office. Macdonald formally offered him the exploration licence without a contest, according to a file note written by a departmental official. The official fee: $22,800.

The paperwork was completed in ten days. No announcement was made. Around 23 December, when the new premier, Nathan Rees, was preparing to fly to New York to marry his girlfriend, Stacey Haines, someone in his office apparently twigged to what was going on. A company controlled by a prominent trade unionist was being issued a potentially lucrative mining licence without any paper trail from the bureaucracy explaining the logic behind the decision.

Macdonald's deputy chief of staff, Jamie Gibson, who had been at the lunch with Maitland six months earlier, issued a plea for help. He sent an email to Graham Hawkes, an official in the department, asking him to retrospectively prepare a memo to explain the decision because someone from 'upstairs' was concerned about the exploration licence. Gibson wrote:

Hi Graham,

Geez mate I am sorry but could we please get a page or 2 of dot points on Doyles Creek training mine – i.e. how good it will be, how it address the skills shortage as pointed out by the ACA, how it will be state of the Art, that $250K goes to Newcastle Uni each year for research and that they are subject to all normal royalty payments etc.

Upstairs have seen it and are having a bit of a panic. if we could get it asap that's another one on my tab!

Thanks,

Cheers.

'Upstairs' was a reference to Rees's office, on the fortieth floor of Governor Macquarie Tower. Macdonald was on level thirty-three. Rees, focused on preparing a budget and his impending wedding, didn't get personally involved. There is no record of the reply to the email from Macdonald's office. But the training mine plan had rung alarm bells among Rees's staff.

Exploration licences are normally advertised before they are granted. News that Maitland's company had been given a green light for Doyles Creek was conveyed to the world in a press release on Christmas Eve. Because few newspapers publish on Christmas Day and most journalists are on holidays, the 24 December press release was almost guaranteed to be ignored by the media, which it was. When lawyers from law firm Clayton Utz searched through the government's files looking for a copy three years later, it wasn't there.

Maitland, meanwhile, was pushing ahead with a plan that would make him wealthier than many of the corporate executives he had spent years fighting.

## Breakfast at Tiffanie's

Craig Murray poked his head into the dining room of Tuscany Ristorante in Sydney's Inner West suburb of Leichhardt and looked around for Ian Macdonald's familiar heavy frame. The managing director of Country Energy, a power utility owned by the New South Wales government, had been asked to turn up to dinner alone on 15 July 2009. The canny Murray had a personal rule about meetings with politicians: don't go solo. He took along his manager of external relations, Bill Frewen, to the out-of-the-way, dimly lit restaurant. Regulars loved the place, although other patrons complained the food was overpriced and that favoured customers got better service.

Among the regulars were Labor politicians and the people who wanted to do business with them. The owner, Frank Moio, boasted of his close contacts in the government and, for a fee, would set up meetings between businessmen and the politicians who could be useful to them.

Murray and Frewen located Macdonald at a small table chatting to the manager. They sat down. After about twenty minutes, restaurant staff brought another table over and placed it next to theirs. It looked like Macdonald was expecting more diners. Murray asked what was going on. Macdonald said the other table was for the food.

After Macdonald, Murray and Frewen ordered, a surprise guest joined them: Ron Medich. The wealthy businessman was a property developer and owner of Rivercorp, a group that provided maintenance services to electricity companies. Medich saw a business opportunity in Country Energy, which was responsible for supplying electricity across 94 per cent of New South Wales. Five minutes later, Rivercorp's chief executive, Kim Shipley, appeared at the table.

Medich's and Shipley's presence put Murray in an uncomfortable position. He hadn't wanted to meet Medich, who launched into a pitch about what Rivercorp could do for Country Energy and complained about the difficulties his company had had trying to get work with the power provider. Rivercorp had gone through Country Energy's normal tender processes for contractors and hadn't been selected. As Medich and Shipley spoke, Macdonald, who had stayed silent, ordered four bottles of wine at $130 each. Adding to Murray's discomfort at being lobbied over a meal, Country Energy's probity rules forbade him from accepting gifts from potential suppliers. That meant he would have to cover the bill for dinner, which was rapidly heading towards $850.

Another strange thing was going on that evening. At a nearby table sat an unusual group: four or five swarthy men in their fifties and sixties and four or five attractive Asian women in tight clothing. Shipley had been sitting with the group before he crashed the Macdonald dinner.

'That's an interesting table you guys have come from,' Murray said.

Medich told him the women were Japanese or Chinese students. 'If you're nice to them, they will be nice to you,' he said. Laughter followed. It was much later before Murray cottoned on to what was happening. Medich had arranged for the women to be present. He offered Macdonald his pick.

Tiffanie, an attractive, petite Chinese woman in her thirties, was one of the group at the table. A few months before the dinner at Tuscany, Tiffanie, bored with her life and married to a man who didn't seem interested in her, started having sex for money. Through her escort agency she met Fortunato Gattellari, a former Australian featherweight boxing champion who worked with Medich.

Gattellari asked Tiffanie to go to Tuscany on that July night. She went along with a Taiwanese friend who also worked in the sex industry. As the men in suits on the nearby table wound up their meal, Gattellari told Tiffanie he had a job for her. He then drove her Honda to the Four Seasons Hotel in Sydney's Rocks district, where they left the car with valet parking. 'You will see some important person for me,' Gattellari told Tiffanie. 'Just treat him well.'

Gattellari picked up the $400 hotel tab, took Tiffanie upstairs to a room and left. She would later describe to a corruption inquiry what happened. Macdonald, overweight and bald, walked in, took off his coat and hung it up. Tiffanie sat on a chair and said hello. The conversation wasn't deep and didn't last long. Macdonald told Tiffanie she was tiny. Tiffanie told him he was tall. Tiffanie undressed to her underwear. Macdonald began kissing her roughly. She could smell wine on his breath from the dinner at Tuscany. She was so repulsed by the huge man that she felt like vomiting, but Macdonald obviously thought he'd made an impression. 'If you knew who I was, you would be very surprised,' he boasted.

Perhaps overwhelmed by his huge meal and an afternoon of drinking expensive wine, Macdonald chose to keep his clothes on. There was sexual contact between the two – neither side has revealed exactly what – which stopped short of full intercourse. Macdonald would later claim he went to the hotel room expecting a neck massage and fell asleep as soon as his head hit the pillow.

Around the time Macdonald was getting to know Tiffanie, Medich and Gattellari were plotting to kill a man, according to court documents. Medich was being sued over a failed property development by Michael McGurk, a former business partner, and was so rattled by the dispute he wanted him dead, according to Gattellari.

Gattellari claims Medich told him: 'I need to put an end to this. I need some help from you. I need you to find someone to kill him for me.'

'Are you sure about this?' Gattellari says he responded. 'Because there is no going back?'

'Yes, I am absolutely sure. If you can find someone, I want him dead.'

Gattellari hired Haissam Safetli to kill McGurk for $500,000, police later alleged. A tough negotiator, Medich initially complained that the price was too high. He agreed to pay $300,000 for the murder and $200,000 for later threats to McGurk's wife, Kimberley, so she would drop the lawsuits.

At 6.25 p.m. on 3 September 2009 McGurk arrived at his home in the posh suburb of Cremorne with takeaway for the family dinner and his ten-year-old son, Luc, in the passenger seat of his Mercedes-Benz. Safetli and Christopher Estephan approached the car, police alleged, and McGurk was shot once in the head. He died in front of his son. A witness heard the boy screaming for his mother.[2]

Sydney was used to suburban slayings, which are covered in sensational detail on the TV news and in the tabloid *Daily Telegraph*. But McGurk's murder stunned the city. There was widespread revulsion that an apparently loving father was shot dead in front of his child. The city's affluent north shore wasn't used to extreme violence – that was normally confined to the poorer suburbs of Sydney's west.

Within days a darker picture emerged of McGurk, who grew up in a tough suburb of Glasgow and moved to Australia as a young man. A property developer and loan shark, McGurk had been charged twice with firebombing houses, including one in affluent Point Piper. The charges were dropped just before he was killed.

McGurk was blackmailing Medich. That February he had secretly recorded Medich boasting he had influence with several government officials and politicians, including former federal minister Graham Richardson, a New South Wales police minister, the director general of the Department of Planning, Sam Haddad, and various state MPs.

Haddad had been paid to rezone land Medich owned at Badgerys Creek, on Sydney's outskirts, the property developer claimed.

McGurk thought the recording, which could threaten the Labor government's very existence, was his ticket to destroy Medich. He made copies and distributed them to friends for safekeeping. He didn't realise the entire conversation was a lie. None of the people discussed by Medich were on the take, and Medich had dropped their names to convince McGurk that he didn't need his help. Both men were playing each other.

'It could bring down the government,' blared the headline on the *Sydney Morning Herald*'s front page two days after McGurk's murder. Journalists Kate McClymont and Vanda Carson had been told about the secret recording which they wrote contained 'revelations about the bribing of senior government figures'. The *Herald* was taking the possibility of an official link to the sensational killing seriously. The rest of the media leapt on the story.

Nathan Rees was desperate to show voters the government wasn't corrupt. But he didn't want to get into a public fight with the *Herald*, which could make his life hell. The article incensed his planning minister, Kristina Keneally. A former theology student who had been in the job only a year, she had heard of Medich through her exposure to the property industry but had no idea who McGurk was. She knew that planning decisions in any large city were vulnerable to corruption. But she trusted Haddad, whose mug-shot-like photo the *Herald* published online next to pictures of Medich and McGurk.

Not long after the story broke, the state's Independent Commission Against Corruption asked for help to investigate the corruption allegations. Rees was receptive. ICAC's commissioner, David Ipp, then formally wrote to Rees seeking changes to the law to allow the commission to use the McGurk–Medich recording in evidence. Because the recording may have been created illegally and wouldn't normally be admissible, Rees discussed the issue with the NSW attorney-general, John Hatzistergos. They agreed, because of the serious allegations, that the law should be changed to let ICAC use the tapes in the McGurk case only. Recordings obtained illegally in other cases would not be allowed in corruption hearings.

New legislation usually has to be approved by government MPs before it is introduced in parliament. At a meeting of the Labor caucus Rees explained why ICAC needed to be temporarily given more authority. Even though such votes are normally procedural, Rees expected some resistance. He got it. Some MPs complained that giving ICAC extra powers, even temporarily, could lead the secretive body to abuse its power. The vote was called for on the voices. Aye in favour. Nay against.

Rees was stunned. Clearly there were more voices in opposition than in favour. Caucus had voted against a law that could clear his government of any connection to a horrific crime. Why would Labor MPs – lawmakers – not want to help fight corruption?

The situation was untenable. Rees's authority was on the line. So was the government's credibility. A second vote was called for, but this time on a show of hands. Any opponents would have to out themselves. This time, the vote passed. Looking at his fellow MPs, a shaken Rees knew there was something badly wrong in the Labor Party.[3]

## A lovely view

The purchase was, according to Eddie Obeid, entirely innocent. The backbencher, former minister, faction leader and businessman didn't buy Cherrydale Park farm for the rich seam of coal running under its grassy fields. It was for the view. 'We went and had a look at it and fell in love with the situation and the farm,' he told the *Australian Financial Review* in 2009.

The seller was John Cherry, an accountant famous in business circles for being Kerry Packer's tax adviser. Cherry had retired to Hope Island on the Gold Coast and no longer needed the 624 hectares, which he had owned for twenty-two years. The beautiful property didn't make any money. A large house sat atop a small, gently sloping hill, surrounded by manicured gardens hidden from outsiders by a carefully planted thicket of trees. A rare, unlimited water licence kept the gardens green. A few fat cows roamed the fields and kept the grass down.

The sale price was $3.65 million. The Obeids agreed to put down $1.02 million in cash and accept a loan from Cherry for the rest. The property was legally transferred to a company owned by the Obeids on 19 November 2007. As part of the deal, Obeid asked Cherry to change the name of the company that owned the farm to United Pastoral Group. Cherry, who was apparently oblivious to the coal under his fields, refused. '[Obeid] wanted to appear as though he wasn't interested in the coalmining,' Cherry later said.

Other friends from Sydney bought nearby, no doubt creating an interesting community in Bylong Valley, which is about 250 kilometres from Sydney by road. Justin Lewis, a friend of the Obeid family, bought a farm next door called Coggan Creek for $2.42 million in late 2008.

Cherrydale Park farm would become the family's base outside of Sydney. Obeid would go there to relax from his busy life in the city, where he oversaw the family's extensive business interests in addition to his political work. His five sons ran the family business from offices at Birkenhead Point, a suburb on the Parramatta River. Each son was assigned his own area of responsibility. Moses, or Mo, was chief executive of Streetscape, which owned the licence for high-tech street poles and sold them to municipalities across the Middle East. He was reportedly involved in the management of the Elizabeth Bay Marina, which has forty-eight moorings on the southern side of Sydney Harbour. He'd also paid $75,000 for access to Russian 'Geo-Radar' technology to locate mineral deposits.

Paul Obeid specialised in property, which was a substantial business for the family. They were involved in the development of a shopping centre at Top Ryde, in north-west Sydney, which opened in 2010 and is Australia's thirty-ninth largest by floor space. They spent $2 million on apartments in Elizabeth Bay and were investors in a modern, $64-million apartment building in Chiswick close to the family offices, according to the *Sydney Morning Herald*. They bought seventeen hectares of rural land near Port Macquarie, 380 kilometres north of Sydney, in the late 1990s, and eventually got regulatory approval to convert it into a housing estate for 5000 people. Once finished, it could be worth about $200 million.

Damien Obeid handled the family's investments in several cafes at Circular Quay, one of the busiest tourist zones in the state. Gerard, Obeid's second youngest, was the family 'gofer' and drove his brothers to business meetings.

The Obeid's purchase of Cherrydale Park was good timing. In 2008 the New South Wales Department of Primary Industries was preparing to sell exploration licences for eleven zones where there was likely to be coal. One of the areas, Mount Penny, was part of an estimated 700-million-tonne deposit – a massive and lucrative target for any coal company – and happened to cover the same land as Cherrydale Park and Coggan Creek.

Unusually, only small and medium-sized companies would be allowed to tender for the licences. The decision, which the industry regarded as unprecedented, locked out mining companies with deep pockets like Rio Tinto, potentially lowering the price. Outraged, the NSW Minerals Council wrote to Macdonald to complain. He didn't respond.

Exploration licences allow mining companies to accurately determine the amount of coal in a deposit, thus greatly impacting their value. Getting an exploration licence was tougher in New South Wales than in some other states. Permission from the mining minister was needed and the licences were restricted to specifically defined areas. Companies applying for the licences had to prove they had enough money to pay for the drilling needed to establish the type and quantity of minerals in the ground. There were huge benefits, though, once this was completed. The next step was a mining lease, which allowed mining to begin.

The state government's plan to sell the exploration licences didn't become public until August 2008. Roughly two months earlier, on 23 June, two of Eddie Obeid's sons, Paul and Gerard, briefed their lawyer about the upcoming tender. They said the government would ask for expressions of interest from mining companies interested in bidding for the licences. The start of the process could have a big impact on property prices in the eleven areas because investors would learn where new mines were likely to eventually be located.

'Once EOI [expressions of interest] issues re Coal Lease land value increases manyfold, three or four times,' the Obeid's lawyer, Chris Rumore, noted in a report of the meeting for his files.

At least one other company had told the Department of Primary Industries it would be interested if any coal licences became available. Struggling Sydney-based Monaro Mining specialised in uranium deposits and was keen to start mining coal, which was in huge demand from Chinese steel smelters.

In the late 2000s, Lehman Brothers, an august Wall Street bank, was trying to establish itself in Australia's crowded investment banking market. Lehman had hired Gardner Brook as a senior vice-president and asked him to drum up some deals. Brook knew Moses Obeid, who offered to help. His father was a politician and could help deliver high-level access to the state's politicians. Moses wasn't exaggerating.

Soon after, Eddie Obeid turned up for a lunch at the plush Lehman headquarters in Governor Phillip Tower in central Sydney. He had three ministers in tow: Ian Macdonald; Joe Tripodi, who was responsible for regulatory reform, ports and waterways, and small business; and treasurer Michael Costa, who also had the infrastructure portfolio. For the executives at Lehman, who hoped to win lucrative government work on big transactions, the lunch was a rare opportunity for face time with the men who controlled the government's purse strings.

The Obeids thought Brook could help them get into the mining game – a plan that could place them among the richest families in the state.

On 15 July 2008, Brook walked into the Monaro Mining offices without an appointment but with an amazing offer. He told

Mart Rampe, Monaro's managing director, he had a source in the Department of Primary Industries. His information backed this up: he had heard about Monaro's contact with the department, which hadn't been made public. Brook claimed he could make sure Monaro won the Mount Penny exploration licence. 'Brook has advised that he can guarantee a transaction for Monaro,' Rampe later wrote in a memo to the Monaro board. 'Mount Penny is the plum containing potentially 600 to 700 million tonnes of coal.'

Brook, who had been at Lehman Brothers less than a year, didn't have any experience in the coal industry. He didn't reveal his government source to Monaro Mining. Nor did he tell the company that two weeks earlier he had met Moses Obeid in a cafe at the Wentworth Hotel, opposite Lehman's Sydney headquarters.

The wealthy Obeids were interested in doing business with Lehman Brothers themselves. Obeid told Brook that his family was preparing a large corporate investment in coal and Lehman might be able to help arrange financing. He revealed that a tender for coal exploration licences was coming up and gave Brook a handwritten list of fifteen companies likely to be invited to participate. Number five on the list was Monaro Mining. After a night out, Brook scanned in the list and sent it to himself at 5.15 a.m. With the exception of two firms added at the bottom by Obeid, the list contained the same names of interested companies, in the same order, as those given to Macdonald by his department.[4]

Nine months after the Obeids bought their farm, an official circular revealed the government planned to sell eleven coal exploration licences. The decision to conduct the tender, which began on 9 September 2008 and was scheduled to close on 24 November, was made by Macdonald. He had overruled the head of his minerals division, Brad Mullard, who wanted more time to estimate the amount of coal in the licence areas. Bigger coal resources could have raised more money for the government. Of the eleven licence areas auctioned, the department, according to Mullard, prepared the details for all but one. Mount Penny was left to Macdonald's office to sort out, he said.

Once the tender process began, the department came under pressure to extend the deadline. Seven letters from mining companies asked for more time to prepare bids. Most of the letters were written by people connected to Cascade Coal, a private mining company which desperately wanted the Mount Penny licence. Cascade was owned by a group of well-connected Sydney businessmen, including Travers Duncan, an extremely wealthy mining entrepreneur who regularly lunched with Macdonald, John Kinghorn, the founder of RAMS Home Loans, Brian Flannery, another mining entrepreneur worth an estimated $600 million, John McGuigan, a former global chairman of international law firm Baker and McKenzie, and John Atkinson, a former partner at the same firm.

Macdonald, who had earlier wanted a quick sale, agreed to the extension. When the department's deputy director-general, Alan Coutts, opposed the decision, he was transferred to the state food authority and given a $10,000 pay cut.

The tender deadline was pushed back to 16 February, which should have allowed all the bidders to resolve any problems. Monaro put in the best bid and was likely to win the Mount Penny licence. Then, four months after the tender closed, it pulled out. The department asked Cascade if it was still interested in Mount

Penny. It was, and on 21 October, Cascade got the Mount Penny licence for $1 million. It was its only substantial asset. The following November, in 2010, a company listed on the Australian Securities Exchange, White Energy, agreed to buy Cascade for $486 million. The two companies already had close links: most of the investors in Cascade were also directors of White Energy.

Under the deal almost everyone involved in Cascade would become rich, or richer. Flannery's Cascade stake, which cost him $640,000 in 2009, potentially would increase in value to $50 million.

Another of the eleven licences went to Andrew Kaidbay, a 36-year-old who worked as a business adviser to the Obeids and at Yellow Brick Road Wealth Management. Kaidbay, who had no experience in the mining industry, flipped most of his interest in the exploration licence six weeks after he was issued it.

The deals and the personalities involved were too colourful to go unnoticed by the press, the Opposition and the New South Wales Independent Commission Against Corruption. The commission began investigating whether Macdonald, Obeid and the main figures in Cascade Coal had rigged the tender for the exploration licence to benefit the Obeid family.

On 17 March 2011, Kinghorn and Duncan were talking about Mount Penny on the phone. 'But John, I have asked a mate of mine in the department and he said the file is totally clean,' Duncan told Kinghorn. 'It's not like NuCoal, where the officers recommended a minister not do it.'

NuCoal appeared to be a reference to the exploration licence granted by Macdonald to the company chaired by John Maitland, the former union leader. Neither Kinghorn nor Duncan knew the anti-corruption commission's investigators, who had found a copy of Monaro's confidential bid on Cascade's computer server, were recording their conversation.

The recording was part of a trove of damaging evidence accumulated by the commission. The Obeids had secretly negotiated to receive a 25 per cent stake in the Cascade-controlled company that won the coal licence, according to the commission. Other documents showed Cascade cut a deal with the Obeids to buy their land for four times its value, a profit for the Obeids of $13 million. Another $1 million to $4 million profit would come from the sale of adjacent properties.

In October 2010, the Obeids agreed to sell their share in the company for $60 million. They got $30 million and were still pushing, in 2012, for the other $30 million. Investigators also found the Obeids had an interest in a separate coal tenement issued by Macdonald, known as the Yarrawa Exploration Licence. Yarrawa could be worth $30 million.

Trusts were used to distribute money to members of the Obeid family as loans. Direct payments would have incurred income tax. Eddie Obeid used some of the money to lease a $300,000 Mercedes-Benz while he was an MP. His wife, Judith, put down a deposit on an $8.5 million house in Woolwich, a wealthy harbourside suburb.[5]

All up, according to the commission, Macdonald's decisions helped generate about $100 million in potential and actual profits for the Obeids. It was potentially one the biggest corruption scams in Australian history – allegedly orchestrated by one of the most powerful men in the state. Unlike other successful politicians who used their power to pursue ideological or political agendas, the evidence suggested Eddie Obeid had a different motivation: he was using his influence over government to benefit his business interests.

Even though he was one of the wealthiest politicians in Australia, the only income he declared to parliament in his last decade there was his $140,000 MP's salary.

## Car crash

On 10 May 2007, Amanda Roozendaal, wife of state minister for roads Eric Roozendaal, was driving along Parramatta Road, one of the busiest in Sydney, when she collided with a bus. Her six-year-old Honda CR-V was a write off. When she told her husband, he knew who to call: his political patron Eddie Obeid. I need a new car, Roozendaal told Obeid.

The Roozendaals liked their four-wheel drive Honda, which was comfortable, practical and not too expensive. Obeid's son Moses, who liked to boast about his contacts in the motor industry, arranged for the purchase of a new CR-V for $44,800. Seven weeks after the accident, Amanda Roozendaal became the registered owner of the car, which cost her husband $34,000.

The $10,800 discount was a great deal for the Roozendaals, who have always maintained the transaction was above board. But as details of the convoluted car purchase emerged, so did a worrying question: was one of the rising stars of the New South Wales Labor government – a man who would later oversee the state's $50 billion budget as treasurer – on the take?

Roozendaal was a new breed of Labor operative. He combined an old-style factional ruthlessness with a new-Labor focus on extracting donations from the business community. State secretary from 1999 to 2004, he drove the party to become more professional at campaigning, researching voters and raising money. The state Labor Party raised $16.3 million while Roozendaal was secretary, in part by giving business figures access to Labor ministers at official fundraisers euphemistically known as business forums.

Roozendaal was extremely loyal to his faction. In 2003 he refused to put John Faulkner, a man respected for his integrity on both sides of politics and Labor's leader in the Senate, on the top of the party's Senate ticket because he was in the Left. The decision was considered overly factional by many commentators, even by Labor standards. Ambitious and intensely private, Roozendaal had no close friends in politics and never discussed his personal life with colleagues in case it was used against him, according to an MP who knew him well.

Roozendaal, who had ambitions to be premier, supported Obeid's Terrigals group when he was party secretary. He was rewarded for his loyalty with an upper house seat in 2004. Within fourteen months he was made the minister for ports and waterways. In 2008 he became treasurer, a job he kept until Labor was swept from office in 2011. Several of the Obeids' business ventures intersected with Roozendaal's portfolios, which included, at different times, ports, roads, commerce, state development and the treasury.

One of Roozendaal's problems was his wife's driving. After the crash on Parramatta Road, Moses Obeid asked a close friend, panel beater Peter Fitzhenry, to find another CR-V for the Roozendaals. Fitzhenry outsourced the job to a car dealer contact, who found a black CR-V at a Honda dealership in Liverpool in western Sydney. It was selling for $38,800, including on-road costs. Fitzhenry and his contact decided to charge $3000 commission each, which bumped up the cost to $44,800.

Obeid told Fitzhenry to go ahead with the purchase. The car was dropped off at Fitzhenry's office in Sydney's Inner West. Four days after it was purchased, Eric Roozendaal picked up the new Honda. The minister responsible for the department that registers cars didn't hand over any money or sign any registration papers. He had already arranged for the car to be insured for $43,000. A little over a week later he paid $34,000 for the Honda.

Strangely, the vehicle wasn't registered in Roozendaal's name, or even his wife's. It was registered to a person he had never met, and someone who had never seen the vehicle: Nata Re, a gemstone dealer. Re's brother was a business partner of the Obeid family. Nineteen days after the car was registered in Re's name, the ownership was transferred to another man, Keith Goodman, who never possessed the car either. After another nineteen days, the registration was transferred to Amanda Roozendaal, who had already been driving the car for thirty-seven days.

From the outside, the transfer of the car through two owners before it got to the Roozendaals made it look like they had bought a second-hand Honda, not a new one. The Roozendaals got a car for $34,000. The Obeids were out of pocket $10,800. The discount to Roozendaal – if that is what it was – never appeared on parliament's pecuniary interest register, a mandatory list of all gifts and external payments to MPs.

Paradoxically, the arrangement probably would have remained a secret if Amanda Roozendaal had been a more honest person. On 30 June, two days after her husband brought home their new car, Amanda was reversing on Buckingham Street, in inner-city Surry Hills. Music blaring, and with no reverse sensors on the low-frills CR-V, she hit a parked Renault hatchback and badly dented the right-hand-side rear door. Amanda opened her door, leant out to check the damage, and drove off.

Her bad luck that day wasn't over, however. Musician Richard Neho, who worked in the neighbourhood, witnessed the bingle. Realising the driver of the sporty Honda was about to make her escape, Neho jotted down the CR-V's registration number, added his phone number, and slipped the note under the Renault's windscreen wiper.

Casey Butler, who lived on the street, owned the Renault. Butler contacted her insurer and was told to report the damage to police. She went to the Surry Hills police station and filed a complaint. When a probationary constable looked up the Honda on the police database, it was registered to Re, the gem dealer who had never seen it. Re got a call from police about the accident. She immediately phoned her brother, Rocco Triulcio, who rang Moses Obeid, who then called Roozendaal and spoke to him for two minutes. Roozendaal then rang his wife.

The police tracked down Amanda Roozendaal at home. Chastened, she agreed to pay for the damage and apologise to Butler. Although the police didn't take any action over what the officer involved described as a misunderstanding, evidence of the misleading registration arrangement was recorded in police records.

Eric Roozendaal was a busy government minister. Moses Obeid was a budding property developer whose dad was an MP. They knew each other but weren't friends. Yet they communicated by phone more frequently than many married couples. The men exchanged forty-eight calls or texts between 17 May, seven days after the

Roozendaals' first Honda was written off, and 31 July, a month after Amanda's second accident.

Moses Obeid would later claim he was caught in a messy dispute between two friends. The $10,800 was needed to bring peace between Triulcio and Fitzhenry, he would say. Roozendaal pleaded incompetence. 'As the minister for roads, I really wasn't au fait with the intimate details of how to register a vehicle,' he later said. 'I was pretty committed to … work … and pretty hopeless with my personal finances.'

The Obeids denied that they expected to be repaid for subsidising the Honda deal. But they weren't shy about lobbying Roozendaal for help with their business interests, contacting him several times over a number of years. There is nothing illegal, or even immoral, about asking a politician for help to resolve a problem with a government department, or for access to public services. But Eddie Obeid's power in the Right may have created the perception that his family had more leverage than an ordinary member of the public.

Moses Obeid tried to get Roozendaal to fix a problem he was having with the Roads and Traffic Authority. Streetscape Enterprises owned a licence to manufacture a new type of street pole. Streetscape had made the shortlist of seven, from thirty-five initial applicants, for an RTA contract to install poles and flashing lights at school crossing zones. But the RTA was refusing to award the contract to Streetscape, which had never done such a big job.

Sitting in his father's parliamentary office, Moses complained to Roozendaal. He accused the RTA of stealing his company's pole designs and wanted an investigation. 'I didn't ask him for a favour, I just wanted to bring to his attention that the RTA were trying to screw one of their small suppliers,' Moses said later. Roozendaal either referred the complaint to his staff or the agency – he couldn't remember which when asked about it by ICAC afterwards. Streetscape still didn't get the contract.

The Obeids had ambitions to become property developers too, which required extensive interaction with the government. One project, which was overseen by Paul Moses, was to build a seventeen-hectare suburb in the Lake Cathie area of Port Macquarie. The project required about $60 million to $70 million in capital and was expected to generate roughly $200 million in revenue. Eddie Obeid had been assigned political responsibility for the area by Labor head office. He asked Roozendaal, as roads minister, to improve a section of the Pacific Highway near Port Macquarie. Improving the road would make access to the suburb easier, potentially increasing its value. Obeid didn't mention his family's financial interest in the area, and Roozendaal later said he was unaware of it.

In 2003, the Obeids paid $2.4 million for the rights to operate three Circular Quay cafes. The land and buildings were owned by state government agencies. In official documents the leaseholder of the cafes – the Arc, Quay Eatery and Sorrentino – was identified as John Abood, Obeid's brother-in-law. In reality, Abood's business acted as a front for the Obeid family, according to court documents obtained by *Sydney Morning Herald* journalists Linton Besser and Kate McClymont. Two years after Obeid bought in, Roozendaal, who was the waterways minister, claimed Obeid asked him to stop a new tender for the cafe leases going ahead because it would have created more competition for his company. Roozendaal refused to go along with the plan to open the leases to tender, but later said he didn't know the Obeids owned the cafes and he was merely putting off a controversial decision.[6]

Obeid was an astute businessman and politician. His businesses and investments were held in trusts or by family members, which allowed him to avoid disclosing them on parliament's compulsory register of MPs' financial interests. That helped avoid unwanted attention from the media and the Liberal Party. Smart as he was, Obeid made a major miscalculation. He was too powerful in the Labor Party to avoid scrutiny. When corruption investigators began examining the Labor government, he became their top target.

## Losing control

Nathan Rees's rugged looks, direct style and practical intelligence should have made him a successful Labor leader. When he became premier of New South Wales, the government was consumed by ill-discipline, rampant self-interest and corruption. He found the job impossibly difficult.

After Bob Carr stepped down as premier in August 2005 and was replaced by Morris Iemma, party headquarters adopted a more American approach. The leader became, even more than in the past, the personification of the government. Emphasising the team was out.

The shift had important consequences. In an effort to distinguish Iemma's decisions from his popular predecessor, party officials criticised Carr's period in office. The comments were mostly made privately to journalists and others. But they were sometimes made publicly too.

As a political strategy, it had merit. Long-term governments in stable, wealthy societies, including Labor in New South Wales, struggle to appear fresh. Portraying the new guy as the leader to fix up the mistakes of the old guy is a trick to avoid voter boredom.

And there is an appetite in the media for the approach. Newspapers, radio and TV news programs, facing more competition for people's time, prefer to concentrate on political leaders at the expense of the examination of policy, which can be tedious.

The leader-centric approach also illustrated the Labor government's greatest vulnerability: party head office, only nominally accountable to the parliamentary leader, was dictating strategy. The premier and his staff didn't control the message.

Initially, the presidential approach seemed to work. Voters embraced Iemma's slightly colourless style after Carr's intellectualism. Despite a dull campaign slogan – 'More to do, but we're heading in the right direction' – Iemma won the 2007 election with the loss of only three seats. It was an impressive Labor win after twelve years in office. But when Iemma tried to sell the state government's inefficient electricity-producing businesses, the union movement turned on him. Bernie Riordan, the state Labor president and secretary of the Electrical Trades Union, refused to support the policy, triggering chaos within the party and destroying the sense of discipline and professionalism built by Carr over seventeen years as leader. Unable to get his own party to back him, Iemma gave up and quit. The Terrigals decided to replace him with Rees, the minister for emergency services.

Rees had the blue-collar-intellectual background of a Labor politician from an earlier era. After leaving school he took on an indentured apprenticeship as a greenkeeper. He then quit, enrolled in an English literature degree at Sydney University and graduated with honours. A top cyclist, he was in contention for the 1992 Barcelona Olympics. A few months before the selection trials a car hit him and he didn't recover from his injuries in time to make the Australian team. He became premier on 5 September 2008.

The fact the Terrigals installed Rees, a member of the Left, as leader was a sign of their utter pragmatism. Rees's integrity would help repair the party's image, they reasoned. Just as importantly, his lack of control over the caucus would give Obeid and the other Terrigals almost complete freedom to run the party without interference.

When yesterday's heroes become today's failures, those who follow are diminished. Over time, the party's decision to undermine the reputation of its previous leaders eroded the mutual loyalty needed to maintain discipline. Cabinet, the ultimate decision-making body, leaked. Instead of fighting for their causes inside the government, ministers gamed the press to kill off policies they didn't like.

It took four days for scandal to hit the new government. Police minister Matt Brown had 'danced semi-naked and simulated a sex act on a female Labor MP at a drunken party at Parliament House', *The Australian* reported. Brown denied the 'titty fucking' incident, as it became known, and said he was getting changed in his office when someone saw him through a window wearing boxer shorts. Unconvinced, Rees made him resign.

It didn't take Rees long to became paranoid about his cabinet. He was convinced senior ministers – including John Della Bosca, one of the top Terrigals and the minister for health, and Eric Roozendaal, who Rees had appointed treasurer – were leaking cabinet discussions to the press. A few months after he became leader, Rees decided to shrink the public service from 160 agencies, trusts and boards into thirteen large departments, a change that would cut a lot of administrative costs. He was convinced someone would leak the plan. The restructure would be portrayed as a threat to government services – which services would depend on the minister who leaked it – killing political support for the change. Senior public servants worked on the plans in secret. Cabinet wasn't told, a fairly radical omission for a complete reorganisation of the government.

When the initiative was ready to roll out in June 2009, Rees rang each minister individually and sought their agreement. All said yes, except one. Della Bosca refused to return the premier's call.

Rees's serious, almost depressed public persona had failed to inspire voters. Friends and advisers told him to lighten up. But his determination to be a decent leader was frustrated by his lack of power over the party. He made some mistakes too. He abandoned selective media briefings of specific government announcements, a decision that made it harder for his communications office to play favourites or punish journalists who attacked the government. When he ordered the state government to stop using bottled water on environmental grounds, there was uproar. What about commuters stranded without water in summer on rail platforms, his advisers asked?

There was a growing stench of impropriety surrounding the government that even the clean-skin Rees couldn't remove. Ian Macdonald, the minister for state development, primary industries and mineral resources, had been dubbed 'Sir Lunchalot' by the press after it emerged that a wine advisory body he had set up, and chaired, spent $150,000 on lunches, dinners and accommodation over six years, including $15,000 to charter a plane for a lunch at a Victorian vineyard. Macdonald had racked up one of the highest bills for overseas travel of any minister in the government. He had appointed people to overseas jobs without going through the premier's office. His decision to create a mining tenement over a farm owned by Obeid worried some of Rees's advisers. Rees didn't trust him. Internal polling showed Joe Tripodi, the minister responsible for finance, infrastructure and ports and another of the leaders of the Terrigals, was widely disliked by voters following a long history of controversies.

A Newspoll in the second half of 2009 showed Liberal leader Barry O'Farrell ahead of Rees 33 per cent to 30 per cent as preferred premier. Labor's primary vote hit 26 per cent, a disastrously low figure that suggested an election wipe out.

Pressure was building on Rees to act. He started thinking about what to say at the party's upcoming state conference. The party's titular decision-making body was scheduled for 14 November at the Sydney Entertainment Centre. Rees believed his speech would be a pivotal moment in his leadership. He needed to assert control. Ministers, MPs and the media – pretty much everyone interested in New South Wales politics – would look to the speech for signs of what Rees stood for and where he was taking the government.

Rees's support base was in the Left faction. The Right controlled the party. How far could he go? On the Saturday two weeks before the conference, Rees called in a small group of party leaders to his office to discuss if he should take a radical step. He was considering asking party delegates to give him the right to hire and fire ministers, instead of the Terrigals-controlled Labor caucus. The meeting was attended by his chief of staff, Graeme Wedderburn, Senator John Faulkner, a leader of the Left, Luke Foley, a head-office organiser from the Left, and Matt Thistlethwaite, the state secretary, from the Right. Senator Mark Arbib, a previous state secretary and a leader of the Right, sent his apologies.

'I am being urged to do this,' Rees told the group. 'What support will there be if I do it?'

'The Left will back you,' Foley told Rees. 'But the question is, what will the Right do?'

The meeting focused on Tripodi and Macdonald. Fairly or unfairly, in the eyes of the public they had come to represent the government's venality. If Rees were given the power to sack them, he would have to exercise it. Thistlethwaite told Rees the Right would support him if he went ahead with the plan.

At huge risk, Rees took the nuclear option. He demanded the conference give him power to select ministers. He announced a ban on political donations from property developers and tougher rules on contact between government officials and lobbyists and developers. Rees drew upon the federal Labor Party's decision to give Kevin Rudd the power to choose his own ministry. 'I come before you today to seek the same authority,' Rees told the delegates. 'Not after an election victory, but in order to win one.' Rudd, who was in Singapore for a diplomatic summit, supported the plan. 'It's a leader's job to select the best executive,' Rudd said. 'Nathan Rees has made that call. I back him 100 per cent.'

In an atmosphere of faint disbelief, the hundreds of delegates at the conference overwhelmingly approved Rees's plan. Thistlethwaite delivered the Right's vote.

Rees, the Left faction and pretty much everyone else in the party who didn't belong to the Terrigals were elated by Rees's historic victory. Finally, after fourteen years in government, a key element of the faction leaders' power had been broken.

But Rees didn't realise that the Right was indulging him. Based on assurances from Thistlethwaite, the faction's leaders didn't expect him to use the new powers against them. They were wrong. Rees fired Tripodi and Macdonald the afternoon of the conference.

Both men issued statements that implied they would go quietly and honourably. Tripodi said he still supported Rees and that claims he might try to remove him as premier were 'ridiculous'.

But the Terrigals saw the sackings as a double-cross and were determined to wreak revenge. Tripodi, Obeid and the Terrigals' leaders decided they had made a mistake appointing Rees. He was too independent. He had to go.

Rees had two choices: begin an all-consuming campaign against the forces in the party opposing him, or try to get on with the work of government. He thought he could hold on as premier if he survived to the end of the parliamentary sitting session, which was three weeks away. When parliament finished for the year, MPs would return to their electorates for the summer and some of the intense emotions created by the sackings would dissipate.

For a few weeks it looked as though Rees would survive. On the final sitting day, a Thursday, Rees proudly briefed the legislative assembly on progress towards the public funding of election campaigns, a change he believed would curtail corruption. 'The task at hand is nothing less than restoring integrity to our political system,' he told parliament.

That night, as he hosted a Christmas party for journalists at Parliament House, Rees got a call from Graeme Wedderburn. The next day would be his last as premier. The Terrigals had called a meeting of Labor MPs and planned to hold a vote for a new leader. There was nothing Rees could do. He refused to cancel a cabinet meeting scheduled for the morning. Only half his ministers turned up. Then, at an impromptu press conference on the footpath outside his office building, he launched an extraordinary attack on the party:

> A malign and disloyal group, well known to the NSW community, has made the business of government almost impossible. Should I not be premier by the end of this day, let there be no doubt in the community's mind ... that any challenger will be a puppet of Eddie Obeid and Joe Tripodi.

Anything Rees said was irrelevant to the Right, which was deciding not whether to replace him, but who to replace him with. The Right had two choices: a Sydney engineer who had served as the city's mayor for twelve years, Frank Sartor; or an American-born woman who spoke with a Midwest accent and entered politics through religious activism, Kristina Keneally. Even though both were competitive, they knew the government couldn't afford any more instability. They reached a private pact: whoever lost would not run an insurgent campaign against the winner.

Sartor had turned down an opportunity to join the Terrigals when he entered parliament in 2003. Never one to miss an opportunity, Obeid offered to make Sartor premier if he agreed to reappoint Tripodi and Macdonald to cabinet, one MP later said he was told by Sartor. Sartor refused, the MP said. (Sartor didn't make any reference to the offer in his book, *The Fog on the Hill*, and declined to discuss the matter.)

Keneally, a loyal Terrigal, won a ballot of Right-faction MPs twenty-five to twenty-two. Given that the Right votes en bloc in the caucus, the views of the Left MPs were irrelevant. Keneally was sworn in as New South Wales's first female premier on 4 December 2009. The *Daily Telegraph* marked the historic day with a cover illustration of Keneally as a puppet. Obeid and Tripodi held strings attached to her hands.

One of Keneally first decisions was to reinstate Ian Macdonald, returning to him his old departments: mineral and forest resources and state development. Keneally also made him minister for major events, which put him in charge of Sydney's New Year's Eve fireworks and the V8 Supercar race at Homebush. Keneally returned Macdonald to cabinet because he was a talented minister who could get things done, according to people familiar with her thinking. Others thought Macdonald's resurrection was part of a secret pact Keneally reached with Obeid to become premier.

Two months after Macdonald returned to his ministerial suites in Chifley Square, the firebrand former union leader John Maitland and other shareholders in the Doyles Creek exploration licence agreed to sell out. A private company called NuCoal Resources purchased Doyles Creek on 5 February and paid in shares. Twelve days later NuCoal floated on the Australian Securities Exchange and was valued near $100 million. For a cash investment of $165,623, Maitland had accumulated a stake worth about $10 million.

## Improbable leader

Kristina Keneally was an unlikely premier of New South Wales. Born in Las Vegas to Republican-voting parents, she met her Australian husband, Ben Keneally, at a religious conference in Poland. She dropped out of a PhD in theology when her second child was stillborn. Her sadness over the girl's death made the solitude of academic research unbearable.

Ben was deeply involved in the Labor Party in Sydney and had his own political ambitions. But his wife's vivacity, and the Labor Party's push to get more women into parliament, delivered her the safe state seat of Heffron in 2003. After four years in parliament, Bob Carr appointed her minister for disability services and ageing. In 2008 she became planning minister. As a minister she combined strong Catholic faith with a heavy dose of pragmatism.

Apart from her intelligence, drive and communication skills, she had another quality the party badly needed: a clean reputation. Early into her premiership, head office was trying to decide how to present Keneally to a public that knew little about her. It scheduled a briefing with Neil Lawrence, the executive creative director of advertising firm STW Group, which was founded by John Singleton. Lawrence was proud of being the creative brains behind the 'Kevin 07' marketing campaign that helped Labor win the 2007 election.

They met in Keneally's office with the party secretary, Matt Thistlethwaite, and her closest advisers. Lawrence ran through his idea to introduce Keneally to a sceptical electorate through a television ad. It would acknowledge Keneally's American heritage and point out that her mother and grandmother were born in Australia. It would emphasise Labor's plans to improve transport, health, education and the environment.

After introducing his ideas, Lawrence paused. 'We need to talk about the elephant in the room,' he said. 'The reputation of the right-wing powerbrokers in the party. If you can't distance yourself from them, I don't think there is any chance of success.'

Although he didn't mention the Terrigals by name, Lawrence wanted Keneally to implicitly distance herself from the group that had made and broken her predecessors Rees and Iemma and installed her in power. Labor would pay for an ad repudiating its record. Staring straight at the camera, Lawrence's script called for

Keneally to say: 'I know many of you have been disappointed with the performance of Labor. So have I. That's why I took on this job.'

Keneally flat-out rejected the idea, although went ahead with a toned-down version of the ad. 'We have to stop rubbishing our record,' she told her advisers. 'If *we* don't believe we are good enough, why will anyone else?'

Instead, the premier with the American accent, distinctive hairstyle and the weight of years of Labor infighting on her shoulders did something unexpected. She governed.

Keneally decided to focus on three main objectives: restore some dignity to the government, demonstrate Labor was listening to voters' concerns, and set an agenda for beyond the election. Her first budget eliminated stamp duty for many buyers of new homes and apartments and reduced payroll taxes, a decision designed to encourage employers to hire. She killed plans for a CBD Metro, a driverless train service linking central Sydney and Rozelle, in Sydney's Inner West. The project, forecast to cost about $7 billion, was bitterly resented by the owners of homes who were being forced to sell to make way for the track. Scrapping it cost the government $330 million.

Keneally wasn't afraid to play hardball with Canberra. When Prime Minister Kevin Rudd said in early 2010 he wanted the federal government to take a bigger role in managing and funding the health system, Keneally held out for more money. Everyone involved knew health funding needed to be reformed. Health costs were growing faster than revenue collected by the state governments, which ran hospitals. Rudd had staked his credibility on finding a solution, which weakened his hand in the negotiations.

As Keneally resisted – and happily let Victorian premier John Brumby take an even harder line – Rudd's annoyance became obvious. Journalists and camera crews were allowed to watch the opening comments of a meeting between the two leaders in Sydney in March 2010. It was the start of a tour by Rudd to nail down an agreement with the states.

As Keneally introduced Rudd around the room, he didn't look at her. When they sat down, Keneally offered a banal but inoffensive welcome. 'So I'm pleased that you've chosen to start here in New South Wales,' she said. 'We see this very much as a historic opportunity. We're very pleased the Commonwealth have taken this step and see the discussions now and up to COAG as very productive.'

Rudd's response was curt: 'Yup, well, let's get on with some health reform.'

The brief exchange got a lot of media coverage. Journalists interpreted Rudd's behaviour as a snub to Keneally. She did think Rudd had been rude. But she knew the incident had played into her hands by making her a sympathetic figure.

Keneally signed up to the health-funding plan when Rudd offered the New South Wales health system an extra $722 million. The state was promised an increase in annual health funding of 8.3 per cent a year and $4.9 billion extra between 2014–15 and 2019–2020 than it would have expected to receive under the previous arrangements.

The day after she cut the deal, Keneally walked in to a cabinet meeting in Sydney to a standing ovation from her ministers. In that moment of elation her thoughts moved to the state election, about nine months away. I can win this, she thought.

The health-funding deal was the high point of Keneally's sixteen months as premier. The government was about to be hit by a barrage of revelations so sleazy it would lose any remaining political credibility. Instead of trying to win the election, Keneally would have to fight to save the party from oblivion.

Ian Macdonald's political career was finally killed by one freebie too many. The *Sydney Morning Herald* reported on 2 June 2010 that Macdonald and three travelling companions, including his wife, Anita, received free business-class upgrades from Emirates Airlines on a trip to Italy via Dubai. Macdonald didn't disclose the upgrade to parliament, a breach of the rules.

Keneally initially doubted it was much of a story. What's the big deal about a couple of airline upgrades, she thought. She asked the head of the premier's department, Brendan O'Reilly, to look over the documents covering the trip. The next day the *Herald* had more details. It estimated the upgrades were worth up to $30,000 and were arranged by the racehorse breeding 'community'. The article drew a connection between the flights and Macdonald's decision to help out the horsebreeding industry during the equine influenza outbreak of 2007 and 2008. Emirates was owned by the Dubai royal family and Dubai's ruler, Sheikh Mohammed bin Rashid Al Maktoum, had a global network of horse studs called Darley, which included a stud in the Hunter Valley.

When the article appeared Walt Secord, Keneally's chief of staff, was on leave because his girlfriend was having an operation. He was in a waiting room at St Vincent's Hospital when his mobile phone started going crazy. There was something seriously fishy about Macdonald's trip to Dubai and Italy, he was told. Secord tried to get clarity from Macdonald about the flights. The answers were vague. Macdonald blamed an adviser. He said he didn't remember. The conversation went nowhere.

The government's internal review into the trip uncovered a more complex picture than initially published in the *Herald*. Macdonald and his deputy chief of staff, Jamie Gibson, clocked up almost $20,000 in expenses on airfares, meals and accommodation at the Le Royal Meridien Beach Resort and Spa in Dubai, which was owned by bin Rashid Al Maktoum. Strangely, Macdonald booked an extra room 'for no specific purpose'. Gibson charged $1594.67 to the hotel but couldn't explain what the bill was for. Emails read by O'Reilly suggested the trip was organised by the Darley group.

Six months after she'd brought Macdonald back from the purgatory imposed by Nathan Rees, Keneally decided to end Macdonald's ministerial career a second time. Secord, who had become expert at extracting ministerial resignations, rang Macdonald one more time from the hospital waiting room. 'Ian, you've got a very tough decision to make,' he told the minister.

To Secord's surprise, Macdonald didn't put up a fight. After a brief silence he agreed to resign. It was the quickest departure Secord had ever negotiated. A few days later Macdonald voluntarily quit parliament. He was out of politics for good.

A few weeks after Macdonald's resignation there was good news for John Maitland, the entrepreneurial former union leader. Maitland was made a Member of the Order of Australia 'for service to industrial relations in the mining sector' and 'social dialogue in developing countries and those undergoing political and economic transition'. Also, the first drilling in twenty years at Maitland's Doyles Creek project had found a lot more coal than previously thought. NuCoal Resources, the new owner of the coal deposit, estimated it now contained 420 million tonnes, up from 247 million tonnes when it bought the site from Maitland and other early investors. The upgrade triggered huge interest on the share market. NuCoal looked like it could be one of the hottest stocks of the year.

It took a while for the new minister for minerals, Paul McLeay, to learn about the existence of the Doyles Creek exploration licence. The training mine wasn't mentioned in any of his initial briefings from his new department. Eventually McLeay heard about it from some senior officials who were clearly uneasy with the secretive way the licence was issued by Macdonald to Maitland's company.

Concerned, McLeay discussed the issue with the Department of Premier and Cabinet. In turn the department hired a small consulting firm, O'Connor Marsden and Associates, to go through the paperwork and determine if something was crooked about the deal. The report, called a 'probity review', was the first sign the government was worried that Macdonald had cut corners to help a political ally win the lucrative exploration licence.

Keneally came into office planning to run a low-drama, professional administration that could regain the confidence of voters. It didn't work out that way. In the four months from 7 May, when Karyn Paluzzano resigned as the MP for Penrith, Keneally suffered one of the worst runs of scandals and resignations in the history of Australian governments. Paluzzano's resignation for rorting her electorate office entitlements triggered a by-election in her previously safe seat, which fell to an anti-Labor swing of 26 per cent. Two weeks later the Seven Network revealed that transport and roads minister David Campbell used his office car and chauffeur to visit a gay sex club. He resigned from cabinet. The minister for juvenile justice, Graham West, resigned as a minister on 4 June, the same day Keneally sacked Macdonald. West was upset the government rejected the recommendations of a report he commissioned on juvenile justice. Kerry Hickey, a former minister for mineral resources and local government, announced in September he wouldn't stand at the next election. The married Hickey had had an affair with an employee at Parliament House. When the woman became pregnant and had a child, he denied being the father. A month later, after being quizzed by the press, he admitted the child was his. In December, the Independent Commission Against Corruption found that Angela D'Amore, the Labor member for Drummoyne, had misused her electorate office entitlements. It recommended she be prosecuted. Keneally sacked her from her role as parliamentary secretary for police. In January the husband of education minister Verity Firth, Matthew Chesher, was arrested after he bought an ecstasy tablet from a drug dealer under police surveillance. Chesher was chief of staff to the roads minister, David Borger. He resigned in disgrace.

Keneally was exhausted by scandal. For the winter school holidays she decided to take her family to Ohio to spend time with her parents. She needed a new strategy for the election, which would be held in March. After hours of working through all the permutations, she ended up at the same place each time: there was nothing she could do to turn around the public's view that the government was irredeemably dysfunctional. It was doomed.

She got on the phone to Secord. 'We can't win,' she told him. 'There's not enough time to turn it around.'

Secord had already reached the same conclusion. Mentally accepting defeat allowed Keneally and Secord to take drastic steps. Along with Sam Dastyari, the head of the party organisation, they agreed on a strategy that would later become known as 'sandbagging', or 'saving the furniture', a phrase Keneally disliked because it implied self-interest.

Keneally, Secord and Dastyari agreed to pretty much give up any electorate Labor held by a margin of less than 12 per cent. The aim was to direct the party's financial and political resources into seats with strong Labor support. If a solid rump of seats remained in Labor hands it would make the task of one day returning to power easier. The party also needed to try to save the MPs who would be capable of serving as ministers in a future Labor government, no matter how far away that seemed.

Every seat was divided into four categories: A, B, C and D. Labor MPs in A seats, like Keneally, would be okay. B seats, which Labor had a chance of winning, would get all the government's attention. Ministers would visit, the candidates would get access to the party's financial resources and, where appropriate, be looked upon favourably for government resources. Members in C and D seats would have to fend for themselves.

Tripodi, a friend of Keneally's, was told it was time to retire. Guy Zangari, a young teacher and father of four from the Italian community, replaced him. Two talented Labor activists – Clayton Barr and Ryan Park – were selected for safe seats.

Keneally, Secord and Dastyari agreed to never concede defeat was inevitable, even though it was. Keneally believed conceding would make it impossible to credibly propose alternative policies to the Coalition. Even acknowledging the probability to other party leaders and ministers was banned. She was certain a private concession would leak, making her look dishonest. The only person she could afford to be honest with, apart from Secord and Dastyari, was her husband, Ben.

Although the phrase 'landslide' is frequently used to describe Australian elections, the reality is voters don't often swap parties. Any swing larger than 10 per cent truly is a landslide, which is why Keneally's decision to prepare for a 12 per cent swing showed she understood how much damage had been caused by the government's winter of sleaze. There was more to come.

A routine check of the internet records of computers in Parliament House by public servants revealed someone in the building was using an office computer to look at online porn. The culprit was McLeay, who was given responsibility for the mining department after Macdonald was fired.

Keneally was offended by McLeay's stupidity. The government had needed a minerals minister who could keep the department and himself out of the news. She had given the thirty-eight-year-old a big promotion. Why would McLeay, the son of former federal Labor MP and Speaker Leo McLeay, do something so easy to detect and so embarrassing for a politician?

Secord, Keneally's chief of staff, asked Keneally to cut McLeay some slack. He had only been a minister nine months. Secord thought the government could tough out what he saw as a minor scandal. The parliamentary report revealing the porn access was public but didn't name who was responsible. The press suspected it was McLeay, but Secord reasoned they wouldn't publish his name because of the personal nature of the infraction and the risk of being sued for defamation. (When a minister in the subsequent Coalition government was caught by police engaging in a sex act in public, the government stuck by him. The press reported vaguely what happened without identifying him.)

Keneally, whose religious beliefs made her less sympathetic to porn than other people, discussed the issue with her husband. The conversation reinforced her conviction that McLeay's actions were unacceptable. Secord thought pretty much everyone in Australia had looked at porn. But he knew it was Keneally's call.

McLeay called his wife and his mother to tell them what had happened. He left his parliamentary office and walked out into the sunshine to confess to the television cameras. 'I am personally humiliated and embarrassed but I accept that it's wrong, and that's why I've offered my resignation as a minister,' he said.

A few days later Secord caught up with Andrew Clennell, the *Daily Telegraph*'s tough state political editor. Clennell told Secord the paper wouldn't have named McLeay if Keneally hadn't removed him. Clennell thought McLeay was the culprit but couldn't prove it. He had planned to pin the porn use on an unnamed 'senior Labor MP'.

Keneally gave responsibility for mineral resources to Steve Whan, a water polo player from Queanbeyan, near Canberra. Two weeks after McLeay's resignation Whan appeared before an obscure parliamentary committee. The Doyles Creek exploration licence had piqued the interest of Coalition MPs, who peppered Whan with questions about the project. Duncan Gay, a Nationals member and former farmer, challenged Whan as to how a project designed to produce 450 million tonnes of coal could be portrayed in any sense as a training facility.

'Does it get to a stage where you believe that a con has been perpetrated on the people of New South Wales and what is meant to have happened is not happening and something very inappropriate is happening?' Gay asked.

A crack opened. Whan didn't express outrage at Gay's serious allegation. Instead, he revealed that McLeay, before resigning, had ordered an independent review of how John Maitland's company came to be issued with the exploration licence.

Whan published the report a week after revealing its existence to the parliamentary committee. It said Macdonald didn't breach his powers under the law when he awarded the lucrative licence to Maitland's company, even though there was no public tender. The report pointed out previous ministers had done similar things. However, the report recommended the communication process for issuing exploration licences be improved – an apparent acknowledgement that other mining companies should have been told the licence was up for grabs. Whan promised to put in place procedures to make the process more transparent in future.

In a sense, the report was good news for the government. Even though it found the matter could have been handled better, it didn't conclude Macdonald had broken the law or overstepped his authority.

But there were several important deficiencies in the report, according to a subsequent investigation by law firm Clayton Utz, which was tabled in parliament. O'Connor Marsden didn't interview Macdonald or Maitland. The firm didn't consider whether Macdonald had a conflict of interest when he awarded the licence to a senior trade unionist. O'Connor Marsden seemed to assume that Macdonald complied with the department's guidelines on mining licences. But the guidelines stipulated licences for mineral deposits as large as Doyles Creek, which aren't part of existing mines, should be allocated through a competitive process. It wasn't. In other words, the probity report didn't do what it was meant to do: determine if the process was ethical and legal, according to Clayton Utz. (When contacted for this book, O'Connor Marsden's managing director, Rory O'Connor, declined to respond to the Clayton Utz findings.)

In October 2010, a few months after Macdonald was told to resign by Walt Secord, Maitland converted more of his NuCoal shares into cash, selling stock worth $1.3 million. In December, NuCoal said it planned to mine and sell coal on the commercial market to raise enough money to set up its training facility for miners. The following day Maitland sold $3.78 million of NuCoal shares. He still owned 6 per cent of NuCoal, a stake worth roughly $15 million. The company founded on a quixotic plan to train miners was worth a quarter of a billion dollars.

# 3

**Kevin 07 – Hard times at the Health Services Union – Craig Thomson and his credit card problem – The Minister for Defence loses his job**

## Out of the wilderness

In early 2006 Labor leader Kim Beazley was struggling to gain traction over John Howard. Australians respected but didn't love the intellectual Beazley, who had been leader from 1996 until 2001 and returned to the job when Mark Latham resigned in early 2005.

A little over a year into the job, Beazley's performance was worrying the factional leaders. Kim Carr, a senator who ran the Socialist Left in Victoria, and Mark Arbib, the secretary of the Labor Party in New South Wales and Right faction coordinator, decided Beazley had become a hindrance. In February and March 2006 Stephen Conroy and Bill Shorten tried, and failed, to replace former leader Simon Crean in his Melbourne seat with one of their own supporters. Beazley didn't intervene, upsetting Carr, who felt

Beazley had a moral obligation to defend the sitting MP even though Crean had once been Beazley's rival. For Carr, it marked the tipping point in Beazley's failure as leader.

Carr's thick beard, glasses and woolly cardigans gave him the look of the 1970s high school history teacher he once was. A superb political organiser, Carr had an ideological commitment to government intervention in the economy. He was strongly in favour of direct payments to the foreign-owned car manufacturers operating in Australia: Ford, Toyota and General Motors. The car companies happened to be big employers of one of his faction's main unions, the Australian Manufacturing Workers' Union.

In early 2006 Carr came up with an audacious plan. The party's self-promoting foreign affairs spokesman, Kevin Rudd, would align himself with shadow health minister Julia Gillard, who had become the Left's most popular MP since winning a lower house seat in 1998. They would challenge Beazley and lead the party back to power.

Carr and Gillard weren't close. But the joint ticket was smart politics for the Left, which would get the deputy leadership slot. With his eye on his faction's long-term prospects, Carr thought Rudd and Gillard could run the party together for ten years and that she would eventually become leader.

Throughout 2006 Carr and Gillard held long conversations with Rudd to work out if they could get along. Rudd, who was adept at saying what his audiences wanted to hear, impressed Carr and Gillard with his commitment to high education standards, a passion of hers, and support for manufacturing subsidies. Sometime between June and October 2006, they formed a secret pact to replace Beazley. To succeed, Carr needed the support of the Right, which had the majority of Labor MPs.

Independent of Carr, Mark Arbib had decided that Beazley's weak public persona was holding back a large chunk of voters unhappy with Howard and contemplating switching to Labor. Party research indicated Labor wasn't gaining as much in marginal seats as it should have been given the unpopularity of the government's WorkChoices law. Arbib agreed to support the new Right-Left ticket.

Arbib wasn't in parliament. But as secretary of the New South Wales division for two years, he held a lot of sway over who was selected for seats, which gave him immense leverage over Right MPs in the state. Arbib's father, who was of Libyan origin, moved to Australia in the 1960s and became a property developer. He died when Arbib was eleven. Arbib joined the Labor Party when he was twenty-one, rose through Young Labor and was given a job at the party's head office in Sydney by the then state secretary, Eric Roozendaal.

Beazley finally killed off his own leadership with a gaffe about a popular TV show host. When the wife of Channel Ten's Rove McManus, actress Belinda Emmett, died of breast cancer, Beazley offered his condolences. Unfortunately for Beazley, he referred to McManus as 'Karl Rove', who was the political adviser to U.S. President George W. Bush. The slip reinforced perceptions that Beazley was out of touch with ordinary Australians.

Rudd called a leadership challenge two weeks later, on 4 December. With an election one year away and three failed leaders behind them, Labor MPs voted forty-nine to thirty-nine to dump Beazley.

Howard called the election ten months later. No-one in the Labor Party doubted his campaigning abilities. But even a great survivor like Howard couldn't overcome the groundswell of anger at

WorkChoices and the popularity of the fresh-looking Rudd–Gillard team. From late 2006, Labor was never behind in the polls.

On election night, Rudd declared victory not long after Howard called him to concede defeat. The next day he told his entire campaign team, with the exception of his two closest aides, they would have to reapply for their jobs. Many were shocked. After months, in many cases years, of loyal work they felt like they had been effectively sacked. Most got jobs in the new government anyway.

The election changed the internal dynamics of the caucus in important ways. Before he became leader, Rudd had secured a promise from the factions that he would be allowed to choose his own ministers. Once he became prime minister, the concession gave Rudd even more authority within the party than the considerable power he would have otherwise had. Being able to choose your own team has obvious advantages, including ensuring loyalty. In Rudd's case it allowed him to skip over newly arrived but already powerful faction leaders for ministerial office, creating resentments that would later fatally undermine his position.

Shorten, forty, Arbib, thirty-seven, and David Feeney, thirty-eight, Shorten's junior factional ally from Victoria, were all elected to parliament for the first time. Arbib and Feeney took seats in the Senate. Shorten, who wanted to be leader one day, was elected to the lower house. All three arrived in Canberra flushed with their rapid rise. Each was a veteran of factional wars at state level. They were used to throwing their weight around. They didn't see themselves as regular, first-time backbenchers. They expected to be taken seriously by Rudd.

The broader party, oblivious to the changing factional dynamics, was electrified by the victory. Rudd was only the third Labor leader to defeat an incumbent government in sixty years. He received more votes, in two-party preferred terms, than Bob Hawke when he beat Malcolm Fraser in the 1983 election. After eleven years in opposition Rudd had restored the party's dignity and opened the possibility of a new, progressive era.

No-one epitomised the party's success better than Maxine McKew. The vibrant television journalist defeated John Howard in the North Sydney electorate of Bennelong. Howard was only the second sitting prime minister, after Stanley Bruce in 1929, to lose his seat in an election. Many Labor Party members regarded Howard's personal defeat as apt punishment for what they saw as his cynical manipulation of tragic events, including inflaming concerns about asylum seekers to win the 2001 election against Beazley. Howard handled the loss with dignity.

Amid the euphoria, few commentators noted the victory of the little-known Labor candidate for the seat of Dobell, a couple of hours north of Sydney. Craig Thomson, a former leader of the Health Services Union, delivered a swing to Labor of 8.7 per cent, two percentage points more than the national swing. It appeared to be another sign of the ALP's effectiveness in selecting high-quality candidates for winnable seats.

McKew later described the excitement of attending her first meeting of Labor MPs in Parliament House, with photos of the party's leaders hanging on the wall and cheers rising as Rudd walked in. 'We all sensed the possibilities, along with the sheer thrill of the privilege and opportunity to govern for all and do good things,' she wrote in her 2012 memoir, *Tales from the Political Trenches*. 'We believed we would build the future, redefine the "light on the hill" and put an end to rancour and belligerence in our public life.'

For the first time in history, Labor was in power in every state and territory *and* at the federal level. The most senior Liberal politician in the country was the lord mayor of Brisbane, Campbell Newman. Labor's triumph was complete.

## Piggy bank

The two men who ran the Health Services Union, Michael Williamson and Craig Thomson, were the old and new faces of the union movement. Williamson was a butcher who had worked in hospital kitchens and decided to become a union organiser. He called people '*maaate*' and loved to rev up his members against the 'bosses' who ran the health system. Thomson, eleven years younger, was hired almost straight out of law school by one of the HSU's predecessor bodies, the Health and Research Employees' Association. He believed unions should be run efficiently and professionally. He also knew the movement offered a reliable path to politics for an ambitious young man like himself.

Several mergers with other health-related unions in the 1990s had increased the union's membership to 60,000. It represented a wide range of occupations from cleaners, cooks, security guards, laundry workers and administrative staff, to nurses, occupational therapists, junior doctors, radiographers, nuclear medicine technologists, radiotherapy technologists, physiotherapists, pharmacists, psychologists and medical scientists.

The sizeable membership made it a player in the Labor Party's factional politics. In New South Wales, where Williamson's authority as secretary was unquestioned, it was aligned with the Right. In Victoria, where the union was split into five divisions, it was with the Left.

Thomson was the most capable organiser in New South Wales and was rising quickly through the ranks. He respected Williamson's street smarts but rated himself more intelligent than the older man. By 2001, after becoming assistant state secretary, Thomson was bugging Williamson to step aside and make him head of the New South Wales division. Williamson, who had bigger plans for himself and the union, came up with an alternative plan: Thomson would move to Melbourne to head the national office. After a suitable period, Williamson would use the union's influence in the party to find Thomson a federal seat. The idea to promote Thomson and eventually put him into politics, which he embraced enthusiastically, was used frequently by leaders in the Labor Party and union movement to get rid of rivals or functionaries who were no longer useful.

In 2002, at Williamson's urging, the union's national executive elected Thomson national secretary, a job that, among other things, required him to represent the union when lobbying governments. The national office had half-a-dozen staff and annual revenue of about $1.2 million, which came from the state divisions that collected all the members' dues.

Thomson's new office was in a poor financial state and lacked basic controls. There were no budgeted forecasts of how much the union expected to spend each year, a standard practice in almost any organisation. Tenders and contracts weren't prepared for large contracts, prices for goods and services weren't compared, there was no formal purchasing system, it was not clear who was responsible for authorising payments and there was no policy covering expenditure on union credit cards.

With Williamson's support Thomson convinced the state divisions to double his budget. He improved the financial controls and invested more in printing, stationery and mail-outs to communicate with members. He boosted his own salary by $30,000 to around $120,000 and gave himself a union-paid car, which didn't seem unreasonable to the state leaders.

Thomson's colleagues in the Victorian divisions mostly liked him. He could be charming and prepared to put politics aside for the good of the union. When there was a push to combine the five Victorian divisions to eliminate wasteful duplication, including separate payroll and computer systems, Thomson helped convince Williamson to support the plan. Initially Williamson was happy for the Victorian divisions to fight among themselves.

There were, however, worrying signs about Thomson's spending. Travel and accommodation costs rose sharply. He liked to combine holidays with work trips and often charged the union for trips for his partner, Christa, who took seventeen flights at a cost to the union of $11,429, including $1086 on a Melbourne-to-Sydney return flight. In September 2005, the couple visited Sydney twice in two weeks. They stayed at the Westin Hotel and Meriton Apartments. The trips, including taxis, meals, car hire and petrol, cost the union $5492.

The longer Thomson was in the job the more comfortable he seemed splurging. Two visits to Italian restaurant Sarti in central Melbourne in 2003 and 2005 cost $1850 and were paid for by the union, even though the dates didn't coincide with any union events. In October 2005, Thomson gave a forty-five-minute presentation to the West Australian Industrial Relations Society conference, held in Margaret River, where he booked a room for four nights at the Quay West Bunker Bay resort, a five-star hotel popular with whale watchers. He drove around the region, which is three and a half hours from Perth, in a hire car, which the union paid for, charging meals and wines from wineries to his union-issued Diners Club.

Thomson's credit card records suggest he decided to begin paying for sexual services with union funds and using credit cards issued by the union to supplement his salary. Records of his spending show that over his five years as national secretary he made hundreds of cash withdrawals from the cards to cover personal costs, from snacks to hotel rooms and prostitutes. In June 2006, Thomson withdrew $500 on an HSU MasterCard from an automatic teller machine on the Central Coast. He headed to Sydney Airport, dropped his union-supplied car into valet parking, which cost $216, and boarded a flight to Melbourne at a cost of $729. In Melbourne he checked in to the Pacific International Suites on Little Bourke Street, at a cost of $658, and called the Miss Behaving Escort Agency. The union picked up the 91-cent cost of the call. Thomson's three-night stay in Melbourne cost the union $2100, nearly three times what most members earned in a week.[7]

Williamson didn't forget his deal with Thomson. In the mid-2000s he approached his two close contacts in the Labor Party's Victorian division, Bill Shorten and Stephen Conroy, and asked if they would find a safe federal seat for Thomson, according to a former HSU official who discussed the approach with Williamson. Struggling to secure seats to keep their own long-time supporters happy, Shorten and Conroy told Williamson that fulfilling Thomson's political ambitions was the New South Wales Right's responsibility.

Then, in 2005, Thomson decided to move the union's head office to Sydney. He chose a Pitt Street office building near Sydney's financial heart and set up house in Bateau Bay, a suburb of The

Entrance, a sleepy Central Coast town popular with retirees looking for good weather and inexpensive property.

Thomson was eyeing Dobell, the federal seat that covered his new home. The electorate encompassed some of the prettiest areas of the state, including long, empty beaches backed by huge sand dunes. Although held by the Liberal Party's Ken Ticehurst, Dobell had many of the attributes of a Labor seat. The region had the lowest median household income in the state and double the national unemployment rate. Labor had a reasonable chance of winning the seat at the 2007 election.

The choice of seat was no accident. Williamson had demanded that the Right leaders Mark Arbib and Karl Bitar find Thomson a seat, according to the former HSU official. Dobell was the best they could do. (Sources close to Arbib and Bitar denied they offered Thomson Dobell.)

Thomson hired an influential player in the local Labor branches, Criselee Stevens, to build his profile in the area. The union paid her. Credit card statements show Stevens shuttled continually around the area, using union funds to pay for printing, advertising, petrol and meals with locals from journalists to surf club volunteers. Like Thomson, she didn't mind racking up personal expenses, including parking, drinks, meals and taxis. On 13 January 2006, she charged $4.45 to her union-funded Diners Club card. Five days later she put 50 cents on the card. She charged the union $382 for a flight from Sydney to Hobart for her son, Joshua. In total, Stevens cost the union $154,713 in salary and expenses.

Thomson hired an aide to help Stevens on the campaign, Matthew Burke, who cost the union $41,707. In March 2007, Burke switched to the staff of Labor senator Steve Hutchins, who allowed him to continue to work on Thomson's Dobell campaign while drawing a government wage. Burke racked up $6705 on a Health Services Union credit card while nominally working for Hutchins.

Day to day, Stevens and Burke ran a community group called Coastal Voice. Using union funds, Coastal Voice was designed to tap into a potentially large group of voters worried about community problems who would be uncomfortable directly associating with the local Labor organisation. Thomson wanted the group to harness community activists and Greens voters to help build his profile. It would also complement the Labor Party's campaign attacking the Howard government's industrial relations policies.

Launched over a barbecue in a park at Terrigal Beach on 27 May 2006, Coastal Voice held meetings, issued press releases and printed T-shirts. A Coastal Voice forum at Wyong High School on youth, drugs and alcohol included speakers from the police force. Burke ran the Coastal Voice website and produced a few newsletters. The group prepared an ad for the local *Sun* weekly newspaper with a photo of Criselee Stevens and the quote: 'My name is Kerry and I have lived on the Central Coast for 17 years. I am involved in the Coastal Voice community group because I want my children to have a voice in the future of our area (Tuggerawong).'

Thomson and his staff set up a charity called Dads in Education. Funded with $10,000 from the union, the group encouraged fathers to visit their children's school during National Literacy and Numeracy Week and read to a class. There was a big public relations pay off when Channel Seven's *Sunrise* program ran an item about the charity on Father's Day, two months before the election. A beaming Thomson was shown on camera.

As Thomson ramped up spending on his Dobell campaign in 2006 and 2007, the drain on the union's finances became disruptive. To cover the money pouring into the seat, Thomson delayed or stopped paying some of the union's regular bills, incensing suppliers, who threatened to sue.

In May 2007, Thomson shut down Coastal Voice, which had been operating for ten months, and put himself forward for the Labor Party vote to choose its candidate for Dobell. The Health Services Union in New South Wales was a big funder of Labor, giving it a lot of sway within the Right, which wanted its own candidate in Dobell. Thomson's spending of union money in the seat pleased head office because it potentially freed up some of its financial resources for other marginal seats. Thomson easily won a ballot of branch members four weeks later, on 13 April 2007, and became the official Labor candidate for Dobell.

The federal election was held six months later on 24 November. Thomson's campaign was professional, energetic and focused on the Howard government's WorkChoices industrial relations legislation. Bob Hawke visited four times. On election day, volunteers from Unions NSW swamped the electorate with anti-WorkChoices posters and banners. At some polling booths they turned up before volunteers from the local Labor branches. In an area with high unemployment, the WorkChoices campaign was potent. Thomson received an 8.8 per cent swing, an impressive result given the national swing to Labor was an already large 5.7 per cent. Kevin Rudd became prime minister because of campaigns like Thomson's.

It was a great victory for Labor. But it came at a huge cost to the members of the Health Services Union who had bankrolled the campaign for a seat most had undoubtedly never heard of. All up, the union spent $267,721 helping Thomson win Dobell. Thomson didn't ask his members whether they were prepared to support his political ambitions. He didn't even ask his fellow officials. The spending never appeared in the minutes of meetings of the union's executive while Thomson was in charge.

Elated at his victory and with a promising career in politics ahead, Thomson stepped down as the union's national secretary three weeks after election day. He continued to spend union money. Six days after his resignation he racked up $550 on his union Diners Club card at the flash Forty One restaurant, located on the forty-first level of Chifley Tower in Sydney's financial district, according to the union's accounts. On Boxing Day, a month after the election, he charged the union almost $500 for a rental car in Adelaide and a newspaper subscription.

By the time he left, the union's national office was a financial disaster zone. Over his period as national secretary, Thomson's personal entertainment expenses charged to the union were $73,849. He had withdrawn $103,338 in cash from ATMs on his union credit cards, money he didn't pay back. In March 2008, as Thomson was settling into life as a politician, the union's national office, now run by Kathy Jackson, owed suppliers $1 million. As Jackson delved into the financial mess she had inherited, she realised Thomson had used the union like a private bank.

## Exposed

When Craig Thomson stood up in the House of Representatives on 19 February 2008 to give his maiden speech, he was looking at a bright political future. Like Bill Shorten, he was part of a new breed of union leaders who had made the jump to politics. Both were educated, young, articulate and intelligent, and both had used their union jobs to build a power base within the party that eased their path into political office. Some people thought Thomson might become a minister one day.

Any politician's first speech to parliament is an important moment for them. It is an opportunity for the fresh MP to articulate their personal philosophy, reflect on their values, and acknowledge the people who shaped their lives. The first person Thomson thanked in his maiden speech wasn't his mother, father or partner, or a mentor from his days in the Health Services Union or university. It was Mark Arbib, the powerful leader from the Right who could make or break Thomson's career.

Favoured by the faction, Thomson was quickly appointed chairman of the House of Representatives economics committee, a great job for a new MP. The position carried extra pay, required him to oversee annual testimony to the committee by senior figures like the Reserve Bank governor, Glenn Stevens, and to review tax, superannuation and other legislation effecting business. Arbib became a parliamentary secretary within eight months, which essentially made him a junior minister. Shorten, who had a higher profile, was made a parliamentary secretary straight after the election. Thomson hired the two party members paid by the union to help him get elected, Criselee Stevens and Matthew Burke, to work in his office.

Thomson's replacement as HSU national secretary, Kathy Jackson, was a gregarious woman with a ready laugh and a thick skin. A member of the Right, she had taken over one of the HSU's Victorian divisions from the Left with the help of David Feeney, giving both a degree of factional clout. Jackson was something of a maverick. She seemed to be more into politics for the fun than the power. Michael Williamson and other HSU leaders thought she would make a great national secretary, mainly because she would shamelessly harass ministers and backbenchers to support the HSU's industrial agenda.

The union's accounts for the 2006–2007 financial year hadn't been filed when Jackson took over in December 2007. Out of normal prudence, the union's national executive ordered up a professional exit audit of the accounts. The result was worrying. The audit uncovered a MasterCard account that had never been approved by the national executive, which oversaw the operations of the national secretary. The records showed Thomson had withdrawn cash from the credit card hundreds of times to cover personal expenses. There were also charges for brothels, personal travel, expensive dinners, perfume and clothing. The office was virtually insolvent. It owed the Australian Council of Trade Unions $350,000, a debt it couldn't pay.

Shocked, the national executive commissioned Slater & Gordon to oversee a deeper investigation by forensic accountants into Thomson's spending. The investigation calculated that Thomson had averaged about $20,000 a year in cash advances on his union credit cards over five years. Worried about the legal implications for the union, the national executive decided to send the Slater & Gordon report to Doug Williams, the industrial registrar and chief executive of the Australian Industrial Relations Commission, for possible legal action. A senior public servant with a background in trade and industry policy, Williams was the ultimate authority in the industrial relations world and had a staff of 240 and an annual budget of $60 million. If a union or employer group was corrupt, it was his job to find out.

Williams wasn't a conspiracy theorist. He wasn't naive about what went on in some unions either. It looked like one of the worst cases of union corruption he'd seen. Williams ordered his staff to start digging almost immediately and asked the federal government solicitor's department for advice on what laws may have been broken. He needed all the help he could get. Even though its job was to regulate unions, the commission had almost no investigatory experience. When unions broke the rules, such as by not filing documents on time, officials from the commission usually sent them a 'slightly assertive letter' of complaint, according to an investigator. Williams knew of only one previous investigation, in 1988, and it ended with a caution issued by the Commonwealth Director of Public Prosecutions.

Williams didn't have much time. As part of a plan to discard the unpopular WorkChoices policies of the previous Coalition government, Julia Gillard, the minister for education, employment, workplace relations and social inclusion, had decided to replace the commission with a body that would embody Labor's desire to bring more fairness into the workplace. She called it Fair Work Australia. The new tribunal would take over the remainder of Williams' powers on 1 July 2009.

One evening Williams' home phone rang. The caller was Ben Hubbard, Gillard's chief of staff. Williams thought the call strange – what was so important that the minister's right-hand man was ringing after hours? Hubbard wanted to know if the Health Services Union inquiry, which hadn't been made public, was focusing on Thomson. Williams told him there was no formal investigation into the MP – the inquiry was still at the preliminary stage – and the commission was examining whether there were appropriate controls over the union's finances. Hubbard didn't try to pressure Williams.

But clearly there were concerns at the highest levels of government about Thomson's past.

Most Australians had never heard of Craig Thomson until 8 April 2009. On that day, a Wednesday, the *Sydney Morning Herald* published a long front-page article accusing Thomson of using union funds to pay for prostitutes, his election campaign in Dobell and day-to-day personal expenses. Jackson, or someone else close to the union, had given a Canberra-based reporter on the paper, Mark Davis, copies of Thomson's credit card statements. Davis picked out four payments to escort agencies and a brothel totalling $3793. He gave copies of the statements to Thomson before publishing. Thomson's explanation, which was quoted at length, was multi-pronged: his expenses were cleared by the union's decision-making bodies, the allegations were triggered by an intra-union feud, the credit card statements given to Davis may have been fabricated, and other union officials had access to his credit cards.

Buried in the last paragraph, the article reported that Michael Williamson was overseeing an audit of Thomson's spending. There was no mention that he was Thomson's political patron. Over the next three days, Davis published follow-up articles that concentrated on Thomson's spending on the 2007 election campaign in Dobell and revealed the Industrial Relations Commission was involved.

The claims raised important questions about the supervision of unions and electoral-funding laws. Yet it was the news that Thomson may have put escorts on his work credit card that caught the public's attention.

Given the government's eighteen-seat majority, the story didn't trigger a huge political reaction. Thomson's future wouldn't alter the political calculus in Canberra. Opposition leader Malcolm Turnbull called for an investigation by the Australian Electoral Commission to examine if the spending on Dobell was properly disclosed. 'I don't know whether [the allegations] are correct or not,' Turnbull said, 'but they should be investigated quickly and certainly Mr Thomson should provide a comprehensive response.'

Thomson went on the offensive. A letter from his lawyers threatened the *Herald*'s owner, Fairfax Media, and Davis with a defamation suit unless they retracted the allegations. Newspapers fear defamation cases, which are expensive to defend and settle. The burden of proof is on the media outlet to prove the suggestions in its articles are correct. Senior editors at the *Herald* weren't certain they could prove in court that Thomson used union funds to pay for prostitutes. All it had was a bunch of credit card statements. Who knew what kind of explanation Thomson would produce in court?

Thomson was aggressive in his denial. As well as threatening Fairfax, he sued the Health Services Union and Kathy Jackson. In the New South Wales Supreme Court he sought back pay for regular and long-service leave he said he was owed. He asked for damages from the union for denying him natural justice, breaching his privacy and violating his employment contract, allegations driven by the leaks to the media about his use of union funds.

Labor Party members in his seat, who were more likely to trust their charming local member than journalists in Canberra and Sydney, largely ignored Thomson's alleged misuse of union money. Many Labor members who had moved to the Central Coast for a quiet, warm retirement appreciated Thomson's friendliness and accessibility. He always had a nice word to say and made an effort to turn up at party functions, no matter how small.

Nonetheless, some local members took the allegations seriously. They included David Mehan, a salesman for a superannuation fund who was Labor's unsuccessful candidate for the seat in 2004. Believing Thomson was vulnerable, Mehan decided to challenge his selection as the Labor candidate. If Mehan could convince most local members that Thomson was a sleaze, and head office didn't intervene, he could contest the seat for Labor at the 2010 election.

When the party's new state secretary, Sam Dastyari, heard about the challenge he asked Mehan to visit him in Sydney. 'Why are you doing this?' Mehan said Dastyari asked him. 'You know he's going to win.' Head office didn't want the adverse publicity of a challenge to a sitting MP. Mehan refused to back down. The party stuck by Thomson. Mehan was defeated 72 to 22 in a ballot of local members.

In the Industrial Relations Commission's final weeks, Doug Williams was determined that the HSU case would survive the transition to Fair Work Australia. He rang Terry Nassios, his chief operating officer and the man who would become responsible for the case at the new body. Williams said he wanted the HSU case upgraded to a full-blown investigation, an important legal step that would give investigators the power to compel witnesses to answer questions. Williams told Nassios that if it looked like the allegations were true, he might have to hand over any evidence to the police. Williams thought there might even be a negligence case against the union's auditor.

Williams didn't have any direct power over Fair Work Australia, but during the call he used his remaining authority to demand a detailed plan of how the investigation would be conducted and what would happen with its findings. He followed up with an email a few hours later to Nassios to make it clear he wasn't just giving advice – he expected quick action. 'I am happy to discuss these directions, but otherwise anticipate that the actions identified will be implemented expeditiously,' he wrote.

The record suggests Nassios wasn't fazed by the tough talk from his outgoing boss. As he began one of the slowest investigations into a union in Australian history, Nassios knew that Williams, in the dying days of his power, was part of the old guard.

## Brotherly love

Joel Fitzgibbon, a working-class auto-electrician who ascended to one of the highest political offices in the nation, should have been a Labor hero. He grew up in the New South Wales Hunter Valley town of Cessnock, where the belief in the rights of the working man was literally forged in blood. Rich seams of coal were discovered in the valleys and hills surrounding the town in 1856. Commercial mining began early the next century and the population exploded from 165 in 1900 to 12,000 in 1926. Men and women from all over New South Wales flocked to Cessnock, where jobs were plentiful but dangerous. An explosion at the Bellbird Colliery in 1923 killed twenty-one men, triggering a push for safer working conditions. On 16 December 1929, police confronted a large protest organised by the Miners' Federation against the use of non-union labour at the Rothbury coalmine. The mine owners had locked out their 10,000 employees for nine months because the workforce refused to accept a wage cut. When the miners attempted to overrun the site and rip up railway lines, the police opened fire. A 29-year-old miner, Norman Brown, was killed and many more were wounded in what is generally regarded as the bloodiest confrontation in Australian industrial relations history. The Battle for Rothbury became ingrained in the town's identity and across the northern coalfields of New South Wales as a symbol of working-class struggle.

Fitzgibbon was a bright boy not too interested in study. He left school at sixteen. The tough and dirty work of going down the coal pits didn't appeal. Instead, he trained as an automotive electrician. When he turned twenty-eight he tired of rewiring cars and got a job with the local federal MP, Eric Fitzgibbon, his father.

The Fitzgibbons created a Labor dynasty in Cessnock. Eric Fitzgibbon was a schoolteacher who ran the local Labor Party branch, was elected to the council, made it to mayor after thirteen years, and eventually took the local federal seat of Hunter when it became available in 1984. He was never a minister or a shadow minister or a committee chairman and retired uneventfully when Labor lost government in 1996. He handed the safe seat to his son, who had spent eleven years as vice-president of the local Labor Party branch.

Joel Fitzgibbon was better at working the factional system than his dad. His easy-going charm was popular around the party. He was smart but indiscreet. He didn't mind taking risks. He would share gossip with friends and colleagues that perhaps he shouldn't have. He liked a beer and a flirt. He became an influential figure in the NSW Right and attracted the attention of a shadowy Chinese property developer, Helen Liu, who told people she was from a wealthy family in the northern Chinese province of Shandong. Liu was a generous Labor Party donor and cultivated relationships with politicians, including Fitzgibbon and his father, who she took to China in 1993 for a week-long trip for the opening of a tourist development. In 2002 and 2005, when Fitzgibbon was a shadow minister, Liu paid for him to take two trips to China, trips Fitzgibbon didn't declare in the official register of gifts to MPs, a breach of the rules. Like many MPs, Fitzgibbon owned a house in his electorate. In Canberra he rented a modest apartment from a relative of Liu's. Liu had also cultivated a relationship with Bob Carr, the former New South Wales premier, who would go on to become foreign minister in the Gillard government.

Two years after he was elected to parliament, Fitzgibbon made it the frontbench. His reward for helping Kevin Rudd remove Kim Beazley as leader in 2006 was the defence portfolio. Defence was one of the toughest jobs for a Labor MP: any sign of weakness about national security or the U.S. military alliance would be exploited by the Coalition. The size of the department, which spent $22.3 billion in 2006–2007, challenged the abilities of the shadow minister and his small staff to follow everything that was going on.

After Rudd won government in 2007, Fitzgibbon was determined to bring the department and defence forces, which had a bungled history of investing in expensive equipment, under greater control. It was the ethics of government that tripped him up.

While Fitzgibbon was making his way through the political world, his brother was moving up in business. After running local councils, including Bankstown in Sydney, Mark Fitzgibbon became the chief lobbyist for the licensed clubs industry. In 2002 he was made chief executive of Sydney-based health insurance company NIB, which listed on the stock exchange in 2007.

In June 2008, Joel Fitzgibbon flew to Brisbane to watch a Queensland versus New South Wales State of Origin rugby league match. He had planned to share an expensive hotel room with Mark. When his brother cancelled at the last moment, Joel

Fitzgibbon put the $450 room on his credit card. Not long after, someone from NIB rang the hotel and said the company would pick up the tab. Fitzgibbon's charge was cancelled without his knowledge. Under parliament's rules, Fitzgibbon was required to disclose the gift. He didn't.

NIB was interested in winning lucrative contracts to provide health cover for existing and retired defence force personnel. It wanted to introduce into Australia the lower-cost private systems developed for the huge U.S. market. NIB had formed an alliance with a U.S. insurance giant, Humana, and was trying to convince the defence department it could provide the service cheaper and more efficiently. In July and August 2008, Mark Fitzgibbon wangled two meetings with Major General Paul Alexander, the commander of health for the military, and officials from the Department of Veterans' Affairs.

On one of the occasions Mark Fitzgibbon turned up at parliament unannounced. Joel was overseas but he got through to his brother's office, which rang the chief of staff to Warren Snowdon, the minister for defence personnel and science. Snowdon, who was Fitzgibbon's junior minister, was responsible for the general health of defence personnel. Alexander, the equivalent of a two-star general, was told by someone in the government to attend the meeting with Mark Fitzgibbon. One of the meetings was held in Snowdon's office in Parliament House. Staff from Joel Fitzgibbon's office were present too.

The outcome of NIB's pitch was inconclusive. The defence department didn't switch to NIB and Humana. But it was helpful for Mark Fitzgibbon to meet Alexander. If NIB were going to win contracts with the defence department in future, it needed Alexander onside. Fitzgibbon was using his brother to get to Alexander.

Meanwhile, Joel Fitzgibbon was embroiled in a public spat with his department. Several hundred soldiers in the Special Air Service regiment had been overpaid due to an administrative error and were being pursued by debt collectors or had had their pay docked. The news triggered outrage when it became public in 2009. The media whipped up anger that the elite soldiers would have to return the money. Fitzgibbon sided with public opinion. He said the soldiers could keep the overpayments and described the department's handling of the matter as 'incompetent', an assessment even some Liberals agreed with.

Tensions between a defence minister and his department aren't unusual. In Fitzgibbon's case they rapidly got out of hand. In March 2009, *The Age* and the *Sydney Morning Herald* reported that the Department of Defence had conducted a secret investigation into Fitzgibbon's friendship with Liu, which it thought was a risk to national security. Officers from the Defence Signals Directorate accessed the computer network in Fitzgibbon's office and got a copy of Liu's bank account number, according to the article.

The news that defence department spies might be spying on their own minister was bizarre. But it was a small lie that did the most damage to Fitzgibbon. In an effort to explain the innocent nature of Fitzgibbon's relationship with Liu, his office claimed that the two families – politicians from the Hunter Valley and property developers from northern China – had a longstanding personal friendship and exchanged small birthday and Christmas gifts. It was a heroic stretching of the truth.

The day the article was published, Fitzgibbon came clean: Liu had sent him on two trips to China when he was in opposition, gifts he hadn't declared. She had also given him a suit, which he said he returned. (There was an even more damaging side to the story that didn't come out at the time. Liu and her then boyfriend had obtained Australian citizenship through sham marriages in 1989 or 1990 with two young Australians, David Shultz and Grace Clague, according to an investigation by *The Age*. Shultz and Clague, who were aged between eighteen and twenty at the time, agreed to the marriages because they were told Liu or her partner would be at risk of prosecution if they returned to China. 'They seemed honest, caring people and I believed their lives were at stake,' Clague told *The Age*, which published the article in April 2013. More than two years after the marriage, Liu signed statutory declarations stating she was in a genuine relationship with her husband and was granted permanent residency.)

An anonymously sourced spy story had morphed into a clear case of ministerial dishonesty. Fitzgibbon's staff trawled through his travel records and discovered that his brother's company, NIB, paid for the Brisbane hotel room when Fitzgibbon went to the rugby league game in 2008. Fitzgibbon admitted the mistake in parliament and apologised.

Rudd, who was on a trip to Washington, was angry at Fitzgibbon's lack of judgement over the China trips. Plenty of MPs accept free flights. Why hide it? Rudd let Fitzgibbon keep his job but warned it was his last chance.

The defence department and the inspector general of intelligence and security, Ian Carnell, investigated whether the department was spying on Fitzgibbon. They found no evidence it was. It seemed someone had maliciously leaked incorrect information to embarrass the minister.

Whoever wanted to take down Fitzgibbon didn't give up. Three months after the minister admitted to the free trips to China, a man dropped an envelope at the entrance to the Senate wing of Parliament House. The envelope, which didn't have identifiable markings, was addressed to the Liberal Party's spokesman for defence, Senator David Johnston. A security guard rang Johnston's office and asked for someone to collect it.

One of Johnston's advisers, Russell Stranger, got to the Senate foyer a couple of minutes after the man left. He asked the guards who the man was. 'We don't know his name but he looks familiar,' they said. Stranger opened the envelope as he walked back to his office. Inside was a one-and-a-half-page unsigned letter suggesting questions Johnston should ask at a parliamentary committee hearing the following day. The topic: Joel Fitzgibbon's brother.

The next day top officials from the defence hierarchy gathered in a Senate committee room for regular budget estimates hearings. It was the only time opposition senators like Johnston got to question public servants in person about spending in their departments. One of the generals taking questions was Alexander, the man who attended the meetings with Mark Fitzgibbon – meetings that had never been made public. After determining that the U.S. insurance company Humana was at the meeting, Johnston asked Alexander who else attended.

**ALEXANDER:** I cannot recall, but I believe there were possibly representatives from another health insurance agency. An Australian health insurance agency.
**JOHNSTON:** Could I suggest that that health agency was NIB Health?
**ALEXANDER:** Yes.
**JOHNSTON:** That is right. And who were those representatives?

ALEXANDER: I believe that the chief executive officer was present at the meeting.
JOHNSTON: Who was he?
ALEXANDER: Mr Fitzgibbon.
JOHNSTON: Mr Mark Fitzgibbon?
ALEXANDER: Mr Mark Fitzgibbon.
JOHNSTON: He, of course, is the brother of the minister.
ALEXANDER: Correct.

At that moment Johnston, who liked Joel Fitzgibbon personally, thought that the defence minister's credibility was finally shot. It looked like Fitzgibbon had pulled strings to get his brother a business meeting with the defence department. It was potentially a major breach of the rules, which prohibit ministers from cutting favours for family members.

Stranger, Johnston's adviser, rang Malcolm Turnbull's office and told the then Liberal leader's staff that Fitzgibbon was in trouble. The next morning Fitzgibbon got a visit from Rudd's chief of staff, Alister Jordan, and John Faulkner, the special minister of state, who oversaw the operation of ministerial offices. Fitzgibbon realised his reputation had been too badly damaged to defend his brother's contacts with the department. He saw Rudd and offered to resign. Rudd accepted.

The source of Johnston's information was intriguing. How many people would have known about a private meeting in a minister's office? In Fitzgibbon's Right faction, some suspected the leaker was Greg Combet, who had been the parliamentary secretary for defence procurement. Combet was an ambitious MP from the Left who regarded Fitzgibbon as intellectually inferior and resented his quick rise, according to people who knew him. On Fitzgibbon's departure Combet became a minister for the first time, and was given responsibility for defence science and personnel. Combet later strenuously denied being the source of the information.

In any event, the evidence pointed elsewhere. The anonymous letter for Johnston was written in highly bureaucratic language, which suggested it was prepared in the public service rather than a ministerial office, where clear communication is paramount. Two people involved in the matter, from opposite sides of politics, said the document probably came from the defence establishment. One of those people singled out the Defence Security Authority, a little-known organisation in the defence department that operates as a kind of internal security service. The authority was involved in the investigation into whether the Defence Signals Directorate spied on Fitzgibbon. (For this book, the defence department said it would not respond to anonymous allegations.)

Fitzgibbon was the first Rudd minister to lose this job. His departure in disgrace was a turning point for the government and undermined the perceived professionalism of the cabinet. His willingness to take gifts from a shady figure like Liu raised serious doubts about his judgement. He became a symbol of the casual disregard some top Labor politicians held for the rules designed to protect government from the culture of providing favours – no matter how small – for mates, relatives and political supporters. The small-town politician was unable to rise to the standards of a national figure. The minister embarrassed himself and damaged the government's credibility. Much worse was to come.

# 4

## The plot to remove Kevin – In the corridors and in the newsrooms – Mining tax, what mining tax?

## We need to talk about Kevin

In 2007, after eleven years in opposition, the Australian Labor Party was led to power by Kevin Rudd. A collective euphoria enveloped the nation. Rudd seemed to be a new kind of politician. A Christian, a family man, a man of intelligence, a man of goodwill, a politician not driven by ideology. His arrival promised an end to the bitter culture wars of John Howard's Coalition government. Australia could finally relax.

The Labor Party's leadership had banked on Rudd to deliver them power. Now, the apparatchiks, union secretaries and factional heads who controlled the party apparatus revelled in the favours, influence, ministries, money, staff, media profiles and almost endless opportunities for patronage that came with government.

Their bet on the intense Queenslander had paid off. But that didn't mean they liked him. Many had derided Rudd behind his back. He was neurotic, self-obsessed, a weirdo, they whispered. Rudd wasn't one of them. He'd never done the drudge work of a union organiser or spent decades accumulating power from the branches up. He wasn't an important figure in either of the party's factions. Almost all Labor MPs belonged to a faction, and these factions competed with each other constantly for control of the party. Rudd, a member of the Right, seemed to dislike factions, as though the grubby business of running a political group was beneath his intellect. When parliament was sitting Rudd never hung out, like his predecessor Mark Latham, at Canberra's bars checking out the pretty young journalists and political advisers. He preferred to focus his brainpower on policy. Not just any policy. The affairs of nations. The Mandarin-speaking former diplomat was an international relations wonk. He was at his happiest – in intellectual ecstasy – discussing the rise of China at the Asia Society in New York or giving a speech to the Oxford Union.

Rudd promised to temper the hard edge of the Coalition government – the tough treatment of refugees, a close U.S. military alliance – with Labor compassion. He vowed to an adoring crowd at Brisbane's Suncorp stadium on election night, 24 November, to heal the conflicts that had split society: 'The old battles between business and unions, the old battles between growth and the environment, the old and tired battles between federal and state, the old battles between public and private. It's time for a new page to be written in our nation's history.' He apologised for the mistreatment of the Aboriginal and Torres Strait Islander Stolen Generations, signed the Kyoto Protocol on Climate Change and legislated more protections for employees in the workplace.

Rudd was, for a period, the most popular prime minister in the history of Australian opinion polls. Yet those who worked for him often found him a difficult man to like: self-centred, abrasive, grumpy and arrogant. As Rudd's ego blossomed after the election victory, his colleagues found he became more and more aloof. Even top ministers and public servants had trouble penetrating his phalanx of advisers. Many turned to his deputy, Julia Gillard, one of the few ministers with direct daily access to Rudd. A lawyer who started in Labor politics as a self-described socialist, Gillard's easygoing personal style hid a steely resolve and sharp mind that had propelled her to the party's top echelons. Gillard become a kind of mother confessor for Labor MPs and ministers, soaking up complaints about their leader.

Rudd's strong polling numbers belied increasing concerns within the government about his judgement. After Australia emerged from the global economic crisis relatively unscathed in 2009, senior ministers became worried he had raised expectations of what the government could achieve so high that voters would be inevitably be disappointed. It wasn't just climate change, which Rudd had called 'the greatest moral challenge of our time', but grand promises about education, health and social security.

Rudd's ideas helped keep his public popularity high, for a while. But they didn't appear aligned to a central theme, which might have created a stronger sense of what the government stood for. They also created a logjam within the government as ministers and public servants valiantly tried to keep up with the torrent of prime ministerial promises. Unable to quickly deliver, some ministers simply put off action by commissioning studies and reports, or asked public servants to do more research. Rudd's press office called it the 'kick the can down the road' strategy. The problem was, the cans, like Rudd's enemies, mounted up.

Rudd had a habit of getting powerful people offside. Bill Shorten and David Feeney were two young MPs with big egos who controlled the Victorian Labor Party. As the national secretary of the Australian Workers' Union before entering the lower house in 2007, Shorten was probably the best-known unionist in the country. His ego was bruised when Rudd chose not to make him a minister after Labor won power. Instead, Rudd made Shorten a parliamentary secretary for disability services, a backwater of policy designed to keep Shorten out of the limelight. Feeney had been the administrative head of the party in Victoria and played a big role in the 1999 state election that removed Liberal premier Jeff Kennett from office, stunning Kennett and the Labor Party. A gregarious personality and a close friend of Shorten's, Feeney was sensitive to personal slights. Not long after coming to power, Rudd met with right-wing Labor MPs who Feeney had organised to make some suggestions to Rudd about government policy. Rudd arrogantly dismissed the advice out of hand. Feeney never forgave him. Stephen Conroy, the communications minister, had had trouble getting time with Rudd to sort out some problems with the national broadband network, according to a person who knew both men. The two opinionated, prickly men didn't get along personally. Rudd would periodically freeze out Mark Arbib, a skilled campaigner and one of the most influential MPs in the New South Wales division of the party. Arbib wanted Rudd to tone down his promises because he believed they were raising expectations that even the most capable government could never fulfil. Rudd didn't like the advice and ignored Arbib's text messages. Don Farrell, a little-known but influential South

Australian aligned with the giant shop assistants' union, resented Rudd for dumping another of the union's MPs, Annette Hurley, as shadow minister for citizenship and multicultural affairs eleven months before the 2007 election.

In December 2009, Rudd convened a meeting at the Commonwealth Parliamentary Offices in Sydney to settle on a strategy for the election, which was expected sometime in the following year. He was joined by a small group of senior ministers and advisers: Julia Gillard, the deputy prime minister; John Faulkner, the leader of the government in the Senate; Alister Jordan, Rudd's chief of staff; Lachlan Harris, Rudd's press secretary; Karl Bitar, the party's national secretary, or administrative head; Wayne Swan, the treasurer; Jim Chalmers, Swan's political adviser; and Mark Arbib.

Bitar spoke first. He recommended Rudd call an election immediately after Australia Day, which was less than two months away. The rest of the group told Rudd they agreed. An early election would probably cost the party a few seats, they thought, but waiting for voters' cynicism to harden throughout 2010 would be far more dangerous. (The latest the election could be held was 16 April 2011.) Rudd agreed and told the group he would go bushwalking with his family in Tasmania over the summer, which would clear his head and allow him to come back refreshed to do what he did best: campaign. Head office booked advertising slots on television and quietly began election preparations.

Back from holidays and faced with polls showing the Coalition line-balling with Labor, Rudd changed his mind. Bitar was told to cancel the advertising slots and end the election preparations at head office. Rudd didn't even bother to explain to the group what had happened. Once again, he had refused to listen to advice.

As predicted, the government's fortunes started to deteriorate. In April 2010, Rudd abandoned plans for an emissions trading scheme (ETS). Given the importance he had placed on climate change, the decision was a huge blow to his credibility. A month later, for the first time, more voters were unhappy than happy with his performance, according to a Nielsen poll. The following month the Coalition led Labor 53 per cent to 47 per cent in the poll. The electorate's great love affair with Rudd was ending. Rudd's political authority had always been dependent on his public popularity, which was fading. Voters didn't know the decision to dump the ETS was made at the urging of Gillard and Swan.

Labor badly needed to regain momentum. Rudd decided to tap into the resources and energy boom through a new tax that the government christened, in a moment of public relations optimism, the Resource Super Profits Tax. The complex tax was designed to generate billions for the government and help smaller mining companies get new projects going.

Announced in May 2010, as part of a response to a review of the taxation system by Treasury secretary Ken Henry, the tax would effectively be a takeover of the inefficient state mining royalty system whereby companies were charged for the amount of minerals produced, not their value. Now prices for iron ore, coal, gold and other minerals had surged. Mining companies were making huge profits.

The plan was intended to make the resources industry pay up when profits were good, and cut it a break when prices fell. The tax would raise $3 billion in its first year, and would fund a cut in the corporate tax rate to 28 per cent from 30 per cent and an increase in employer superannuation contributions to 12 per cent from 9 per cent. Most companies and all working Australians would benefit. 'Politically it shouldn't be too difficult for the government to sell,' an accounting firm, RSM Bird Cameron, declared the day after the tax was announced. 'There are more winners than losers.'

Rudd and Swan could have expected the mining industry to be on side. Mining executives had long wanted a profit-based royalty system. That would mean they wouldn't be punished when production was high and prices were low, or during the early phases of a project when they were spending a lot on equipment and labour.

Naively expecting the industry to support the tax, Rudd and Swan didn't prepare it for the sticker shock: a 40 per cent rate, which it would have to pay in addition to the regular corporate tax. The tax sent shockwaves through the industry, which was facing a massive, overnight reduction in the value of assets because of the much higher taxes it would have to pay. Some Chinese companies that had recently invested in Australia would take a hit. Fortescue Metals Group, which was building a large iron ore mine in Western Australia's Pilbara region, was worried it wouldn't be able to meet the interest payments on its billions in U.S. loans after paying the tax, or afford to borrow more money. The company's chief executive and founder, Andrew Forrest, was advised that if the tax became law he might have to warn his lenders that Fortescue could be in breach of its loan agreement, a dramatic step that would shake confidence in the company.

The mining industry launched a ferocious campaign to kill the tax. From the start of May until late June the Minerals Council of Australia, BHP Billiton, Rio Tinto and the Association of Mining and Exploration Companies spent $22.2 million on an advertising and public relations campaign designed to make the tax so politically toxic it could never be implemented. The government started running its own pro-tax ads too.

Amid a barrage of daily hostile headlines, the government tried to negotiate a compromise. Complicating the discussions with the industry, there were two tracks of talks. Treasurer Wayne Swan led formal negotiations with the Minerals Council and the major mining companies. At the same time Rudd hoped to reach a deal with Fortescue that would undercut opposition from the other big mining groups.

Forrest, now ranked among Australia's richest men, and Rudd had a personal connection. One of Forrest's pet schemes was to create 50,000 jobs for Indigenous Australians through his GenerationOne project. He had grown up with Aboriginal children on his family's cattle station near Onslow in Western Australia and saw many die young. In 2008 Rudd agreed to support the plan if Forrest could convince other employers to participate. He did.

The mining tax was a make-or-break issue for Fortescue. Rudd was willing to listen to Forrest, who told him the tax would put Fortescue's existence at risk and make it harder for other mining companies to get started in Australia. Over a series of phone calls and meetings that dragged long into the night, Fortescue executives pushed Rudd and the Treasury to change the tax. Instead of the money going to the government, they wanted companies to be required to spend it on infrastructure. They would then own that infrastructure, but it could be used for the public good. For example, Fortescue, which had ports and train lines servicing its iron ore export trade from Port Hedland in Western Australia, would have to allow other companies to use its facilities, and would be paid a reasonable fee. Eventually, Fortescue argued, mining companies would invest in infrastructure all over Australia.

Fortescue's biggest competitors had different plans. In talks with Swan, BHP Billiton, Rio Tinto and Xstrata sought a simple but important change to the way the tax would be calculated. They wanted to deduct the existing value of their mines from what they would owe the government under the tax. High prices for coal and iron ore had driven up the values of their mines to incredible levels: BHP Billiton and Rio Tinto's Australian assets were worth roughly $120 billion each. If they could deduct even a small portion of this from their tax bill each year, the amount they would have to pay would be negligible.

Forrest flew to Canberra from Perth on Sunday, 20 June, and met Rudd at the Lodge, the prime minister's official Canberra residence. They started to thrash out a deal that would keep the tax at 40 per cent and allow Fortescue to spend the money on infrastructure rather than handing it to the government. Forrest and one of his advisers explained why the tax would make it all but impossible for Fortescue to raise debt overseas. Forrest was convincing but Rudd wanted more advice before committing to a redesign of the tax.

While Rudd was engrossed in the negotiations, an important government player was becoming even more frustrated with his leader. Mark Arbib was scheduled to see Rudd the same day to discuss the government's fortunes. Rudd cancelled. The meeting was rescheduled to the following day. Again Rudd cancelled. Focused on a mining tax deal, he was oblivious to a threat looming within his own ranks.

On the Monday night Forrest returned to the Lodge to thrash out the final details. The meeting was cut short by news that an aeroplane wreckage had been found in Cameroon in western Africa with no survivors. Several of the men on the flight were directors of a West Australian mining company, Sundance Resources, and were known to Forrest. He and Rudd had already wrapped up the key points of their agreement and agreed over a handshake to go ahead with the reconstituted mining tax. Forrest left for Perth to be with his family.

Rudd planned to triumphantly announce the deal on the Friday. Forrest thought the other big mining companies would take a couple of weeks to digest the new scheme and come out in support. Treasury officials had participated in the talks the whole way, which meant that Wayne Swan must have known about the deal, Forrest later said.

Meanwhile, tensions were building within the government. Earlier on Monday, a senior Labor figure had approached Simon Crean, the former leader who had become trade minister. Crean was told about internal party research that said voters saw Rudd as 'not of the people' and Gillard as 'trustworthy' and 'visionary'. Crean was shocked at the implication: the party would be better off if Gillard took over as leader. 'You are not seriously suggesting we challenge, are you?' he said. The other person said no.

Earlier, Gillard had sent an email to Rudd complaining he hadn't carried through on a promise to take a tougher approach to the thousands of asylum seekers making their way to Christmas Island by boat from Indonesia. Unable to get time with Rudd, several Labor MPs had complained to Gillard that Rudd's refusal to act on the issue was hurting the government in marginal seats with large immigrant populations, including western Sydney. In the email, Gillard bluntly expressed her frustration to Rudd. That night, after a cabinet meeting, she made her views clear in person. In a tense, fifteen-minute conversation on a couch outside the cabinet room in Parliament House she emphasised the importance of finding a new way to discourage the asylum seekers. Trying to calm Gillard, Rudd assured her he was aware of the problem and working to solve it.

The next day Tuesday, 22 June, Forrest put the compromise tax deal he had agreed on with Rudd to the Fortescue board. He planned to publicly endorse the new tax, which would be portrayed as a massive Labor-led and privately funded infrastructure investment program. Forrest later estimated it would have led to $200 billion investment in five years. 'It would have been a huge legacy for a Labor government,' he told the *Financial Review*.

Since April there had been murmurings about Rudd's leadership when he dumped a plan for an emissions trading scheme. But a challenge seemed inconceivable. No modern Labor prime minister had been removed by his own party in his first term.

Rudd thought rumours he would be replaced were 'absurd', according to one person who knew him well. Gillard was the only person with enough authority in the party to take Rudd on, and she had ruled out a challenge. Plus she was from the party's Left, which had never had enough MPs to elect one of its own members as leader.

On Tuesday morning, Labor MPs gathered at Parliament House for a regular scheduled meeting. No-one directly complained about Rudd's leadership. Bob McMullan, one of Labor's most experienced MPs, said the polls showed the party could win the election. In Rudd's office, there was relief. If there was going to be a challenge, there would have been signals at the meeting – posturing or positioning against Rudd, or a direct attack on his performance. No dissent was visible.

That afternoon Rudd and Crean met for a previously scheduled meeting to talk about the government's progress. Crean didn't think Rudd should be dumped because of Labor's poor polling, which he knew could bounce around. But he was concerned about Rudd's highly centralised management style, which he worried was making the government less flexible in response to urgent problems. He urged Rudd to resolve the main three problems sapping the party's support: the mining tax, asylum seekers and carbon emissions. For once, Rudd seemed to listen to advice.

Rudd and Crean didn't know Gillard had already, very gingerly, started testing her support to replace him. After the meeting of Labor MPs, Gillard called Kim Carr, the industry minister and a leader of the Victorian Left, into her office. She criticised the government's performance and cited the internal polling that showed a new leader would improve the party's support. 'We are sleepwalking to defeat,' she told Carr.

Gillard wanted intelligence from Carr about any possible plot in the Right to replace Rudd. Carr was in a position to know. He had a working relationship with Shorten and Conroy through an alliance – dubbed the 'Stability Pact' – they had formed to control the Victorian Labor Party. Because he was from the Left, Kim Carr would add legitimacy – and numbers – to a Gillard challenge.

Carr knew that the Right was preparing a petition to trigger a spill, but didn't tell Gillard. It was clear to Carr the plot had probably been in train for weeks. (Gillard later denied she raised a leadership challenge with anyone the day before it occurred.)

That night Rudd was the main speaker at the Business Council of Australia's annual ball. In a pugnacious mood over the mining industry's attack on the government, he expressed his displeasure with what he saw as an overly partisan approach by the business community to the government. Some Labor ministers thought the speech was way over the top. 'Why would he be out there insulting the business elite?' one minister later said.

The government was greeted the next morning, Wednesday 22 June, by an explosive headline on the front page of the *Sydney Morning Herald*: 'Rudd's secret polling on his leadership.' The article reported that Jordan, Rudd's chief of staff, had spoken to more than fifty Labor MPs to see if they still supported Rudd. *Herald* journalists Peter Hartcher and Phillip Coorey concluded that Rudd 'does not necessarily fully trust the public assurances of his deputy, Julia Gillard, that she is not interested in the leadership'.

After returning from an early morning soccer game to his office, Arbib got a visit from Feeney. Both later told journalists the article about Jordan ringing around MPs was the 'final straw'. After years of dysfunctional leadership, Rudd had finally gone too far by calling into question the one person who had stood loyally by him: Gillard.

Whatever the truth of their explanation, there is no doubt Arbib and Feeney decided that morning it was the time to launch the push to remove Rudd. One of their first jobs was to brief Don Farrell. He could deliver MPs aligned with the shop assistants' union. In a quick presentation, they gave Farrell the pitch they would use with devastating effect over the next twelve hours: the party's support is fading and Rudd can't win the election. Farrell was in.

Arbib, Farrell, Shorten, Conroy and Feeney then met in Feeney's office in the Senate wing. Fuelled by a mixture of personal animosity towards Rudd, frustrated ambitions, ego and a genuine belief that his removal would be good for the Labor Party and the government, they agreed Rudd needed to go. That resolved, there was one key question on their minds: could Gillard win the election for them? No woman had ever come close to being Labor leader, let alone prime minister. In a society becoming wealthier and less ideological, Gillard's roots in the socialist Left could be a liability. But Shorten, Conroy and Feeney were Victorians, the state where Gillard lived and was widely admired. They had faith her popularity would survive the difficult task of removing Rudd. Being from South Australia, where Gillard grew up, Farrell knew his state would go gaga over one of its own becoming prime minister. Arbib, who liked Gillard, thought Rudd would lose the election anyway. Badly.

One of the most important meetings in the modern history of Australian politics was brief. It took about twenty minutes for the five men to agree that Gillard would be a huge electoral plus for the party. What they didn't know was whether she would take the prize if offered it.

Concerned that Gillard was offended by the implication in the *Herald* article that Rudd no longer trusted his deputy, the prime minister's office scheduled a meeting with her and Rudd that day. The catch up was postponed. Rudd then tried to reach his deputy on the phone. Gillard was too busy to take the call. But she did have time to see the plotters.

That afternoon Arbib, Feeney, Farrell, Shorten and Carr gathered in Carr's office to brief Gillard. Everyone was on edge, aware of the high stakes. Over about half an hour, they tried to convince Gillard that a challenge was necessary to save the government from a catastrophic loss at the election. Arbib told her all the New South Wales Right MPs and most of its Left MPs would support her.

Conroy and Shorten were confident they could deliver the Victorian MPs. Farrell promised the shop assistants' union's vote.⁸

(Some newspapers later reported Arbib and Feeney told Gillard that Jordan's ring-around was a breach of trust and that she was highly offended by it. But one person present said Jordan's conversations didn't come up or weren't a significant part of the discussion.)

Offered a shot at political immortality, at becoming prime minister of Australia – a position never held by a woman, let alone a childless, unmarried, feminist atheist from the Socialist Left – Gillard played it cool. I'll go and have a chat with Kevin, she told the men. They had no idea what she was going to do.

As the afternoon wore on and phone calls started pouring into Rudd's office, it became clear to Rudd and his staff that something serious was going on. Was it a leadership challenge? They didn't know. Harris, Rudd's press secretary, walked over to the second floor of the Senate wing of parliament to see if anyone in the media knew what was happening. He ran into the one person outside the plotters and their supporters who did: Mark Simkin, the ABC's chief political correspondent.

A few days earlier Simkin had been tipped off by a source in the New South Wales Labor Party that he should look into the leadership rumours. For days Simkin tried to break the story. He spoke to all of the main plotters except Farrell. They refused to reveal anything substantive. That morning, though, one faction leader asked Simkin's ABC colleague Chris Uhlmann a seemingly innocuous question at the Parliament House coffee shop: do you think we can win with Gillard?

Uhlmann raced back to the office and told Simkin. The election was looming. Gillard had ruled out challenging Rudd. Why would someone so senior even be discussing Gillard as a possible party leader with a journalist? Both men thought something was going on. What they needed was confirmation. Uhlmann reached one factional leader who told him to ring back at 8 p.m. for the full story. 'But the news is at seven!' Uhlmann replied. The politician hung up.

Simkin was working on another story that day about the war in Afghanistan. At 6.40 p.m. he was in one of parliament's courtyards preparing to film his report. All day he'd been calling a key source about the leadership, who hadn't picked up the phone. Simkin decided to give it one more shot. The MP answered and agreed to talk on one condition: every answer would be yes or no.

'Are you moving to replace Rudd?' Simkin asked.

'Yes.'

'Are there cabinet ministers involved?'

'Yes.'

'Has Gillard committed?'

'No.'

The call lasted about five minutes. Simkin's heart raced. He had a huge scoop. He was also in a delicate position. There was no certainty Gillard would agree to the challenge. If she didn't, the plotters would likely retreat into the shadows and deny everything. If he put the story to air — and the evening bulletin started in about fifteen minutes — he could be embarrassed in front of millions of people. The ABC was the national broadcaster. It couldn't afford to get a big story like this wrong.

Simkin ran up to the ABC studio. Harris, Rudd's press secretary, saw him in the corridor. Sensing Simkin's urgency, he asked: 'What are you up to?' 'You'll have to watch the news, I'm afraid,' Simkin replied.

The member for Maribyrnong. Shorten said he won the seat by knocking on more doors than anyone else and shrugged off criticism that factional deals were behind the victory.

Bill Shorten and Kathy Jackson at a union meeting in 2005. Later, Jackson would compare Shorten's role as Minister for Workplace Relations to 'Dracula being in charge of the blood bank'.

The so-called faceless men on both sides of the coup against Kevin Rudd. *Left to right, top to bottom:* Mark Arbib, Paul Howes, Stephen Conroy, Kim Carr, David Feeney, Don Farrell, Alister Jordan and Bill Shorten.

Kevin Rudd in fine form on YouTube. Rudd delivered power to the ALP after eleven years in opposition. Highly popular with the electorate, he was disliked by many MPs within his own party, who saw him as aloof, grumpy and arrogant.

Kristina Keneally put on a brave face when Julia Gillard announced a carbon tax during the NSW election campaign. In private she was aghast at the damaging decision.

*Above*: Eddie Obeid arrives at the ICAC hearings, where he was accused of engaging in a corrupt coal licence deal with Ian Macdonald (*left*), a former NSW mining minister and his close political ally.

Obeid's son Moses ran the family's street pole business which was sued for millions by City of Sydney Council.

Eric Roozendaal, a former NSW treasurer, leaves ICAC where he was accused of receiving a discounted Honda SUV from the Obeids.

Michael Williamson, former ALP president and once the most powerful figure in the Health Services Union.

Police removing a bag of evidence seized from Michael Williamson during a raid on the HSU.

After a long campaign protesting his innocence, Craig Thomson was arrested and charged over his abuse of travel entitlements as an MP. 'I've done no wrongdoing,' he said after his arrest.

Thomson's accuser and successor as HSU national secretary, Kathy Jackson, found herself under siege from the media and her rivals in the union and the party.

One of Jackson's accusers, Andrew Landeryou, political blogger from the site Vexnews. Vexnews also took on Jackson's husband, Michael Lawler, dubbing him a 'hopelessly compromised, Koolade swilling judge'.

Walking contradiction. Peter Slipper in regalia as Speaker of the House. Slipper thrived on public formality. His private text messages revealed a very different side.

Anna Bligh's campaign to retain power in Queensland was fatally undermined by her claim that her rival would go to jail for corruption.

After weeks of public speculation, Simon Crean backed an attempt by Kevin Rudd's supporters to reinstall him as prime minister in March 2013. Realising he didn't have the numbers, Rudd did not stand. The fallout from the coup that never was saw the government ridiculed and several ministers demoted to the backbench.

Bureau chief Greg Jennett rang the ABC's network centre in Sydney and told them Simkin needed ninety seconds of airtime at the start of the news. The ABC has different news readers in each state, who speak at their own pace. That made it impossible to coordinate the exact moment Simkin could appear live on air. It would have to be pre-recorded. With only minutes to go, and with a broken autocue, Simkin turned to the camera and began speaking.

'Federal government sources have told the ABC that MPs are being sounded out about a possible move against the prime minister,' he said. 'Ministers have been asked for their support and the push is apparently coming from Victoria.'

When the story aired, there was an eerie silence. Simkin had expected Rudd's office and Gillard's office to call and angrily denounce his report. They didn't. The story was true.

## The takeover

When the leadership challenge was revealed on the ABC News bulletin, Kevin Rudd was giving a speech for Tasmanian Senator Nick Sherry's twentieth anniversary in parliament. A crowd had gathered in a lounge in the Senate's ministerial area. Rudd was fresh, seemingly relaxed. There was no hint in his delivery or body language of the crisis enveloping him.

After the speech, about 7.20 p.m., Gillard finally arrived at Rudd's office adjacent to the ministerial courtyard in Parliament House. John Faulkner, one the party's most experienced and respected MPs and by now the minister for defence, sat in. Neither Rudd, Gillard nor Faulkner has ever described what happened. But it is clear that Gillard explained to Rudd the party was unhappy with his performance and was prepared to replace him with her immediately. Rudd promised to change and asked for more time.

The talks went for a long time. One person whose office was nearby said it felt like it lasted three hours. Others said it was shorter, probably two. The tension made every minute seem interminable.

At one point Gillard agreed to call off the challenge and give Rudd until October to turn around the government's fortunes, according to three people with knowledge of the conversation. She then left the room, called Stephen Conroy and told him about the arrangement, according to one source. 'You can't cut the deal,' Conroy told her. 'It's too late.'

Gillard walked back in. She told Rudd he would get no more time. He needed to go now. They kept talking. The tension got so great that one of Rudd's supporters, Anthony Albanese, the minister for infrastructure, burst into the room and urged them to make a decision.

Meanwhile, the plotters were anxiously marshalling support behind Gillard. The stakes couldn't have been higher. Arbib, Carr, Conroy, Farrell, Feeney and Shorten still didn't have confirmation that Gillard was a willing candidate. If she refused to go ahead the challenge would collapse, Rudd would probably survive and the government would be badly damaged, perhaps fatally. Known for a willingness to settle a score, Rudd would almost certainly have his revenge. If not immediately, then later. The plotters' political careers – the power and prestige they had spent their lives working for – hung in the balance.

As news of the challenge spread, the core group had expanded to include Tony Burke, the minister for population, agriculture, fisheries and forestry, Jacinta Collins, a Victorian senator from the shop assistants' union, Brendan O'Connor, the minister for home affairs, Warren Snowdon, the minister for defence science and personnel, and Gary Gray, a former national secretary of the party. Others joined as the night wore on. One person present estimated twenty MPs, packed into a row of small offices normally used by Gillard's advisers, were working their mobile phones to reach the other ninety-five Labor MPs spread across Canberra. We can't win with Rudd, was their basic message. Collins and Snowdon kept track of who was supporting whom on pieces of paper. Arbib, Conroy and Shorten were bombarded by calls from MPs and journalists desperate to find out what was going on.

After her meeting with Rudd, at about 9 p.m., Gillard returned to her office and called in a small group of supporters from her Socialist Left faction. She told them there would be a leadership vote at 9.30 the following morning. Rudd hadn't agreed to go quietly. Under the party's rules, all federal Labor MPs would get to vote if they made the meeting. Gillard then, finally, updated the main plotters on what was going on, according to one person present. They had crossed the Rubicon.

Simon Crean, the trade minister, had attended Rudd's farewell speech for Sherry earlier in the evening. He then took a car to Canberra's swish Ottoman Restaurant for a long-scheduled dinner with Bernie Ripoll, Laurie Ferguson and several Coalition MPs to celebrate their twenty years in the House of Representatives. Everyone's phones were going crazy with news of the challenge. Crean got a call from one of the plotters and ducked outside for the conversation. They asked for his support. Crean wasn't going to agree to remove a prime minister over the phone.

When the dinner finished, around 9.15 p.m., Crean returned to Parliament House and went straight to Gillard's offices. Alone with Gillard in her conference room, he confronted her over the challenge. He objected to what he saw as the ambush of Rudd and argued an internal debate was necessary before taking such a drastic step. Removed as leader in 2003 without being allowed to contest an election, Crean knew how traumatic the change would be for Rudd, the party and the nation. As he spoke to Gillard he realised that whatever he said was no use. She had made up her mind. He quickly left.

Paul Howes, the national secretary of the Australian Workers' Union and an important, emerging figure in the party, had heard vague references about dissatisfaction with Rudd all week. But he didn't realise a challenge was brewing until that afternoon, he later told journalists. Howes drove to a hotel near the union's Sydney office and met with the AWU's national president, Bill Ludwig, who was one of the most influential players in the Queensland division of the Labor Party. The two men talked for about half an hour and agreed to support Gillard. Howes then told Gillard about the union's decision. Howes and Ludwig started ringing around about a dozen Labor MPs who owed their seats to the union and urged them to support Gillard.

Leadership challenges in parliamentary democracies normally unfold over weeks or days. Gillard's plotters used the media to create an irresistible sense of momentum in a matter of hours. The ABC, Sky News, radio stations and the major newspapers' websites swarmed over the story. Howes, a 28-year-old media charmer, decided to appear on the ABC's *Lateline* program, which went to air at 10.30 p.m. He supported a leadership switch and complained that the reported ring-around of MPs by Rudd's chief of staff, Alister Jordan, in the previous weeks was an insult to Gillard's loyalty.

'Having staffers going out and canvassing support for the prime minister, insinuating that there has been some type of challenge mounted by the deputy prime minister in the last couple of days ... I think that that was a grave mistake,' he said.

Howes' criticism of Jordan was part of a calculated ploy by the plotters to portray his calls to MPs, on behalf of Rudd, as the final act of treachery that triggered the challenge. In the coming days and years numerous journalists would be told by the plotters, including Arbib, that a challenge wasn't under consideration until he and the others read about Jordan's calls on the front page of the *Sydney Morning Herald*. It was a spontaneous uprising, they said.

Jordan was wounded by the criticism, which he thought grossly unfair. As the person running the prime minister's office, it was his job to maintain an open line of communication to ministers and other Labor MPs, whom he spoke to on a daily basis. He told associates the suggestion he rang around testing Rudd's support was untrue. For his part, Howes regretted the *Lateline* interview, which created the impression his union had a big role in Rudd's removal.

Rudd held a defiant late-night press conference. But as the night wore on his remaining backers left him. Once Swan decided to switch to Gillard, the plotters knew Rudd had no chance. Even Health Services Union leader Michael Williamson, who was in his last months as president of the Labor Party and would later become infamous for his involvement in a corruption scandal, urged MPs to vote for Gillard.

Rudd realised he was finished. His wife, Thérèse Rein, and daughter Jessica comforted him in his office. His shocked staff couldn't believe that events had moved so quickly. There was also a weird sense of excitement. They were in the middle of history.

Gillard was going to be appointed leader the following day. That was certain. But the move against Rudd was so unusual – Labor hadn't dumped a sitting prime minister since Bob Hawke in 1991, and that was after four elections – the longer-term consequences for the government, the party and the nation were unclear.

The calls from Gillard's office stopped at 2 a.m. The final tally: seventy-two had committed for Gillard, which left Rudd with forty-three. The margin was more than enough to cover any MPs who had lied about who they planned to vote for. The plot had succeeded.

The next morning Labor MPs gathered for their meeting at Parliament House. On the way in, Conroy flashed a huge grin at Rudd's crestfallen political adviser, Bruce Hawker. In the meeting, Rudd gave an emotional speech about his achievements as prime minister and acknowledged he didn't have enough support to remain leader. He didn't contest the ballot.

In the days and weeks after Rudd's removal the men behind the plot worked hard to shape perceptions of what triggered the change and how events unfolded. They largely succeeded. A conventional view formed that Labor MPs and ministers, no longer able to bear Rudd's dysfunctional leadership, staged an unplanned uprising, which Gillard reluctantly agreed to front when she saw there was no alternative.

There were three specific triggers for the removal of Rudd, according to the plotters. In background briefings and on-the-record interviews with journalists, Gillard and other Labor figures suggested or stated that Rudd's micro-management made it difficult to make decisions and implement policy, new leadership was needed to resolve the mining tax crisis, and Rudd had questioned Gillard's loyalty by asking his chief of staff to conduct a kind of straw poll of ministers and backbenchers.

The reasons given for Rudd's removal contained a mix of fact and fiction. The manufactured sense of outrage about Jordan's calls was used to flip culpability for the challenge from the plotters onto Rudd. There was little Jordan could do to defend himself. As a political appointee he didn't want to get into a public spat with the elected representatives who had removed his boss. 'History is written by the victors,' he later said.

Did Rudd deserve to be removed? Too many stories emerged of his egocentric management style to be untrue. *Australian* journalist John Lyons wrote a 2008 article headlined 'Captain Chaos and the workings of the inner circle' that revealed Rudd had kept the chief of the defence force, Angus Houston, and foreign affairs and trade secretary Michael L'Estrange waiting in a corridor for four hours. ABC TV host Barrie Cassidy described in *The Party Thieves: The Real Story of the 2010 Election* numerous examples of Rudd's staff bullying ministers.

Even his friends could see Rudd needlessly alienated people. 'He is a leader who makes few allowances for people who don't share his own obsessions or can't work to his timetable,' former Labor MP and Rudd loyalist Maxine McKew wrote in *Tales from the Political Trenches*.

A lot of the criticism used to justify Rudd's removal from office was self-serving and overly personal. *The Party Thieves* described a plan by Stephen Conroy to spend a night in London with relatives as part of a business trip to Germany. Apparently aghast at the indulgence of adding on the personal detour, Rudd's office called the communications minister at the airport and ordered him to take a direct flight to Germany the following day, according to the book. Rudd's staff even got the airline to pull Conroy's luggage from the flight without his prior permission, the book claimed, without citing a source for the anecdote. (A Qantas spokesman said it would not be common practice to remove a passenger's baggage at the request of someone else without the owner's approval.) A source with direct knowledge of Conroy's travel arrangements said the incident never happened.

Conroy was no puritan when it came to perks. He had a reputation for being receptive to free tickets to sporting matches from media companies, which he was responsible for overseeing as part of his portfolio. Parliamentary records show Conroy was given tickets to the Australian Open, test cricket, many AFL games, the Melbourne Formula One Grand Prix and the World Cup soccer tournament in South Africa, which was paid for by SBS, the public broadcaster.

Lindsay Tanner was one of four ministers who made most of the government's key decisions. The others were Rudd, Gillard and Swan. Tanner believes the centralised approach worked well during the 2008–09 global economic crisis, when a small group could commit the time and intellectual focus needed to devise a cross-government plan to avoid a recession. By 2010 the 'gang of four' was trying to do too much, too quickly, he said, and should have left more decisions to others. That didn't mean Rudd was incompetent or deserved his humiliating removal, though. 'Removing a first-term elected Labor prime minister by a caucus vote, ostensibly because of his management style, is such an extreme thing to do that those involved have found it necessary to enormously exaggerate the deficiencies in Kevin Rudd's leadership,' Tanner wrote in *Politics With Purpose*, a collection of speeches and articles.

The greatest unresolved question is whether the challenge was premeditated. Even three years later several of the main plotters swore they made up their mind to remove Rudd on the day. By claiming the challenge was spontaneous, they made themselves look like they were reacting to a situation that was spiralling out of control rather than working behind the scenes to bring down a democratically elected prime minister.

The evidence the challenge was prepared before the events of 23 June is overwhelming. Attorney-General Robert McClelland said pro-Gillard MP Brendan O'Connor showed him the Labor-commissioned research that looked bad for Rudd a week before the challenge. O'Connor denied the claim. Kim Carr also saw copies. Someone raised the research with Simon Crean. John Faulkner confirmed the research was distributed to MPs. 'I consider this was just sheer bastardry,' Faulkner told *The Australian*. One former cabinet minister believed planning began as early as April, when the government's decision to drop the emissions trading scheme was leaked.

Did the plotters play Gillard or did she play them? Arbib, Feeney, Shorten, Farrell and Conroy wanted to use Gillard to get rid of Rudd, who they saw as an impediment to their own ambitions. But throughout the day, when asked to commit, Gillard wouldn't give a straight answer. Given the main plotters, all leaders of the Right, had already began the coup, the personal consequences for them of failure would have been dire. An aborted challenge would have destabilised the government and triggered recriminations from Rudd and his supporters.

Some people involved believe ABC journalist Mark Simkin was briefed in order to force Gillard to declare her position. His report was broadcast shortly before the meeting between Gillard and Rudd began. At that point some ministers, including Simon Crean, didn't even know the challenge was happening.

The plotters needed Gillard to get rid of Rudd. Gillard needed the plotters to become leader. On Tuesday, 22 June, the day before the challenge, she went to Kim Carr's office to discuss the government's election prospects. She wasn't just talking politics. She was considering whether to challenge Rudd. Carr was from the Left. Knowing she would likely have the Right behind her, she needed to know if the Left, or parts of it, would back her too.

In reality, there were many factors driving Rudd's removal. They included his personal style, the government's declining popularity, and the sense of crisis created by the mining industry's ad campaign. If Rudd had rewarded the factional leaders before they turned on him, he may have been able to survive. Ultimately his biggest mistake was refusing to bow to the power structures of the party.

One of Kevin Rudd's best speeches as prime minister was his last. Standing in the courtyard outside his office after he was removed as leader, Rudd listed his government's achievements, including changes to the way hospitals are funded, an increase in the age pension, and the apology to the Stolen Generations of Aboriginal and Torres Strait Islander people. Choking up, voice at times unsteady and his family proudly standing beside him, Rudd appeared sad but not self-pitying, regretful but not angry. Even veteran journalists like Laurie Oakes thought his farewell press conference brave. After being in charge of 240,000 public servants and military personnel, Rudd became a backbench MP. He was entitled to six staff.

Julia Gillard's first decision as prime minister was to cancel the government ads promoting the mining tax. She asked the industry to suspend its campaign too, which it did. 'We've been stuck on this question as a nation for too long,' Gillard told reporters. 'It's also essential we have a stable and a coherent government and a positive basis for trust, and I believe we have established that this week.'

Eight days later Gillard announced she had struck a deal with the resources industry. The new tax, which was renamed the Minerals Resources Rent Tax, would be applied at a 22.5 per cent rate rather than Rudd's 40 per cent.[9] Many fewer companies would pay and it would apply only to iron ore and coal.

Gillard portrayed the deal as a huge victory for the government and her pragmatic negotiating skills. Andrew Forrest believed she was being disingenuous. The main sticking points in negotiations between BHP Billiton, Rio Tinto and Xstrata and Treasurer Wayne Swan were already resolved when Rudd was removed, according to the Fortescue chief executive. Gillard knew this when she extended an olive branch to the mining industry on her first day as prime minister. 'She already had in her back pocket that truce,' Forrest told 3AW in April 2012. 'Swan was doing a different deal in secret.' Swan denied Forrest's claim and accused him of believing in conspiracies. Gillard said the claim was 'more rehashed old nonsense'.

One change had a big impact on the operation of the tax. Instead of getting a refund for the royalties they paid state governments, mining companies would receive a credit for the minerals tax. If prices and profits were low they would still carry the cost of state royalties, which defeated one of the main objectives of the original option. Officially, the government estimated the tax would raise $10.5 billion over the first two years, only $1.5 billion less than Rudd's version. No-one following the issue closely believed the lower target was achievable, given the concessions made by the government. The critics were right. Gillard's mining tax, which she portrayed as an example of her superb negotiation skills, would turn out to be a colossal financial failure and damage her credibility.

# 5

## Julia Gillard's first election – Campaign leaks – Power outages in Victoria and NSW

## The leak

Replacing Kevin Rudd with Julia Gillard seemed, at first, to be smart politics. Australia's first female prime minister, who combined a steely determination with personal warmth that was rare in many male politicians, intrigued the public. She quickly resolved the biggest policy problem bedevilling the government when she cut a deal with the multinational mining companies for a new minerals tax at a lower rate than planned by Rudd. In the following weeks Gillard promised more money to stop asylum seekers reaching Australia, which she illustrated by taking a Labor MP from western Sydney, David Bradbury, to Darwin to watch Navy patrol boats practising boarding rickety wooden boats. Many voters in Bradbury's electorate were hostile to policies sympathetic to people travelling to Australia to claim refugee status. Gillard's visit, accompanied by television cameras, sent a message: I'm going to be tougher on asylum seekers than Rudd.

After the trauma of the leadership challenge, equilibrium seemed to return to the government. The trashing of Kevin Rudd's reputation by Gillard and other ministers had convinced many voters that the decision to remove its once loved leader was justified. Previously facing a big election defeat, Labor jumped ahead of the Coalition by 55 to 45 per cent. Gillard's personal rating was almost forty points higher than Rudd's in his final months.

Then, twenty-three days after Governor-General Quentin Bryce swore her in, Gillard drove to Government House once again, on a freezing Canberra morning, and asked Bryce to prorogue parliament to allow an election to be held on 21 August. The polls looked good for Gillard.

At the first press conference of the campaign Gillard introduced her campaign slogan: 'Moving Australia Forward'. It was an unsubtle attempt to distance her leadership from Rudd's. In case anyone didn't get the message, she used the phrase 'moving forward' twenty-four times in five minutes.

Gillard used to joke about the difficulty of being a female politician without children. Her first event of the campaign was a barbecue for parents of newborn babies in Brisbane. About 250 parents turned out. Dressed in a black suit with pearls, Gillard looked at babies, held babies and talked to parents about their babies. Babies make the most hardened operator look kind, gentle and caring. The event was the first of many designed to create positive images for television to make Gillard, the lifelong political activist who began her career as a self-declared socialist, come across as a regular person.

In policy positioning, Gillard had shifted to the right to appeal to conservative working- and middle-class voters. Labor officials preferred to call it 'moving to the centre'. On her trip to Brisbane on the first full day of the campaign, she repudiated one of Rudd's signature policies, a 'Big Australia' strategy to manage an expected increase in the population to 36 million by 2049. Rudd didn't set the target, but embraced it, which echoed the post-World War II European immigration overseen by Labor immigration minister Arthur Calwell. A lover of international power plays, Rudd argued the extra wealth created by a bigger population would make Australia a more important player in the Asia-Pacific.

Gillard had a better grasp of the politics on the issue than Rudd. She knew many Australians who lived in poorer suburbs served by crowded highways hated the idea of millions of extra people, who they feared would be immigrants competing with them for jobs and government resources. 'I do not believe in the idea of a big Australia, an Australia where we push all the policy levers into top gear to drive population growth as high as it can be,' Gillard told voters. Rudd, who was stung by Gillard's comments, later privately expressed contempt at the U-turn and complained that voters in western Sydney – a hive of marginal Labor seats – shouldn't be allowed to dictate national policy.

Did Rudd have his revenge? It looked as though he did. On Tuesday, 27 July, veteran Channel Nine journalist Laurie Oakes dropped a bombshell that ripped apart Labor's campaign. He reported that in cabinet Gillard had opposed two policies that were an important part of Labor's pitch to voters: government-paid leave for new parents and an increase in pensions. The leave scheme, which was scheduled to begin the following year, would pay parents eighteen weeks salary at the minimum wage, which was $570 a week. It was hard to think of a policy more Labor than giving working-class mothers the financial support to stay at home with their new baby. The pension increase, as high as 10 per cent in some categories, was introduced in 2009 and benefited 3.3 million elderly and disabled people, carers and military veterans. The government had touted it as the biggest change to pensions since they were introduced 100 years earlier.

Oakes sought comment from Gillard before going to air. She didn't deny the allegations but tried to deflect the story by accusing the Liberal Party of being Oakes' source. How the Liberals would know what happened in a Labor cabinet wasn't explained.

Oakes slapped Gillard down. 'Prime Minister, you know this information didn't come from the Liberals,' he said straight to the camera. 'You'll need to look closer to home.'

Rudd instantly became the number one suspect. The focus on him hardened the next morning when journalist Peter Hartcher – who was respected by the former prime minister for his grasp of politics and foreign policy – published an article in the *Sydney Morning Herald* that amplified Oakes' piece from the night before. Gillard, as deputy leader, had apparently opposed both policies on political grounds. She argued that people too old to have children would resent the leave scheme, and that age pensioners didn't vote Labor.

Initially, it was unclear what was more damaging: Gillard campaigning on policies she opposed or someone revealing conversations between ministers. Very quickly the media homed in on the leak, which was the first public sign that the bitterness created by Rudd's removal hadn't subsided.

'PM rocked by Labor leaks amid bitter divisions,' Michelle Grattan wrote in *The Age*. Grattan had called her cabinet sources, who didn't remember Gillard opposing the policies – which was surprising given the billions they would cost and Gillard's central position in cabinet. Grattan thought that could mean Gillard's comments were made in the committee that oversaw many of the government's most important decisions. It only had four members: Rudd, Gillard, Treasurer Wayne Swan and Lindsay Tanner, the finance minister.

Presumably Gillard didn't leak against herself. Tanner denied being Oakes' source. Given Swan became deputy prime minister when Gillard replaced Rudd, he was unlikely to have tried to blow up the government's campaign. That left Rudd, or his supporters. If Rudd was the source, it was an act of disloyalty so damaging it threatened Labor's chances of winning the election.

Campaigning that day in his Brisbane electorate, Rudd said little. 'I fully support the re-election of the government and I fully support the election of Prime Minister Julia Gillard,' he told reporters. The former Labor leader had removed any reference to the Labor Party from his campaign posters.

By the weekend the Coalition was in front 52 per cent to 48 per cent, according to a Nielsen poll. Although unclear at the time, in hindsight the leak was the first attack in a guerilla campaign against Gillard that would consume the government for years.

Hit by leaks, falling polls and facing an increasingly sceptical press, Gillard decided to press the re-set button. She announced, in a front-page exclusive with her hometown tabloid, the *Herald Sun*, that she would personally take control of Labor's campaign. Her appearances would be less stage managed, more spontaneous and she would interact more with voters. 'I think it's time for me to make sure that the real Julia is well and truly on display,' she told journalist Phillip Hudson on board her Air Force jet. 'So I'm going to step up and take personal charge of what we do in the campaign from this point.'

Gillard was promising an approach the press would have normally welcomed because it could make the campaign more interesting. Yet the critical response to what became known as the 'real Julia' strategy was universally negative. Even though the 'real Julia' reference was a shorthand description for a shift in campaigning, the comment was interpreted literally. By repudiating her own leadership style over the previous weeks, Gillard made it look like she'd been acting. 'Suddenly and remarkably, Julia had made herself a fake,' Barrie Cassidy wrote in *The Party Thieves*. In politics, words count.

True to her promise, Gillard delivered her speech at Labor's official campaign launch, on 16 August, without a written text. Most political leaders today use autocues for major speeches. Gillard didn't, she said, because she wanted to speak from the heart. As Labor members and supporters gathered in the Brisbane Convention Centre, Kevin Rudd's arrival was met with frisson. He sat at the end of the second row next to John Faulkner, who acted as a sort of kindly minder to the former prime minister. The other former leader present, Bob Hawke, gave Gillard an energetic introduction. In her distinctive nasal voice, Gillard described her humble upbringing in Adelaide by immigrant parents from Wales. She emphasised the government's achievements, particularly in her previous portfolio, education. The speech portrayed Gillard as a legitimate successor to past Labor prime ministers like Ben Chifley, but was a sign that Gillard and her advisers felt they had to overcome public concerns that her sudden appointment as prime minister made her a less legitimate leader than Rudd, who had won a general election. The speech went down well with the audience and the journalists covering the launch, who noted nothing happened to further embarrass Gillard. Rudd left immediately afterwards and had no formal role in the event.

The campaign, which ran for thirty-five days, was one of the shortest in Australian history. Election night started badly for Labor and got worse. It was unclear who would win. Tensions were high on both sides. Bill Shorten got snarky on a Channel Nine panel when pushed about the decision to replace Rudd. 'Julia Gillard is a Labor rock star,' he said, defensively. At 9 p.m. Maxine McKew, the celebrity candidate who took John Howard's seat in 2007, became the first MP to publicly state the obvious: removing a first-term prime minister might not have been the act of political genius his executioners thought at the time. It soon became clear Australia would have its first hung federal parliament since World War II.

After the big victory three years earlier, Labor lost its parliamentary majority. Advances by Labor in Gillard's home states of South Australia and Victoria were outweighed by bigger swings against the party in New South Wales, where voters were disgusted by the behaviour of the state party, and Rudd's home state of Queensland, where there was a backlash against his removal. Nationally, there was a 2.6 per cent swing away from Labor, which received 30,527 more votes than the Coalition out of the 12.4 million cast. In 2007 Labor received 671,636 more votes than the Coalition. Labor won seventy-two seats, the Coalition won seventy-three, the Greens won one and four independents were elected: Andrew Wilkie, Tony Windsor, Rob Oakeshott and Bob Katter. Seventeen days later Oakeshott became the last of the four to declare his allegiance. He chose to keep Labor in power. In return, Gillard promised to introduce sixteen policies

Oakeshott wanted. Many related to transport, health and education spending in and around his political base of Port Macquarie, on the mid-north coast of New South Wales. Others would allow him to claim credit for important national policies, including a referendum to recognise Aborigines in the constitution. To appease Oakeshott and Windsor, Gillard and Swan agreed to an $800 million spending splurge over five years in rural areas, promising to build new roads, bridges, town halls and sports grounds.

The hung parliament even triggered criticism of Governor-General Quentin Bryce. The problem: her connection to Bill Shorten, her son-in-law. (In late 2008 Shorten acknowledged that he had split from his wife, Deborah Beale, and was in a relationship with Bryce's daughter, Chloe, a publicist for the cement industry who had two children from a previous marriage. Fourteen months later, with Chloe Bryce eight months pregnant, the couple married at their home in Moonee Ponds, a suburb in Shorten's electorate.) With the outcome of the election uncertain and experts raising the possibility of a constitutional crisis, Bryce became more central to the political process than any governor-general since John Kerr, who famously sacked Gough Whitlam in 1975. As head of state, she faced the possibility of choosing between her daughter's husband's party and the Coalition, which had won more seats than the government.

Given the speculation that Shorten could succeed Gillard, Melbourne QC Peter Faris said Bryce's relationship to him was a conflict of interest under a definition adopted by the High Court. He took the extraordinary step of calling on her to resign. 'When she accepted the position, on 5 September 2008, it is difficult to know if she knew Shorten was having an affair with her daughter, but given that the marriage occurred 14 months later, it is probable that she did,' the criminal-law barrister wrote in *The Australian*. 'Australia is entitled to a governor-general who is independent and above politics. We are also entitled to a governor-general who does not have the appearance of bias.' Bryce didn't respond publicly but asked the government's solicitor-general, Stephen Gageler, to clarify her position. Gageler advised that her relationship to Shorten did not affect her ability to appoint the next prime minister or their ministry.

Gillard and her ministry were sworn in at the governor-general's residence in Canberra on 14 September. The plotters were rewarded. David Feeney was made parliamentary secretary for defence, a kind of junior minister. Don Farrell became parliamentary secretary for sustainability and urban water. Shorten was promoted from parliamentary secretary for disabilities to assistant treasurer and minister for financial services. It was a big step up. He got oversight of the tax office, which had 45,000 employees, and the superannuation and savings system, which was responsible for $2 trillion of investments. Mark Arbib got three ministries: employment and economic development, social housing and homelessness, and sport. The job placed him in an important portfolio for any Labor government – employment policy – and one with a lot of inbuilt perks – sport. Many of the minor plotters received promotions too.

Gillard fulfilled a promise to give Rudd a senior job. Rudd, who turned up to be sworn in at Government House with his own priest, Frank Brennan, was made foreign minister, a job that would keep him out of Canberra a lot. As other ministers enjoyed the ceremony and talked among themselves, Rudd sat silent. It seemed as though his colleagues were shunning him for the leak during the campaign.

With the election over and Labor back in power, many exhausted government advisers decided to leave. Among them were Swan's chief of staff, Chris Barrett, and his press secretary, Matthew Coghlan. Their exits illustrated one of the rorts of ministerial office – advisers who resigned got termination payments and often large sums for leave they had clocked up in the heat of political office.

Barrett got a $183,640 payout. About six months later, Swan appointed him ambassador to the Organisation for Economic Co-operation and Development in Paris, a well-paid and low-stress job that included a large apartment in the Australian embassy complex near the Eiffel Tower. Coghlan got $97,767 and went travelling. Seven months later he was back in his old job.

On 27 November, three months after the federal election, another Labor government faced voters. Victorian premier John Brumby was the favourite to win a second term for himself and a fourth term for the Labor government. Their state's economy was the fastest growing in Australia, apart from resources-driven Western Australia. *The Age* called on voters to support Brumby because of his 'vigorous advocacy of this state's interests'. Many Victorians felt differently. Upset by the botched introduction of a train, tram and bus ticketing system by transport minister Martin Pakula – Shorten's former ally in Young Labor – voters in Melbourne's east and south-eastern suburbs turned on the government. A 7 per cent swing against Labor cost it twelve seats and delivered government to Liberal Party leader Ted Baillieu, who had re-united his party with the Nationals after a nine-year break. The Labor Party was stunned by the loss in what had been one of its strongest states. If voters would do that to a government that had demonstrated mild ineptitude, imagine what could happen in New South Wales, party officials thought.

## Landslide

New South Wales premier Kristina Keneally had no idea it was coming. On 24 February 2011, the day of the first televised debate of the state election campaign, Julia Gillard dropped a bombshell: despite her promise before the 2010 election there would be no carbon tax, Gillard planned to introduce laws enacting a price on carbon. Companies that emitted greenhouse gases, from airlines to power stations, would have to buy carbon permits if they wanted to stay in business. Gillard, who didn't use the word 'tax' during her announcement at Parliament House, later that evening acknowledged the system was a form of taxation on the creation of greenhouse gases.

Keneally was furious. She didn't doubt the science of global warming. But she knew a carbon tax that would drive up power prices was toxic to her campaign, which was based on helping poor and middle-class voters manage everyday costs like electricity.

She had few options. Complaining privately would be pointless. Opposing the tax publicly would create a media firestorm that would likely envelop her entire campaign. 'What was I meant to do?' she said later. 'Ring up Julia and say, "What the fuck?"'

The carbon price was a gift for Barry O'Farrell, the NSW Liberal Party's deceptively uncharismatic leader. At their debate that night, O'Farrell cited government advice that he said showed a carbon tax would increase power bills by $500 a year for some families. Keneally said a carbon price was the most 'efficient thing the nation can do'.

There were conspiracy theories about Gillard's timing. A long-time columnist at *The Age*, Kenneth Davidson, believed the announcement was designed to distract attention from the resignation of Australia's Chief Scientist, Penny Sackett, halfway through her five-year term. Sackett's story, although it received little national attention, troubled the scientific community.

Sackett was a rare scientist: a leader in her field and a strong administrator. American born and educated at the University of Pittsburgh, she made her way through the male-dominated world of astrophysics. Kevin Rudd, as prime minister, decided the government needed a full-time chief scientist to advise him on science, technology and innovation. He hired Sackett, the director of the Research School of Astronomy and Astrophysics at the Australian National University and head of the Mount Stromlo observatory in Canberra.

Sackett, who warned not enough was being done to slow global warming, worked hard but struggled to get the high-level access needed to change government policy. She only had one meeting with Rudd, who didn't include her in the Australian delegation to the United Nations climate change summit at Copenhagen in 2009. Gillard never met her. Eventually, Sackett gave up and resigned on 17 February. A week later she revealed to a Senate committee her limited contact with the two prime ministers.

The carbon tax was the lead article in the *Sydney Morning Herald* the next day and most other newspapers and news bulletins. A shorter article also on the front page of the *Herald* covered Keneally's debate with O'Farrell. The premier was the clear winner, it said, according to a poll of the audience.

Premiers of New South Wales don't get to choose when to fight their elections, which are held every four years on the last Saturday in March. This time the election was to be on 26 March, which meant the government would go into caretaker mode three weeks earlier, on 4 March. Under the Westminster conventions, once an election campaign officially starts ministers are required to stop everything except routine work. The public service shouldn't be locked into any big decisions that may be opposed by the incoming government.

As the Keneally government began winding down and preparing for the election campaign, the premier's office got a request. Tony Kelly, the planning and lands minister, wanted to approve a major land development two hours before caretaker mode kicked in. Sensing it would look like the government was trying to rush through a decision at the last moment, Kelly was told to nix the idea.

A week later, one of Kelly's top public servants got a call offering up a property Kelly had long had his eye on for the state: a collection of historic holiday homes on Sydney's beautiful Pittwater called Currawong. Allen Linz, one of the owners of the site, rang Warwick Watkins, the chief executive of the body that oversaw the government's property holdings, the Land and Property Management Authority. Linz asked if the government was interested in buying. Currawong was well known inside and outside the government because Unions NSW, the umbrella group for the state's unions, previously owned it.

The government had long been interested in turning the site into a state park. Linz initially wanted $20 million. Watkins offered $11 million to $12 million. On 10 March they agreed on $12.2 million. The contract was drawn up and signed five days later, a very short time for such a big transaction.

The expensive purchase raised alarm bells among Keneally's advisers, even though they were preoccupied with the campaign. Her deputy chief of staff, Tony Pooley, told Kelly's chief of staff,

Stephen Fenn, the deal shouldn't have been done during the caretaker period. Brendan O'Reilly, the director-general of the Department of Premier and Cabinet who had witnessed most of the Keneally government's scandals up close, was concerned the deal was a serious breach of protocol. The purchase hadn't been authorised by cabinet. Kelly's role in the transaction was murky.

O'Reilly told Keneally, a former planning minister herself, about the deal. Keneally hit the roof. She was fighting to save the New South Wales Labor party from being wiped out and Kelly's department was going around behind her back buying holiday cottages for huge sums. Watkins was stood aside as chief executive of the Land Authority and an investigation ordered by the state's Internal Audit Bureau, which specialised in combating misconduct, fraud and corruption. Keneally rang Kelly and told him the purchase would be referred to the Independent Commission Against Corruption, a serious step that would damage Kelly's reputation even if he were cleared. Watkins was in deep trouble too. A forty-year public service veteran, he had risen to become the New South Wales surveyor-general and was a Member of the Order of Australia.

Over several phone conversations on the morning of 18 March, a Friday, Watkins and Kelly came up with a plan to cover their tracks. That afternoon Kelly met Robert Costello, another official in the Land Authority, at a Lindt Chocolat Café in central Sydney. Surrounded by delicious Swiss chocolate, Costello showed Kelly a one-paragraph letter drafted by Watkins that gave Watkins approval to buy Currawong. The letter was made to look like it was written by Kelly, who signed it on the spot and wrote in the date 28 February 2011, four days before caretaker mode began and eighteen days before this meeting.

The letter seemed to prove that Kelly and Watkins lined up the deal before the election campaign officially got under way. When an investigator from the Internal Audit Bureau asked Kelly if he knew the purchase was going to be completed in the middle of March, during the election, Kelly told her he approved the deal in writing before caretaker mode kicked in. The Audit Bureau investigator checked out the letter fabricated by Kelly and Watkins and concluded it was genuine. She cleared Watkins of buying the property without permission.

Not everyone was convinced. O'Reilly, the head of the premier's department, tried to verify whether the letter was genuine. When he couldn't, he sent it to ICAC.

Keneally claimed she slept soundly on election eve and got up early to tour her own electorate, Heffron. It was the first time during the campaign she had visited the seat, which takes in working-class suburbs around Sydney Airport. The rest of the day she travelled around western Sydney visiting electorates she knew Labor couldn't win. She wanted to thank the candidates and MPs who had worked hard to salvage Labor's vote. She made a point of seeing her education minister, Verity Firth, who was in a tough fight with the Greens and Liberals for the seat of Balmain, a gentrifying Inner West suburb regarded in Labor legend as one of the birthplaces of the party. The last seat she visited was Maroubra, held by Labor MP Michael Daley, because it was where she lived. Labor volunteers on polling booths lit up when Keneally arrived. Her sunny personality provided respite from the grim parade of voters who refused to accept Labor's how-to-vote cards. Keneally never let her smile slip. But she and everyone she met had no doubt the day would be one of the party's worst.

She went home to eat and prepare for a heart-wrenching night. A few of her advisers, including chief of staff Walt Secord, came around and worked on her speech. Sam Dastyari, the party's administrative head, called and urged her to lead the party from opposition.

After dinner, Keneally, her husband Ben and her staff left for the Labor Party's election-night reception at the nearby Randwick Labor Club. Keneally's two sons, aged ten and twelve, stayed home. She didn't want them to have the painful memory of being pulled onstage to witness their mother acknowledge a humiliating defeat.

Unsurprisingly, the mood at the event was subdued. Supporters ate sausages, chips and salad. As a monotonously long list of seats fell, including many previously considered safe for Labor, a cheer broke out a little after 7 p.m. when a TV commentator declared Keneally wouldn't lose Heffron.

The result was the landslide everyone predicted. In the lower house, the Liberal Party and Nationals received a swing of 11.6 per cent and won sixty-nine seats, for a combined vote of 51.2 per cent. Labor won twenty seats and got 25.6 per cent of the vote, a swing away from it of 13.4 per cent. The Australian Greens won one lower house seat and 10.3 per cent of the vote. Of the twenty-one upper house seats decided, Labor won five.

It was one of the worst defeats in Australian political history. Not since the dismissed New South Wales premier Jack Lang lost the 1932 election had so many of the state's voters turned to the opposition parties, according to ABC election analyst Antony Green. The last time Labor won fewer seats in the state parliament was 1904, Green wrote.

Despite the size of the loss, Secord and Dastyari felt vindicated. Their 'sandbagging' strategy to direct resources to a handful of seats that could realistically be held seemed to have worked. Some commentators had thought Labor would be left with as few as seven seats in the ninety-three-seat parliament. Secord and Dastyari felt Labor had a core of good MPs who could form the nucleus of a future Labor government. With the nervous tension finally draining, Secord and Dastyari hugged.

Few other senior figures saw the bright side. On the ABC television's broadcast, Labor organiser Luke Foley referred to the election as a catastrophic loss. Dastyari called Foley on his mobile and told him to stop using such strong language. Foley told Dastyari to fuck off and hung up.

Even though she regarded the sandbagging strategy as effective, Keneally couldn't pretend the election wasn't a disaster. As she prepared her concession speech, she knew she needed to strike a delicate balance: acknowledge that the behaviour of figures inside the government had damaged the party *and* create a sense of hope for Labor by signalling the outcome could have been worse.

At the Liberal Party's election-night reception at the Parramatta Leagues Club, the atmosphere was unrestrained joy. Television camera spotlights perched on a raised dais along one side of the room created a glamorous glow. Shadow ministers were fawned over by wellwishers. Hundreds of supporters, including CEOs, former federal MPs and the relatives of ex-Liberal ministers, got drunk. When early counting made it look like Liberal Party candidate James Falk would win Balmain, cheers erupted from the crowd. (The result wasn't decided for several weeks. Falk got the most votes but lost on preferences. The Greens' Jamie Parker won.)

A quiet settled across the room when Keneally appeared on a large video screen. When the defeated premier blamed the behaviour of some Labor MPs for the party's failure, there were gasps. When she declared 'we have kept Labor intact' there was mocking laughter. By the time Keneally confirmed she intended to step down as leader and go to the backbench – to cries of 'no, no, no' from her Labor audience – most people at the Liberal victory party had turned away from the screen.

Liberal leader Barry O'Farrell arrived at the club about an hour after Keneally conceded. His twelve-minute speech was interrupted by applause roughly every thirty seconds. Apart from a thank you to his wife and two sons, who were on stage with him, the line that got the biggest response wasn't related to state politics at all. It was a promise to 'take up the fight to Canberra' against a carbon tax. He promised not to disappoint traditional Labor supporters who had switched to the Coalition out of disgust with Keneally's government.

Soon after taking power O'Farrell increased the budget of ICAC. The new government wanted the commission to conduct a thorough investigation into Eddie Obeid, Ian Macdonald and any other Labor minister who may have been involved in corruption. An investigation and public hearings by the commission would remind the public of Labor government sleaze and make an opposition comeback even harder.

To stop the commission being used as a political weapon, it is up to parliament not the government to order ICAC investigations. Chris Hartcher, the new resources and energy minister, asked law firm Clayton Utz to review the awarding of the coal exploration licence to John Maitland's company by Macdonald, and Eddie Obeid's purchase of a farm over a lucrative coal deposit. The law firm examined all of the paperwork associated with the Maitland deal. It didn't find any documents proving corruption. But it argued the circumstances were so strange a special commission of inquiry was needed to determine what happened. Hartcher asked parliament to refer Macdonald to the Independent Commission Against Corruption, a step that would automatically trigger an investigation. 'At every level this was rort upon rort upon rort that only the Labor Party would have believed it could get away with in a democratic society,' Hartcher told parliament. 'Only the Labor Party would have done such a deal. Only the Labor Party did that deal.'

Labor MPs felt they had no choice. They voted for the ICAC investigation.

The commission was already investigating Kelly, the former planning minister, over the unauthorised purchase of the holiday resort on Pittwater. ICAC had tapped phones and interviewed witnesses. On 6 June, three weeks before Kelly was due to take the stand in public corruption hearings, he quit parliament.

Kelly's appearance at the ICAC hearings, which were public, didn't go well. Giving vague answers, he denied the backdated letter was written to deceive investigators examining the deal. ICAC commissioner David Ipp didn't believe him.

ICAC's report, which was completed at the end of 2011, found Kelly and Watkins guilty of a cover up. The two men engaged in 'corrupt conduct' during the investigation by using the backdated letter that made it look like Kelly gave Watkins permission to buy Currawong, ICAC determined. The decision was devastating for Kelly, who was expelled from the Labor Party. But he got a break. The commission didn't find anything corrupt about the purchase itself. With Kelly out of politics and Labor in opposition, the media viewed the hearings almost as a non-event.

There was more interest in the latest drama involving the Obeid family. On 1 February 2012, the Supreme Court ruled on allegations against Streetscape, the company controlled by Eddie Obeid's son Moses, which was being sued by the City of Sydney Council.

Streetscape had won a contract to manufacture street light poles for the council in the early 2000s under the name 'Smartpole'. The poles were constructed from ribbed aluminium tubes, which made it easier to mount equipment like road signs and traffic lights. Streetscape had bought a licence from the council to sell them within Australia, New Zealand and Spain. Moses Obeid then went behind the council's back and sold the technology to government authorities in Singapore and across the Middle East, according to allegations made in court, generating at least $40 million in profit. When Sydney Council found out it sued. Moses Obeid appealed and told the court he didn't have the money, despite evidence he drove a Range Rover, employed a maid, and lived in a $4.5 million house in Vaucluse, one of Sydney's most expensive suburbs. The judge didn't believe him and said the Obeids appeared to exemplify the line 'How to live well on nothing a year' from the novel *Vanity Fair*.

He ordered Streetscape to pay the council $16.6 million, a figure that included interest and the council's legal costs. To avoid paying, the Obeids put Streetscape into administration, a step before bankruptcy. On 9 August 2012, Streetscape's creditors voted to accept one cent of every dollar the Obeids owed them – a decision that wiped out 99 per cent of the money owed to the council.

Due to a quirk of the law, every creditor had one vote no matter how much they were owed. Sydney Council was outvoted by Moses Obeid's sister, Gemma Vrana, his business associate Rocco

Triulcio, the office cleaner, the local newsagent, the Obeids' long-time accountant, Sid Sassine, the family's lawyers, Colin Biggers & Paisley, and a former employee, John McLeod, according to the *Herald*.

The Obeids' original breach of the deal with the council and their blatant avoidance of the court-ordered compensation illustrated the family's contempt for the legal system and disregard for the effect of their actions on their own reputations. Coverage of the court case added to the notoriety surrounding the family. Although Eddie Obeid wasn't directly implicated, many people would wonder how the son of a former Labor minister became caught up in such a brazenly unethical scheme.

It would get much worse. Within a year Eddie Obeid and his five sons would find themselves in a witness box at ICAC. The hearings into a plan to dig for coal on the Obeid farm would reveal the family's inner workings, their links to government, and a web of companies and property investments worth tens of millions. The revelations would be devastating for the Labor Party.

# 6

## Craig's little problem gets bigger – Kathy Jackson steps in – Bill Shorten, Minister for Industrial Relations

## The entrepreneur

The question sweeping through the gossipy world of politics was: how could Craig Thomson have been stupid – and so venal – to charge bills for sex services to a union representing thousands of low-paid women. It was one thing for Thomson to deny the allegations publicly. Almost all politicians will lie when their careers are on the line. In private, when asked by the factional leaders about the allegations, Thomson was even more emphatic that he was a victim of a smear campaign by his enemies in the union and the *Sydney Morning Herald*. To demonstrate his innocence, he decided to sue the *Herald*'s owner, Fairfax Media. He also went after Kathy Jackson, his successor at the Health Services Union, for her involvement in compiling the evidence against him.

As a union official and MP, Craig Thomson was well paid. But the cost of funding a complex and high-stakes lawsuit against a big company was beyond him. Bankrupts can't be members of parliament. If Thomson lost the lawsuit and couldn't cover the legal costs of the case, he could be expelled from parliament. The seat would almost certainly fall to the Liberal Party in a by-election, threatening Labor's thin hold on power. The only way he could pursue the law suit was because Labor head office in Sydney agreed to cover his rapidly escalating legal bill.

Fairfax Media fought. The HSU caved. On 5 August 2010, almost three years after Thomson resigned from the union, the HSU national executive met to vote on whether the union should settle Thomson's claim and pay him off. His political patron, Michael Williamson, chaired the meeting. When he called the vote, Williamson didn't bother to ask if anyone opposed the payment. The meeting's minutes noted the vote was carried unanimously. Thomson got $129,955 for unpaid leave – of which $45,194 was paid to the tax office – and $30,000 to settle his allegations against Jackson and the union. Williamson never explained publicly why he chose to pay out Thomson when the union's audit said he had misused hundreds of thousands of dollars in union funds. Williamson may have decided the case would cost too much to defend in court. His rivals in the union suspected it was a favour for an old mate. Whatever the reason, Thomson's victory over the union seemed to convince him that he could also defeat Fairfax and clear his name.

As his case against Fairfax wound its way through the legal system, the company's lawyers forced the union to hand over documents from Thomson's time as national secretary. Fairfax executives were amazed at the trove of evidence: there were credit card receipts made out to brothels and records of calls from Thomson's phone to escort agencies from hotels. They couldn't work out why Thomson was going ahead with the lawsuit when the case against him was so strong.

Jackson was the national secretary of a union with political clout. She had a fancy work car: a new Volvo four-wheel drive. She was dating Michael Lawler, a deputy president of Fair Work Australia and the son of an eminent public servant under Prime Minister Robert Menzies, Sir Peter Lawler. Her closest friend in the Labor Party was David Feeney, a senator married to Liberty Sanger, a top lawyer at Maurice Blackburn, Bill Shorten's old firm. Jackson and Lawler had become a prominent couple in a clique of union officials, politicians and labour lawyers at the heart of Melbourne's clubby industrial relations world.

Jackson's influence, though, was less than it seemed. Even though she was nominally head of the entire union, the real power in the Health Services Union had always resided with Williamson, the secretary of the New South Wales division. Within New South Wales, the biggest division, his authority was unquestioned. Jackson referred to him as 'God'.

Like many unions, the HSU was more of a federation than a single entity. The state branches collected revenue from their members, gave some to head office and pretty much controlled their own affairs. State secretaries had more power than the national secretary and were usually influential players in the state divisions of the Labor Party.

For eleven years, every official supported by Williamson in New South Wales was elected unopposed. By 2010, thirty-seven of the forty-eight HSU officials holding elected office in the state had never faced a vote, according to Jackson's calculations. They had their jobs because Williamson chose them. He placed loyalists — often family members — in key jobs, including the all-important finance department.

Williamson was an influential figure in the Labor Party too. He was on the party's national executive, a powerful body that adjudicated disputes over the selection of Labor candidates and other administrative matters. Prime ministers Kevin Rudd and Julia Gillard were members along with each state secretary and other top union leaders. Williamson's daughter, Alexandra, worked on Gillard's private staff and had been publicly thanked by Gillard for her hard work. She shared an apartment in Canberra with Mark Arbib. In 2009, Williamson was appointed president of the Labor Party, a largely ceremonial job only given to the most senior and loyal members, including former science minister Barry Jones, Queensland premier Anna Bligh and Carmen Lawrence, the former premier of Western Australia.

Both members of the Right, Williamson and Jackson had formed an alliance of mutual convenience. According to the rival Left's Chris Brown, who was then head of the union's Tasmanian division and later became national president, Williamson provided financial support to Jackson and her allies in 2009 when they seized control of the biggest of the Victorian HSU divisions, the Number 1 branch.

In 2010 Williamson and Jackson agreed on a restructure of the union that would give both of them more power and pay. Williamson's New South Wales division would merge with the two Victorian divisions aligned with Jackson and her allies, the Number 1 and Number 3 branch. A new super-division called HSU East would be created. Williamson and Jackson would be the biggest players in an even bigger organisation. The change was pitched as part of the trend towards bigger unions with more financial clout and lower costs. Jackson's rivals believed she was slyly pushing the merger as part of scheme to eventually push out Williamson and replace him. 'She wanted to take over the whole union,' said Brown. Jackson later denied she supported the merger to increase her power and said she became less influential because Williamson and his allies had more representatives on the combined division's governing council.

In early 2011, urged on by Williamson and Jackson, HSU officials in Victoria and New South Wales overwhelmingly voted in favour of merging and creating a new entity called HSU East. When the merger was completed on 24 May 2011, Jackson's salary as national secretary was bumped up to $286,976 a year from $173,314 to reflect her additional role as HSU East executive president. Within the HSU, only Williamson's $394,675 annual pay was higher.[10]

By union standards, the pay packets were extraordinary. Williamson was probably the best-paid unionist in Australia. Paul Howes, the national secretary of the Australian Workers' Union and one of the highest-profile unionists in the country, was paid $146,000 a year, which was less than many of the people he represented. Williamson had turned the Health Services Union into a money-making machine – for himself.

Before the merger of the Victorian and New South Wales branches, Jackson didn't have access to detailed accounts for the New South Wales division. Around the time the two organisations were being stitched together she pulled four months of bank records from the New South Wales division's files. Payments to four companies looked strange. Mah-Chut Architects, a little-known Sydney architecture firm, was on an annual retainer of $88,000. Over the four-month period Mah-Chut was paid $283,250 even though the union hadn't needed an architect around that time and wasn't planning any building work. Two printing firms were also on the payroll and seemed to have received excessive payments, Communigraphix and Access Focus. The union's computer-systems provider, United Edge, was also being paid a lot. Access Focus got $5,013,543 between October 2007 and September 2009, six months after the first newspaper reports of abuse of union funds by Thomson. The reason for the payments was unclear. The company was a mystery. It didn't have a phone number or website. It didn't exist at its registered office. No-one from the union would explain what it did. Payments to the four companies over the four-month period totalled $1,266,365.

There didn't seem to be any legitimate reason for the spending. Jackson later said she developed a growing suspicion that Williamson was at the centre of 'major corruption' in the union. Williamson and his allies had firm control over the union's finances, and the payments were so large it seemed inconceivable they could have been made without his approval. Where was the money going? Jackson started to believe the money, perhaps millions, was being secretly funnelled back to Williamson. If that were the case, the misconduct in the union was far, far worse than the allegations against Craig Thomson suggested.

Others doubted Jackson's motives. Chris Brown later claimed his rival wasn't surprised by Williamson's apparent profiteering and saw an opportunity to advance her own career, a charge Jackson denied. 'She may not have had concrete evidence, but Kathy Jackson knew about the corruption,' Brown said. 'She wanted to make Williamson look like a crook and take the union over.'

Towards the end of summer Jackson invited an HSU official from Sydney who wasn't part of Williamson's clique, Gerard Hayes, to a barbecue at her Melbourne home. The only other person present, initially, was Lawler.[11]

'Gerard, I have something very important to raise with you,' Jackson said she told Hayes. 'I have come to the view that Michael Williamson is corrupt and that the corruption is real and large.'

She went through the evidence, including the large payments to the architecture firm. 'So will you support me in dealing with Williamson's corruption?' she asked.

'I know he is a crook but there is nothing we can do,' Hayes replied, according to Jackson. 'He is just too powerful. Look, he will be gone in a couple of years. When he retires we can make him CEO.'

'Oh, for fuck's sake!' Jackson said. 'CEO! You think he should be the chief executive officer in retirement? We are not a big company, we are a union.'

Later in the conversation Hayes offered some help, according to Jackson.

'Look, I can support you quietly behind the scenes, but I can't come out in the open,' Jackson said Hayes told her.

Hayes later said he didn't remember the conversation and was so drunk at the barbecue he could barely walk. In an affidavit signed the following June, he said he didn't regard Williamson as a crook at the time and it would have been illogical to appoint him chief executive because, in effect, he already held the role. Hayes did acknowledge advising Jackson to be cautious. 'Hold your line,' Hayes said he told Jackson. 'Williamson's due to retire soon. Just let things take their course.'

Jackson later said she was reluctant to go to the police because Williamson 'was likely to do everything in what I assumed to be his considerable power to destroy me'. 'He would certainly succeed if I did not have hard evidence,' she said.

Jackson spent another four months agonising about what to do. Unsurprisingly, she turned to Lawler for advice. Lawler was a barrister who prosecuted fraud cases in Canberra when he worked for the Director of Public Prosecutions. He knew police fraud squads around the country were under-resourced and disliked cases involving unions. 'They have a reputation for being awful to investigate,' he told her. 'What you need is evidence of a quality that will leave the cops with no option but to conduct a proper investigation.'

Lawler suggested Jackson hire a private detective, Nicholas Mamouzelos, to compile enough information to convince the police to investigate Williamson. Jackson agreed. Mamouzelos began digging. After asking a lawyer if it would be illegal, Jackson began surreptitiously recording meetings with other senior HSU officials. At the same time, Kate McClymont, the *Sydney Morning Herald* investigative reporter, had got a tip that Thomson wasn't the only person who might be abusing the HSU members' trust. She started poring through corporate and government records too.

Mamouzelos and McClymont separately established that under Williamson the HSU was being run more like a family-owned enterprise than a regular trade union. Williamson's 26-year-old son, Chris, worked at the union as a media officer. Michael Williamson's brother, Darren, was the HSU's recruitment and marketing manager. Williamson's sister-in-law, Monique Irvine, was the lead organiser. Half-brother Struan Robertson was an organiser. Williamson's friend, Cheryl McMillan, was the procurement manager, a sensitive role given the large sums being paid to contractors. McMillan's sister, daughter and niece worked at the union.[12] Williamson's wife, Julieanne, was paid $384,625 from December 2005 to June 2009. The money went through a private company, Canme Services, named for the initials of the Williamson children: Chris, Alexandra, Nicholas, Madeline and Elizabeth. After the payments became public it was claimed she worked for the union as a paid archivist collecting folders, dismantling them and collating them for scanning. No-one in the union seemed to have seen the archiving carried out. Even if Julieanne Williamson was working 37.5 hour weeks going through the paperwork, which seemed unlikely, she was receiving $34 an hour for basic clerical work.

Williamson's architect was on the union payroll. Ron Mah-Chut, who ran a Sydney practice a little north of the Harbour Bridge, received $3.74 million between March 2007 and September 2011. His firm, which was deregistered in 2008 because of unpaid bills, modernised the union's Sydney headquarters in Pitt Street. McClymont tracked down local government building records from 2008 that identified Mah-Chut as the architect of a holiday house Williamson was building at Lake Macquarie. Mah-Chut cut Williamson a discount on the job because of the volume of work coming from the union. He also worked on the 2001 renovation of Williamson's large home in Maroubra, a Sydney beachside suburb. Mah-Chut's annual retainer covered the cost of spending one day a week scouting for sites suitable for the union to build retirement villages or holiday accommodation.

Two companies had been paid to provide separate record-keeping computer systems. One was partly owned by Williamson and received $1.3 million a year between April 2008 and September 2011.

There were unusual property deals. In 2006 the union bought a building in Sydney for about $800,000. Williamson's son Chris took control and converted it into a commercial recording studio, which he rented to bands.

An obscure couple living on Sydney's picturesque northern beaches – John Gilleland and his wife, Carron – were making good money out of the HSU too. From their home in Palm Beach their Communigraphix printing company was paid $3.44 million from the union between March 2007 and September 2011 to produce the union's regular glossy magazine for members. Other unions were paying one-tenth of that for similar newsletters. John Gilleland had a dubious background. In 1984 he was charged by the Federal Police, along with his brother, Ian, for printing counterfeit deutsche marks. A jury acquitted John in 1986. Ian was found guilty and sentenced to five years' jail, according to the *Herald*.

The private detective's information, combined with the strange payments set out in the union's financial records, suggested Thomson wasn't the only official in the HSU who had misused union funds. He may have been copying his mentor.

While Jackson was delving deeper into the union's finances, the Liberal Party decided to go on the attack over what was emerging as a national scandal. On 19 August 2011, Senator George Brandis, the shadow attorney-general, rang the New South Wales police minister, Mike Gallacher, a fellow Liberal, and discussed the need for a police investigation of the HSU. Brandis then wrote to the head of NSW Police, Andrew Scipione, and asked for the police to act. Scipione said the police needed a complaint from the union's national office, which threw the onus onto Jackson.

The pressure was building. Jackson was receiving hundreds of emails, phone calls and text messages a day. Labor Party colleagues accused her of being a traitor.

Early on the morning of 26 August 2011, while Jackson was asleep, there was loud banging outside her house. Scared, she waited before going to investigate. A shovel was lying on the porch. Newspapers later said it was underworld code for 'dig your own grave'.

A week later white powder was discovered in an envelope at Feeney's office in Melbourne, prompting an evacuation. The powder was harmless and no-one was hurt. Many people in the union movement and Labor Party suspected a connection between the powder and Feeney's friendship with Jackson. Not long after the shovel incident the pressure became unbearable for Jackson, who suffered a mental breakdown and spent five days in Austin Hospital's psychiatric unit. She had no idea things were going to get a lot worse.

## Shunned

In private, Craig Thomson declared victory. He boasted to fellow MPs that Fairfax Media had settled his defamation lawsuit over the original *Sydney Morning Herald* articles that accused him of misusing union funds. Instead of fighting to defend the accuracy of its report on the spending scandal within the Health Services Union, the media company folded before Thomson's lawsuit got to court, he said. Thomson used the apparent settlement to try to head off the Fair Work Australia investigation into his HSU spending. In an email to the industrial tribunal on 18 May headed PRIVATE,

CONFIDENTIAL and NOT FOR PUBLICATION, he wrote: 'Fairfax publications has also agreed to a confidential settlement of the defamation action I brought against them.'

Thomson had told Fair Work Australia that his travel records, backed up by witnesses, proved he wasn't in Sydney on the days the *Herald* reported his credit card records were used to pay for escorts. Because the agreement was confidential he couldn't explain why Fairfax had settled. He did, however, drop a couple of hints about the evidence he could produce to shoot down the allegations: his now ex-wife, Christa, was prepared to testify she was with him at the precise times prostitutes were being racked up on his credit cards; and his signature was forged and he could produce a handwriting expert to prove it.

Thomson was lying. Fairfax didn't agree to settle with him. He agreed to settle with Fairfax. Thomson's legal position was so weak his lawyers offered Fairfax a 'walk-away' deal – each side would give up and pay their own costs. Fairfax refused. A trove of documents, including credit card statements and phone records obtained by the company through the court process, seemed to prove Thomson did use union funds to pay for prostitutes. As the case neared a point where some of the evidence would become public, Graham Richardson, the former Labor minister and factional leader, approached Thomson. Richardson told Thomson to cut a deal with Fairfax and end the lawsuit.

In April 2011, Thomson agreed to cover Fairfax's legal costs of $240,000 and drop the defamation claim. Both sides resolved to keep the settlement private. Thomson dropped the lawsuit against Mark Davis, the reporter who wrote the original articles. Davis had taken a job as press secretary to Greg Combet, the climate change minister. Fairfax was still conducting his legal defence. On 6 June Fairfax, in response to a subpoena, handed over its Thomson evidence to the Fair Work Australia investigative team.

Thomson's greatest asset was the threat his removal posed to Labor's tenuous hold on power. The minority government couldn't afford to let Thomson go bankrupt, as that would mean he'd be expelled from parliament and the party would probably lose his marginal seat in a by-election. Labor figures in the New South Wales division decided they had no choice but to cover Thomson's settlement bill. In addition, the party paid out $108,366 to cover Thomson's other legal expenses and some of its own costs for the case. Saving Thomson was cheaper than fighting an election.

Thomson got a break on 8 September 2011. The New South Wales police fraud squad decided it didn't have the jurisdiction to pursue him over the allegations because most of the relevant documents originated in Victoria. The case would be referred to Victoria Police. Journalists were briefed on the decision. A memo from the squad conceded the Victorians were unlikely to prosecute.

The police seemed eager to drop the case. The fraud squad spent less than two weeks sifting through thousands of Thomson-related documents. Unable to find a 'smoking receipt', it gave up. *Sydney Morning Herald* reporter Dylan Welch believed the decision would go down well with the force's hierarchy. 'Police Commissioner Andrew Scipione would have been uncomfortable having such a politically explosive matter under his purview,' he wrote.

The next day the *Herald*'s Kate McClymont blew the story wide open. Without revealing where she got the information, McClymont published details of the evidence uncovered by Kathy Jackson's private detective, Nicholas Mamouzelos, and from her own investigations. The article accused Thomson and Michael Williamson of receiving secret commissions from Communigraphix, the printing firm used to produce the union newsletter. It seemed that in return for inflating the value of the printing contract, Communigraphix had agreed to cover some of Thomson's and Williamson's day-to-day living expenses. McClymont reported that two American Express credit cards issued in their names were attached to an account belonging to the printing firm's owner, John Gilleland.

Gilleland's wife, Carron, had complained to union officials at a function in 2011 that Williamson had 'run amok' with the Amex card and used it to pay for his children's private school fees, McClymont reported. 'This was not part of the deal,' she told the officials. After years of big payments by the union to Communigraphix, the relationship seemed to have soured.

The kickback allegations triggered a media frenzy. They were much more damaging to the union and the government than anything before. Thomson had always argued that the expenses he racked up on his union credit cards, including flights, accommodation and food, were properly authorised. (He denied using prostitutes.) Given Thomson was the head of the union and approved his own spending, it was a credible defence. But accepting kickbacks from a union supplier was clearly illegal. Thomson and Williamson faced jail time. If convicted, Thomson would be ineligible to remain an MP. The government, which held power by one seat, was on the precipice.

News photographers camped outside Williamson's and Thomson's houses. Neither man would speak to the press. But there were signs the media pressure was getting to the Williamson family. His son

Chris, who ran his music studio out of a union-owned building, posted a message on Facebook: 'What are they going to blame for next? The gfc?'

Four days after the *Herald* article, Jackson met with an assistant commissioner at the police headquarters in Parramatta. She accused Williamson, Thomson and the union's printing contractor of corruption. That afternoon the police established Strike Force Carnarvon, staffed by six detectives, to investigate the union. After three years of trying to hold someone accountable, Jackson had finally convinced police to devote the resources needed to expose what she was convinced was her union's corrupt culture.

Later that week Jackson got a call from David Feeney. The senator had a warning and an offer. He said he had spoken to Sam Dastyari, the administrative head of the Labor Party in New South Wales, according to Jackson. Dastyari had proposed an 'amicable divorce'. The HSU would be broken up into its original divisions in New South Wales and Victoria. Jackson would retreat to Victoria and give up the campaign against her opponents in New South Wales. If she refused, she would face the full power of the party hierarchy in New South Wales, Feeney said, according to Jackson.

'You are not strong enough to take on the whole of Sussex Street [referring to NSW Labor's head office] and that is what an all-out fight against the Williamson forces will entail,' Jackson said Feeney told her. 'They know that Williamson is gone but they will not stand for any risk of them losing control of the HSU's votes.'

Jackson said she replied: 'Well, I'm happy to talk but I will not put up with a cover-up. I am not going to let this get swept under the carpet. They have done it with Craig Thomson and I am not going to put up with another cover-up.'

She said Feeney responded: 'Of course, I'm not suggesting otherwise. I'm just saying that you should think about whether you can get proper treatment of the corruption as part of an amicable divorce.'

Jackson said she agreed to consider Feeney's plan. (Dastyari later said he had no recollection of the conversation and questioned Jackson's motives. Feeney declined to discuss the call.)

A week after the kickback allegations were published Williamson got good news. The union had agreed to cover his legal costs for the ensuing investigation by police.

About 7 a.m., on 2 December 2011, Jackson's mobile phone beeped with an incoming message. She was in the shower. Curious about the early morning text, her partner, Michael Lawler, picked up the phone. One of Jackson's few confidantes in the union, Carol Glen, was so sick of the infighting she had decided to quit. The message sent a shock through Lawler. Glen's departure would be a huge blow to Jackson. The women were close. They liked to socialise outside of work, often at Jackson's house. Jackson had confessed the stress she was under to Glen and cried in front of her several times. Glen was a member of the HSU national executive, which was split 4–4 between Williamson's group and Jackson's allies.

Fearful of his partner losing an important personal and professional ally, Lawler rang Glen straight away to say her resignation would be a catastrophe for Jackson. Lawler later said he calmly tried to convince her to stay, and said she would be entitled to a medical certificate for stress leave. Later, Glen didn't dispute the substance of the conversation but had a very different take on its tone. According to her, Lawler said:

You can't do this. This will put Kathy back in hospital and give Michael Williamson the option of putting [his ally] Stuart Miller in your position. You can fuck off and take sick leave if you don't want to do the work and still be paid, but you can't resign.

Jackson rang Glen as soon as she got out of the shower. Glen didn't pick up. By 10 a.m. Glen's work email account was shut down. The formal notification of her resignation was sent out at 1 p.m. Jackson and Glen never spoke again. Four days later Glen wrote a letter to Lawler's superior at Fair Work Australia, president Geoffrey Giudice, and accused Lawler of harassment. The letter was embarrassing for Lawler, who was a deputy president on the industrial tribunal and had the same legal protections as a judge. Giudice didn't do anything about the complaint.

Around the time of Glen's resignation, Jackson attended a big superannuation conference in Brisbane. Many former union officials join the boards of industry super funds and Jackson recognised scores of people. Over two days, not one union or Labor person spoke to her. The campaign to destroy Jackson's reputation was working.

## Stepping up

The Labor Party ended 2011, Julia Gillard's first full year as prime minister, debating if gay people should be allowed to marry. The body with the power to definitely settle the party's position, its three-day national conference, was held over the first weekend of December. Four hundred delegates from unions and Labor branches around Australia gathered at Sydney's creaking Exhibition Centre in Darling Harbour for a political version of the Big Day Out.

Any uncertainty about Gillard's ideological journey from the left to the right of the party was sealed by her opposition to same-sex marriage at the conference. The belief that only a man and a woman could be married was an important point of principle for many of those MPs who made her leader in 2010, including Don Farrell and the Catholic Church-aligned shop assistants' union. The Left, and most delegates, regarded gay marriage as a basic human right and insisted the party support a private member's bill from Labor MP Stephen Jones that would make it law. Gillard locked in behind her conservative supporters.

Still, the vote in favour of gay marriage passed easily. Enough delegates from the Right, which had an overall majority, supported the motion without the need for a count.

There was a catch. Some MPs from the Right so strongly opposed gay marriage they would likely vote against the law in parliament, triggering a damaging schism in the party. Supporting Labor policies in parliament is one of the party's bedrock rules. To avoid a split, right-wing factional leaders asked for a rare conscience vote on gay marriage. All federal Labor MPs, including Gillard, would be given a free pass to vote against the party's policy.

The Left thought the carve-out ridiculous. 'A conscience vote on human rights is not conscionable,' Senator John Faulkner said. The Right overruled him. Conference delegates tallied 208 to 184 in favour of a conscience vote. The arrangement condemned the gay marriage law to failure – there weren't enough votes to overcome Liberal Party and Nationals opposition.[13]

Tepid moves to make the party more democratic at the conference didn't go far either. Delegates decided not to give the national president, a position first elected by the membership that year, a vote on the national executive, which runs the party on a month-to-month basis. The members' representative would continue to have no formal say on the party's governance.

Gillard had been prime minister for sixteen months. To the surprise of many she had led a stable minority government. After the 2010 election she had felt obliged to promote the plotters who made her leader. Those men continued to support her. But they weren't close to her personally. By December 2011, Gillard had established enough personal authority to reshuffle the ministry on her own terms.

A week after the Labor conference, she rewarded two women she trusted and liked, strengthening her position in cabinet. Minister for health and ageing Nicola Roxon was made attorney-general, a dream job for the ex-lawyer. Tanya Plibersek, the minister for health services and social inclusion, became health minister, a big promotion that gave her a seat in cabinet. Mark Arbib was made assistant treasurer. Robert McClelland and Kim Carr were demoted. Both became staunch enemies of Gillard's.

Gillard, knowing she wouldn't be in the job forever, appeared sensitive to the ambitions of two of the men who might eventually replace her. Bill Shorten and Greg Combet were both promoted, a decision that avoided creating the perception one was her preferred successor. Combet, the climate change minister, got the industry portfolio too, which made him responsible for billions in subsidies to the foreign-owned car-manufacturing industry. Shorten was appointed to Cabinet and made minister for employment and workplace relations. Once a trainee union organiser, he was now responsible for the entire industrial relations system. He kept financial services too.

Critics said Shorten was being stretched too thin across two big jobs. Others thought keeping financial services was a smart move. If Shorten had wanted to give up the portfolio, Gillard presumably would have agreed. There were plenty of ambitious ministers interested in expanding their power. The ability to control changes to superannuation rules and corporate regulation allowed Shorten to exert huge influence over the business world. Workplace relations gave him oversight of the union movement, a powerful platform to build up favours with the union leaders who controlled the Labor Party's finances.

With his ascent to cabinet, newspaper articles piled up predicting Shorten would eventually become prime minister. Even he joked he was getting tired of the positive coverage. In his own mind, he had sacrificed the top political office in his home state for a chance to seize a bigger prize. 'I could have been premier of Victoria,' he told one person who had regular meetings with him not long after he was appointed assistant treasurer. Shorten believed that if he had taken the Victorian state seat of Melton, which the Labor Party offered him when he was thirty-one, he would have been a minister in Steve Bracks' government and probably would have succeeded Bracks, who retired in July 2007 when Shorten was forty.

Shorten's cabinet promotion allowed him to raise his profile even further. He became one of the government's main voices. In press appearances at Parliament House and his electorate, and in numerous television interviews, he took questions on almost all the main political issues, including the carbon tax, asylum seekers, the budget surplus and the Labor leadership.

Pounding the opposition came naturally. Shorten loved nothing more than ridiculing his opponents. The difference now was he was focused on those in another political party. A criticism by Tony Abbott about union-dominated superannuation funds was flipped back at the Liberal leader. Abbott had repeated a common complaint that former union officials with no financial-industry experience were getting cushy positions on super fund boards. In parliament, Shorten pointed out that many employer bodies appointed representatives to the same funds, including Master Builders Australia, the National Retail Association and the National Farmers' Federation, groups broadly sympathetic to the Coalition. 'What did these organisations ever do to be maligned, attacked and defamed by the leader of the Opposition and his caucus room?' Shorten asked in question time on 14 March.

Shorten deployed aggression as a tool of self-promotion. The attacks on the Coalition were part of a strategy to boost Shorten's leadership credentials with the backbench. As a minister, Shorten had quickly developed a reputation as a dangerous man to cross. If a lobbyist criticised one of his decisions publicly, he would often ring and bluntly express his displeasure, sometimes swearing to hammer home the point. The financial services industry was used to a friendlier relationship. When Shorten's predecessor as financial services minister, Chris Bowen, planned to publish details of a new policy, he would personally ring industry leaders a couple of days before to let them know what was coming. Sometimes he would hand over briefing papers explaining the decision. The notice gave the groups time to prepare their responses for the press and keep their corporate funders feeling informed.

Shorten's approach was different. His aides would often ring industry representatives at the last moment before a new policy document was released. It was a power play that kept the industry on edge and gave Shorten greater control over public debate about his decisions. When he thought the Financial Services Council had leaked tentative government plans to the *Australian Financial Review* about reducing tax concessions on superannuation for the wealthy, Shorten threatened to cut off the group's access to his office. Such a move would have been disastrous for the council, which needed access to Shorten and his staff to push the interests of its members, which included most of the biggest superannuation funds in the country. (The Financial Services Council denied it was the *Financial Review*'s source.)

As minister for workplace relations, one issue would consume Shorten's time like no other in the coming months: the corruption engulfing the Health Services Union. Allegations about the leaders of the previously obscure union would become a national scandal that would tarnish the labour movement's reputation and threaten the government's very existence. Shorten, who led the government's political response, had personal interests at stake. One of the protagonists, Michael Williamson, was his factional confederate. Another, Kathy Jackson, was a sworn enemy. As the affair unfolded Jackson and Shorten, both determined political operators, would inflict terrible damage on each other.

# 7

## The return of the king – a Queensland campaign goes wrong – Blackout in the Sunshine State

### Families are off limits

In April 2011, eleven months before the Queensland election, Labor's Brisbane headquarters were in full-time campaign mode. Labor faced a potent new opponent, Campbell Newman, the former Brisbane lord mayor. Campbell, who wasn't even an MP, was trying to lead the opposition to an election victory from outside parliament. The polls showed he was popular and trusted.

After a decade and a half in government, Labor was losing its grip on power. The party and its exhausted leader, Anna Bligh, were getting desperate. Bligh's team began probing Newman's record for vulnerabilities.

Bligh was intelligent, popular and calm. A descendant of William Bligh, the notorious captain of the *Bounty*, she was born in Warwick, a medium-sized town 130 kilometres south-west of Brisbane, and grew up on the Gold Coast. Her father, Bill Bligh, was an alcoholic with a gambling problem who separated from her mother, Frances, when Bligh was thirteen. A smart and diligent student, Bligh was drawn to leftist causes by her difficult family circumstances. She got into an arts degree at the University of Queensland in the 1970s, where she was elected student union vice-president for women's rights. Her first job after graduating was in a women's refuge. An active player in the local Labor Party branches, she won the seat of South Brisbane at age thirty-five. Her work ethic and serious approach to policy was noted and she was quickly promoted. In 2001 she became Queensland's first female education minister. Four years later, and a decade after entering parliament, Premier Peter Beattie appointed her deputy premier. 'She's deputy premier and treasurer and every other piece of shit I didn't want,' Beattie was caught on tape telling New South Wales premier Morris Iemma at a meeting in 2006. When Beattie retired in 2007 after nine years as premier, no other Labor MP stood against Bligh to replace him. In 2009 she became the first woman to lead a party to victory in an Australian state election.

In a crisis, Bligh was a superb communicator. More authoritative than Kristina Keneally and more down-to-earth than Julia Gillard, Bligh's leadership skills were demonstrated when a cyclone and floods in December 2010 and January 2011 turned three-quarters of Queensland into a disaster zone. Thirty-five people were killed. The economic damage was estimated at $4 billion. About 19,000 kilometres of roads and 28 per cent of the state rail network was damaged.

Bligh spent hours in front of television cameras explaining the government's response and reassuring the community. As the flood swept through central Brisbane and other parts of south-east

Queensland, cutting power to 118,000 homes, the emotional force of the disaster became overwhelming. Towards the end of a press briefing, after delivering an unemotional summary of events, Bligh briefly lost her composure as she tried to rally the state. 'I want us to remember who we are,' she said. 'We are Queenslanders. We are the people that they breed tough north of the border. We are the ones they knock down and we get up again. This weather may break our hearts – and it's doing that – but it will not break our will.' Bligh 'has become the embodiment of a whole state's resilience', author John Birmingham wrote.

Bligh wasn't the only politician who emerged from the disaster looking good. As lord mayor, Campbell Newman helped lead the response to the flooding, which had turned central Brisbane into a lake. A former officer in the Army Corps of Engineers, his practical style was a hit with voters too.

Two months after the water subsided, Newman engineered one of the most audacious manoeuvres in Australian political history. On 22 March he resigned as mayor and simultaneously put himself forward as a candidate for a state seat. In a coordinated move, the existing leader of the Liberal National Party, John-Paul Langbroek, agreed to step aside for Newman, who became the first Australian to lead a major political party without even being an MP.

Newman was the new face of the Liberal National Party. One of the reasons Labor had held power for twenty years out of the previous twenty-two was because Brisbane voters didn't like National Party or Liberal National Party leaders from country areas. They were too conservative.

Newman's appointment as LNP leader upended Queensland's political equilibrium. For the first time, a city-bred Liberal led the conservative opposition. The polls showed Queenslanders were taken with the new LNP leader, who wasn't that different from Bligh, or her predecessors, Wayne Goss and Beattie. His engineering degree, training as an army officer and his leadership of the city council went down particularly well in Brisbane, which had 40 per cent of all Queensland seats.

Newman wasn't just another suburban councillor. Both his parents, Kevin and Jocelyn Newman, had served as ministers in separate federal Liberal governments. As the mayor of Brisbane City Council since 2004, he had the most important municipal job in Australia. The council covered about half the metropolitan area, provided services to one million people, employed 8500 staff and had an annual budget of $2.28 billion.

Newman's elevation triggered consternation at Labor headquarters. Bligh's main political advisers, who included Andrew Fraser, the state's treasurer, Labor state secretary Anthony Chisholm, his deputy, Jackie Trad, Bligh's chief of staff, Nicole Scurrah, and her director of policy, Matt Collins, urged her to go negative.

Initially, Bligh was reluctant. 'I can give this guarantee,' she told the media not long after Newman became leader, 'I won't be at any stage insulting or criticising any member of Mr Newman's family.'

Newman's father-in-law, Frank Monsour, was a wealthy oral surgeon and property developer. In September *The Australian* reported that a company set up by his family soon after the floods, Majella Global Technologies Asia Pacific, applied for a $29 million contract to provide technology to the Queensland Reconstruction Authority, which had primary responsibility for rebuilding the state's infrastructure. Newman's wife, Lisa, was the firm's company secretary for the first three weeks of its existence. At the time, her husband hadn't revealed his plan to switch to state politics.

Even though the Monsours' company didn't win a contract with the authority, the article was highly embarrassing for Newman. It looked like his family was trying to cash in on the disaster that had propelled him to the party leadership.

The election was due in the first half of 2012. The exact date was dependent on the conclusion of an official investigation into the floods. Bligh knew voters would want to learn the findings of the inquiry before they decided how hard to punish Labor after fourteen years in power.

Bligh had plenty of material with which to attack Newman. Chisholm had prepared a television ad about the Monsours' failed bid for the flood contract. But she didn't want to break her promise not to go after Newman's family. Chisholm wrote a series of attack lines for Bligh to deploy at a debate with Newman organised by *The Courier-Mail* in November at Brisbane's Customs House. Because Newman didn't have a seat in parliament it was the first time the two leaders had appeared on the same stage to answer questions. Bligh pushed a plan to spend taxes from the burgeoning gas industry on schools. She used only one of Chisholm's lines. Newman looked confident and calm.

Clearly Bligh's tactics weren't working. If Labor were going to avoid a New South Wales-style disaster, she would have to reconsider her no-attack pledge.

## Bad timing

Anna Bligh's promise not to attack Campbell Newman's in-laws lasted until four days before the start of the formal election campaign.

In parliament, on 15 February, Bligh singled out the shady company owned by Newman's wife's family that had pitched for the $29 million flood-recovery contract. An American competitor had accused Majella Global Technologies of illegally accessing its technology. The U.S. Federal Bureau of Investigation was reviewing the allegations, according to a media report. Newman's brother-in-law, Seb Monsour, ran Majella. Newman had denied he and his wife were involved in the company.

In parliament, Bligh accused him of lying. Corporate records showed Lisa Newman was a shareholder in the company and Newman was entitled to a share of his wife's assets because they were married, she said. Bligh didn't use the word corruption. But she suggested Newman might have been involved in corrupt business dealings through the Monsours.

Newman wasn't a member of parliament and couldn't defend himself in person. The Opposition was outraged at Bligh's personal attack. When a Liberal National MP, Jeff Seeney, referred to Gordon Nuttall, a Labor minister jailed in 2009 for receiving bribes and committing perjury, Bligh ratcheted up her rhetoric. 'Those people are behind bars and Campbell Newman will end up there as well,' she said.

Newman's response later in the day to this incredible claim – that he would be convicted of corruption and sent to prison – was measured. He accused the government of smearing his family's reputation – which was true – and didn't respond to the detail of Bligh's allegations. 'I don't know anything about this,' he said. 'I'm not involved in [Seb Monsour's] business dealings and neither is my wife.'

Bligh's jail claim wasn't premeditated. Caught up in the moment, she went further than had been agreed with her advisers beforehand.

Once it was said, she couldn't back down. The consequences wouldn't become clear until almost the end of the campaign.

Kevin Rudd has a foul temper. When he gets annoyed, he swears. Few Australians realised how fond Rudd was of obscenities until someone posted a clip on YouTube on 17 February, three days after Bligh's attack on Newman's family. The video contained outtakes from a message in Chinese given when Rudd was prime minister. In the video he expressed frustration with the complexity of the text prepared for him by the public service. 'Tell those dickheads in the embassy to give me simple sentences,' he said. 'Just fucking hopeless. I fucked up the last word.'

No-one knew who posted the embarrassing video. On YouTube they identified themselves as 'HappyVegemiteKR' – a reference to Rudd's standard answer when asked if he wanted to be prime minister again. 'I'm a happy little Vegemite being foreign minister,' he would say. The provocateur must have had high-level access, which suggested a minister or their staff. Rudd thought the leak came from Julia Gillard's office. She denied any involvement.

Posting the video was a juvenile act that simultaneously made Rudd look like a difficult person and the victim of dirty tricks. It also suggested the deep tensions in the government that triggered the 2010 leadership change hadn't been resolved. Gillard's supporters perceived Rudd as an ongoing threat. They believed he hadn't accepted his removal as leader and was defying her authority.

The Queensland election campaign officially kicked off on 19 February 2012, when Governor Penelope Wensley dissolved parliament. Labor's polling predicted a 16 per cent swing against the government, a result that would reduce the number of Labor MPs from fifty-one to fewer than ten in the eighty-nine-member parliament. Labor's only sliver of hope was Ashgrove, the Brisbane electorate Campbell Newman was trying to win. Support for Labor was, amazingly, improving in Ashgrove at the start of the campaign, according to internal party polls. If Labor could convince the public it had a credible chance of retaining Ashgrove, it could legitimately raise doubts about whether Newman would get elected to parliament. Newman needed a not inconsiderable swing of 7.1 per cent to win the seat in north-west Brisbane that took in the Enoggera Army Barracks. If Newman weren't elected, the Liberal National Party would probably revert to its roots and choose a conservative, rural-based leader. That would worry a lot of moderate voters in Brisbane and the state's south-east and possibly spook them into voting Labor.

Government strategists figured if they could get the anti-Labor swing down to about 8 per cent, they would retain about twenty seats. Even though that would be a landslide victory to the LNP, it would leave Labor with a cadre of MPs large enough to be a reasonably effective opposition who could rebuild the party's support.

The strategy hinged on stopping Newman personally. Anna Bligh, who hadn't wanted to run a grubby campaign, had a choice: take the high road or the low road. She chose the low road.

Five days after Bligh's going-to-jail attack on Newman, the Labor Party was embarrassed by one of its candidates. Peter Watson, a nineteen-year-old running in a Liberal National seat, had posted homophobic and neo-Nazi rants in a blog as an adolescent. Watson wrote that homosexuals were degenerates who should be 'wiped out'. Another post promised to share information about other Labor Party members as part of his 'long battle against the commies in the branch here in Warwick'. He was quickly removed as the candidate and expelled from the party.

Watson's teenage musings created a brief flurry of media interest but had little impact on the campaign. In the background a far bigger story was brewing. Federal Labor was about to go to war with itself, destabilising the government and overshadowing the campaign in Queensland.

On 21 February, three days after Rudd's YouTube video was posted, regional development minister Simon Crean brought into the open the resentment towards Rudd within the top echelons of the Labor Party. 'He's clearly been disloyal internally,' Crean said on ABC Radio. 'I know he's been talking to other people.' Crean said Rudd should be sacked or resign unless he committed to supporting Gillard.

Rudd, who was in the U.S. on his way to Mexico for a meeting of the Group of 20 nations, didn't immediately respond. Australian journalists gathered at his Washington hotel until 2 a.m., when he appeared behind a podium in a small function room. It was early afternoon in Australia. The reporters in the room were exhausted. Sky News carried the press conference live. In typical Rudd style, he had a bombshell to drop.

Rudd announced his resignation as foreign minister. A letter had already been sent by fax to Gillard, he said. The reason for this stunning decision: the prime minister's disloyalty. Rudd argued that Gillard's failure to rebuke Crean and other ministers for criticising him meant she must share their views. He said he was shocked by the personal attacks against him and that they had no place in Australian politics. 'The truth is I can only serve as foreign minister if I have the confidence of Prime Minister Gillard and senior ministers,' he said. 'When challenged today on these attacks, Prime Minister Gillard chose not to repudiate them. I can only reluctantly conclude that she therefore shares these views.'

Rudd's chutzpah was astounding. All the signs pointed to Rudd for leaking damaging details of cabinet discussions during the 2010 election, which contributed to the loss of Labor's parliamentary majority. Since then, in private, Rudd was critical of Gillard's policies in meetings with journalists, including her repudiation of his 'Big Australia' policy. Whatever the merits of Rudd's position – and most Labor MPs didn't agree with him – Rudd's loyalty to Gillard and the government was highly questionable, at best. Yet he portrayed himself, and was largely unchallenged on this point, as a victim of disloyalty by Gillard.

In a tactical move, Rudd didn't announce a challenge. He wanted to get home and work on his support among Labor MPs first. Labor looked like it was heading for a big loss under Gillard – the latest poll showed it six percentage points behind the Coalition – and Rudd clearly believed he was the party's best chance. He left Washington the next day for Australia.

It was Gillard, who was on a trip to Adelaide, who formally declared there would be a leadership vote. At a press conference a few hours after Rudd's, Gillard said a ballot would be held in four days time, a tight time frame that limited Rudd's ability to run a public campaign to drum up votes. Gillard promised to go to the backbench and never challenge again if she lost. She asked Rudd to do the same. Then she ripped into him.

'It is now evident to me and I think it is evident to the Australian people that there has been a long-running destabilisation campaign here to get to this point, where Kevin Rudd is clearly going to announce that he wants to seek the Labor leadership,' she said.

'Having lived through the days of the Rudd government, it became absolutely clear to me that one of the overriding problems of the government that Kevin Rudd led is it was very, very focused on the next news cycle, on the next picture opportunity, rather than the long-term reforms for the nation's interests.'

Gillard was deputy prime minister under Rudd for three years. She knew his work style as well as anyone in cabinet. At the press conference she said Rudd was a difficult, dysfunctional and chaotic leader obsessed by headlines and opinion polls. He lacked the temperament to hold his nerve when the polls turned against him, she said, even though it was her supporters who had used opinion polls as a reason to remove him as leader.

Gillard portrayed herself as a leader who could rise above populism and keep the government working no matter how tough the political environment. Most seriously, she accused Rudd of being responsible for cabinet leaks during the 2010 election campaign. Gillard, who was usually implacable in public, became annoyed when an insistent reporter from *The Australian*, Michael Owen, implied Gillard was hypocritical because of what he said was her manoeuvring to replace Rudd when he was prime minister. 'I'm not going to have you just speak to me like this,' Gillard told Owen. 'End of sentence.'

Owen kept pushing. 'So you just fell into the leadership?' he said.

'Your question is internally inconsistent,' Gillard told him. 'If you stop talking then I'll give you an answer, but I can't give you an answer if you keep talking.'

Owen later apologised.

The competing press conferences framed the leadership contest. They also illustrated the bitter split in the senior ranks of the party. When Treasurer Paul Keating challenged Prime Minister Bob

Hawke in 1991, both men were perceived within the community and by their peers to be highly capable leaders with legitimate claims to the job. They avoided personal attacks against each other.

The battle between Gillard and Rudd was entirely different. Gillard questioned Rudd's basic competence. She portrayed him as managerially unfit to head the government. She accused him of unethical behaviour.

The Gillard–Rudd conflict was a paradox. Gillard was well liked by most Labor MPs and disliked by most voters. Rudd was loathed by most Labor MPs and vastly more popular with the public. The parliamentary party had to choose between electoral star power and unloved dependability.

## Wipe out

Anna Bligh was campaigning in Townsville when news broke that there would be another leadership vote in Canberra. Her stress levels, almost maxed out already, rose further. 'I don't have a vote, I'm not going to speculate about it, but I am going to say get it fixed,' she told reporters.

Based on his soundings of federal MPs, Anthony Chisholm, the secretary of the Queensland Labor Party, didn't think Rudd could win. He was certain Queenslanders would take their frustrations out on Bligh if the Labor Party rejected Rudd a second time. He knew Bligh and the Queensland Labor Party needed a new plan.

Chisholm got the next available flight to Townsville and met Anna Bligh at her hotel to work out their response. Their original plan that week was to establish in voters' minds Labor's achievements in government. That had already been obliterated by the massive media attention on federal Labor. The party's nightly polling showed the challenge was doing even more damage to Labor's Queensland campaign than the disruption caused by the carbon tax during the New South Wales election a year earlier. The swing against the state government was a huge 16 per cent – a gap growing by the day. *The Courier-Mail*, Brisbane's only daily newspaper, had pulled its reporters from travelling with Bligh and Newman as they criss-crossed the state campaigning. The decision, which saved on travel costs, also reflected the lack of substance in the staged media events of both sides. Chisholm and Bligh knew it was impossible to compete with the drama in Canberra. They agreed to take a desperate step: launch an all-out attack on Newman's family.

On the morning of 27 February Labor MPs gathered in Canberra to choose their leader. Unlike Rudd's removal in 2010, there would be a vote. The tense atmosphere was mixed with a healthy dollop of excitement. Rudd wasn't expected to win. Exhaustive lists of which Labor MPs supported Rudd and Gillard had appeared for days in most newspapers. It was clear a majority would back the prime minister. But would the victory be large enough? A narrow win would wound the prime minister, perhaps fatally.

The public was conflicted. Forty-seven per cent thought the party should stick with Gillard, according to a Newspoll, and 48 per cent wanted a change to Rudd.

Labor MPs had a clearer view. He lost seventy-one to thirty-one. Gillard's decision to call a quick vote had worked. Rudd didn't have time to build support. In the nineteen months since he was removed as leader, Rudd's support among Labor MPs hadn't budged. Gillard triumphantly left the caucus room flanked by two Queenslanders: Treasurer Wayne Swan and trade minister Craig Emerson.

Rudd's loss again illustrated the power of the factional leaders. Of the six men who led Rudd's removal in 2010, only one had swapped sides: Kim Carr. Their own careers and reputations on the line, Bill Shorten, Stephen Conroy, Mark Arbib, Don Farrell and David Feeney had stuck solidly behind Gillard, locking in most of the caucus with them. Even though the polls showed Labor was heading for a disastrous loss under Gillard, the five leaders of the Right couldn't bring themselves to admit that Rudd's bloody removal had turned out to be an electoral miscalculation.

The outcome was great for Gillard, who looked like she had finally vanquished her rival. It was a disaster for Bligh, who knew Queensland voters would be resentful their home son had been humiliated twice. Bligh's predecessor, Peter Beattie, summed up the state's frustration. 'In my thirty-seven years in the Labor Party I have never felt such anger in the community towards the ALP,' he said. The disgust at the party's internal turmoil was national. Labor's support, on a two-party basis, fell from 47 per cent to 43 per cent in the month after the leadership ballot.

In an appearance on the ABC's *7.30* program the night of the vote, Shorten played the role of party statesman. 'The message out of today is that the Labor Party is uniting behind Julia Gillard,' he said.

Adding to the drama, Mark Arbib said he would resign from the Senate and drop out of politics. The forty-year-old was one of the toughest operators in parliament. His resignation triggered speculation he was in some kind of legal trouble. Arbib said he wanted to spend more time with his young family.

\*\*\*

In Queensland, Labor went after the Newmans through a television ad campaign. The ads weren't subtle and, in some cases, contained untruths and factual distortions. One ad said it was Lisa Newman who applied for the $29 million flood contract – even though Bligh presented an email in parliament that showed her brother, Seb Monsour, had approached the Flood Reconstruction Authority.

The ad also referred to what it called 'The Dodgy Deal', a decision to rezone land while Newman was Brisbane lord mayor. The ALP said the decision could generate millions of dollars for the Monsours. The Brisbane City Council had approved apartment buildings of up to eight storeys in Woolloongabba, the inner-city suburb that is home to the Brisbane Cricket Ground. Newman was mayor but abstained from voting on the rezoning, citing a conflict of interest because he was a member of an RSL club in the area. The rezoning took effect on 29 March 2011, five days before he resigned as mayor. The Monsour family then purchased land in the area and applied for permission to build ninety-one apartments well after Newman left the council. Newman said he didn't know about the land deal. The ad finished with slow-motion footage of Lisa Newman staring lovingly at her husband while a voice said: 'Hmm, wasn't that nice of him.' The land-deal allegations worked well with men, according to Labor research.

The Woolloongabba developments triggered more Labor attacks. In late February and early March, *The Australian* reported a property developer, Philip Usher, donated $60,000 through at least five separate companies a year earlier to the re-election fund for Newman's team on the council.

Bligh threatened to ask for an investigation by the Crime and Misconduct Commission, Queensland's anti-corruption authority, into the donations. Newman said he wasn't aware of them and promised to relinquish all financial interests and positions in private companies within ninety days of the election if he became premier.

The personal attacks seemed to work, at least initially. On 6 March an automated telephone poll of 742 people who lived in Ashgrove showed the outcome was too close to call – a remarkable situation given the huge shift against Labor across the rest of the state. Chisholm's nightly polling of 300 people in six electorates estimated the swing against the government had improved to 10 per cent from the 16 per cent at the start of the campaign. The change, if sustained, would save Labor about twelve seats and have a big impact on its ability to rebuild after losing office.

Two weeks before election day, Chisholm switched to the final phase of the party's strategy. He started running ads that questioned whether Newman would even get elected to parliament, an attempt to stoke fears in Brisbane of a figure reminiscent of Joh Bjelke-Petersen becoming Liberal National Party leader and premier.

Then, just as Labor was pulling its campaign together, Bligh made a fatal concession. On 13 March, eleven days before the poll, a group of reporters pinned her down on the campaign trail. They wanted to know if the government had carried through on its threat to seek an investigation by the Crime and Misconduct Commission into the political donations to Newman's campaign. 'No,' Bligh said. 'Right now, all I have is questions.'

The acknowledgement that Bligh didn't have enough information to make a formal complaint about Newman's conduct – an issue she had placed at the heart of Labor's campaign – destroyed her remaining credibility. Bligh's advisers were shocked by the political ineptitude of the concession. They felt it was a sign she was exhausted by fourteen years in government and the emotional weight of the deadly floods a year earlier.

Apparently sensing it was being used for political purposes, the Crime and Misconduct Commission decided to act. The day after Bligh's concession, a commission spokeswoman said it was conducting an assessment of the case – a preliminary step that could trigger a full-blown investigation. The review was sensational news: ten days before polling day the alternative premier was being examined by the anti-corruption authority. There was speculation the outcome might not be known until after the election. No-one seemed to know what impact it could have on the vote.

The commission's investigators examined Brisbane City Council files and records of the donations, which had been publicly declared. Among the evidence was an audio recording of the council meeting that approved the apartment. Newman wasn't present at the meeting. Two days later, without even speaking to Newman, the commission said there was no evidence of official misconduct by him when mayor and that the allegations would not be pursued further.

Legally, Newman was in the clear. Politically, Labor's target-the-leader strategy was dead. In the five days following Bligh's concession that she didn't have firm evidence of misconduct by Newman, the anti-Labor swing widened from 10 per cent to 17 per cent, according to the party's internal polling. A seven-point swing in such a short time is extremely unusual. In the last days of the campaign it was devastating.

On the last Sunday before the election, Bligh said Labor had no chance of winning. She was stating the obvious. But the concession demoralised Labor Party members, who were expected to work up to polling day shoring up support for the government.

The election made history. The 15.7 per cent swing against Labor was the biggest in Australian history, according to the federal parliamentary library. In no seat did Labor receive more than 50 per cent of the vote. Labor was left with seven seats in the eighty-nine-seat parliament, a number not high enough to qualify for status as a political party. Knowing a more effective opposition would promote good government, the new premier, Newman, granted the ALP party status. 'Everyone thought it was going to be bad, but no-one thought it would be quite this dire,' wrote journalist Mark Ludlow in the *Australian Financial Review*.

Newman won Ashgrove with nearly 52 per cent of the vote and became the first premier to be elected from outside parliament. The Liberal National Party won seventy-eight seats, the largest parliamentary majority in Australian history. There is no upper house in Queensland and the new government had unfettered legislative power. Bob Katter's Australian Party, which received $250,000 from casino owner James Packer, won two seats. Many traditional Labor supporters were attracted to its protectionist message. Two independents were elected. The Greens didn't win a seat.

Bligh retained her seat of South Brisbane. Her deputy and treasurer, Andrew Fraser, lost his seat, Mount Coot-tha. Most of the cabinet were thrown out. Bligh insisted throughout the campaign she would serve a full term if re-elected. Two days after the vote she called a press conference in Brisbane and said she planned to retire from politics immediately. She acknowledged she was a political liability. 'I simply don't believe that Labor can develop an effective opposition … if it has me as part of its public face,' she said.

Bligh took personal responsibility for the unpopular decision to sell off some of the state's biggest commercial assets and said she was sorry she couldn't convince the community it was good policy.

Labor supporters had reason to be angry with Bligh. Her over-the-top attacks on Newman backfired. Her decision to retire, which contradicted her previous public position, triggered a by-election in her electorate of South Brisbane, a by-election the defeated party barely had the energy to fight. With Fraser no longer an MP, Labor didn't have an obvious leader to turn to.

Remarkably, the swing was larger than the 13.4 per cent against Kristina Keneally's government in the New South Wales election a year earlier. There were similarities between the two governments. Credible and admired women headed both. Both governments had been in power a long time and were seen to have broken faith with the electorate on privatisation of public assets.

There was a crucial difference. Labor in New South Wales was racked by corruption and maladministration scandals. Labor in Queensland wasn't seen as corrupt. But many voters were turned off by Bligh's attempt to tar her opponent with the taint of corruption. She had predicted Newman would be convicted and sent to jail, a claim shown to be outrageous. Bligh then suggested she would refer Newman's conduct to anti-corruption investigators, and backed away from the threat days later.

A review by the federal parliamentary library cited Labor's negative campaign as a big turn-off for many voters. The Labor

Party's official post-election review said the tone of the campaign was one of four main factors behind the loss. The others were the privatisations, the cost of water, public transport and other necessities, and the government's long time in office. Most people join political parties because they want to make a positive contribution to society, the review observed. Many were repelled by their leaders' behaviour.

The voters of South Brisbane replaced Bligh with Jackie Trad, a Labor ministerial adviser, unionist and party functionary. The by-election, held two months after the general election, delivered a further 3 per cent swing against Labor. Bligh relocated to Sydney, where her husband, Greg Withers, was appointed head of strategy and government relations for Arts NSW, which oversees arts funding in the state. The seven Labor MPs left in Queensland unanimously chose a new leader, Annastacia Palaszczuk, a 42-year-old who inherited her seat from her father, Henry Palaszczuk.

# 8

**Smears, scandals, sexual harassment and a Speaker called Slipper – Who controls the HSU? – Julia, files and union slush funds**

## The takedown

There was a good reason Peter Slipper was known as 'Slippery Pete' in political circles. First elected as a federal MP in 1984 in Queensland as a National, Slipper switched to the Liberals in 1993, and became an independent on 24 November 2011, when Julia Gillard offered to make him speaker of the House of Representatives if he turned on his party. Slipper agreed and Labor's speaker, the widely respected Harry Jenkins, moved to the backbench. Slipper's betrayal gave Labor an extra seat in the finely balanced parliament.

Within the political world the appointment was seen as another example of Gillard's ability to outmanoeuvre Tony Abbott. Prising Slipper away from the Coalition ensured the government's slim hold on power got a little safer. But as the opposition pointed out, Labor had bought him. Now they owned him. Members of his own party, unhappy with his seeming inability to avoid negative publicity, had tried to kick him out of politics in 2010, and failed.

Slipper was a walking contradiction. He loved the Queen, the royal coat of arms and parliamentary ceremony. As speaker, he reintroduced formal robes and a daily, public procession for himself, traditions previously abandoned because they were seen as old fashioned. He was proud of his Christianity and was an ordained minister in the Traditional Anglican Communion, a breakaway group from the Anglican Church that opposed female priests. He was fascinated with homosexuality. He was a flirt and could be exceptionally crude.

In 2009 his expenses were higher than any other federal MP from Queensland, apart from Kevin Rudd, who was prime minister. Slipper had racked up $16,038 in taxi fares in six months and $1764 on magazine subscriptions, for titles including *Australian Aquarium Keeper*, *Men's Fitness* and *Harper's Bazaar*.

Slipper had enough self-awareness to realise he was very lucky to reach high office. 'Frankly, I have got to admit that I am not perfect and I have made some mistakes, as some of the colourful stories about me reveal,' he told parliament the day he was appointed.

The speakership is one of the most coveted jobs in politics. It comes with a big salary – $323,750 – lots of travel, a large staff, status and little real responsibility. On the official order of precedence, which governs things like seating arrangements at official banquets, the speaker ranks above all cabinet ministers except the prime minister. The administrative duties of the job are undemanding. The speaker and the president of the Senate oversee the Department of Parliamentary Services, which manages the parliament's operations, including its library, gym, gift shop and well-watered grounds.

Slipper decided to hire a press secretary, James Ashby, to help protect his public image, which was taking a battering from his former Liberal Party colleagues. Slipper knew Ashby from Queensland political circles and was impressed by the way the younger man confidently handled the media. Ashby had spent time at Slipper's Sunshine Coast home, often late at night, and got to know his second wife, Inge, a real estate agent.

Ashby had a wild streak. Earlier in his career he was fired from a radio station in Townsville for threatening a rival DJ over the phone. Slipper and Ashby liked to gossip and discuss political strategy by text messages. Other politicians might have restrained themselves when expressing their thoughts in writing. Not Slipper. On 10 October 2011, before Ashby joined his staff, they discussed by text a plan to make a YouTube video about Mal Brough, Slipper's long-time political rival. Slipper described Brough as a 'cunt' and said it was funny to use the word in a pejorative sense when 'many guys' liked them. 'Not I,' Ashby replied. Slipper kept up the anatomical references. He said female genitalia looked like 'a mussel removed from its shell'.

> SLIPPER: Look at a bottle of mussel meat! Salty Cunts in brine!
> ASHBY: So tell me, do u want to run again or do u want to step up to speaker of the house and not bother with pre selection. I wanna know how much fight u have in u and whether I put my tactical brain into action to see u give Mal a carving up.

After a couple more exchanges about politics, Slipper returned to women: Been to thw fish shop yet to buy the bottle of shell less mussels?

ASHBY: Not likely:o
SLIPPER: Make Pete's Spicy Pickled Beetroot yesterday!
ASHBY: Yeah, u were saying. Goes the carbon tax vote going? Said NO yet

Slipper was interested in Ashby's sex life. Two weeks after the conversation about mussels, Slipper raised, in a text, Ashby's latest boyfriend. He asked if Ashby had 'lost his maidenhead again?' with the man. 'What's that?' asked Ashby, who then sent Slipper a message about public use of a caravan park.

SLIPPER: Your virtual hymen
ASHBY: You're weird

Two weeks later Slipper asked if the relationship with the man had been 'consummerated'.

By November Slipper had obtained the man's phone number – it is unclear how – and sent him a text message asking if he was still in a relationship with Ashby. Slipper wanted to know their plans for the following weekend.

Confused, the man asked Ashby how to respond. 'Do I tell him we're going on a road trip or wot?' he wrote to Ashby. 'It feels weird himtexting me, not sure wot to say or NOT say.'

'Yeah he's asked me too many personal questions so I don't talk to him bout you anymore,' Ashby replied.

Ashby began working in Slipper's offices in Parliament House in the first week of 2012. He quickly found out Slipper wasn't a regular boss. At Slipper's insistence, Ashby agreed to stay at Slipper's Canberra apartment. On their third day together Slipper complained of a sore neck. That evening at the flat, clothed only in shorts, Slipper asked Ashby to massage his neck. He began groaning as though in sexual ecstasy and suggested Ashby have a shower with the door open. Ashby declined.

As a press secretary, Ashby was an asset to Slipper. He knew which journalists could be beneficial and used social media to promote Slipper's work as speaker. He wanted to pursue his career as a political adviser and was interested in working for the new Queensland state government. But Ashby wasn't naive. Working for a turncoat like Slipper would count against him in the Queensland Liberal National Party.

On 2 February, without Slipper's knowledge, Ashby privately met Queensland energy minister Mark McArdle, a former leader of the Queensland Liberal Party and a friend. The following month he was also in touch with Mal Brough, the former Howard minister who was gunning for Slipper's seat. Ashby had already decided he wanted to take down Slipper. He told Brough that Slipper was sexually harassing him and he wanted to take legal action. Brough set up a meeting with barrister David Russell, a Queen's Counsel who was influential in the Queensland National Party.

Slipper had no idea what was going on behind his back. On 26 February he had received a text message from Ashby that said: 'I am more than loyal, we are all working for your re-election, I have no respect for Mal Brough and never will.'

On 10 April Ashby called in sick and told Slipper he was urinating large quantities of blood. In reality, he flew to Sydney and was put up in the Sebel Surry Hills hotel by News Limited, the parent company of the *Daily Telegraph* and Rupert Murdoch's other Australian newspapers. He met Steve Lewis, a political reporter at the *Telegraph* with a record of breaking big political scandals.

Afterwards, the two men stayed in touch through texts, including one from Lewis that said: 'We will get him.' Ashby photocopied pages from Slipper's diary and emailed them to Lewis and Brough.

Ashby's lawyers filed a sexual harassment lawsuit against Slipper in the Federal Court on Friday, 20 April. It accused him of 'unwelcome sexual advances, unwelcome sexual comments and unwelcome suggestions of a sexual nature'.

Slipper learned Ashby had turned on him during a visit to New York when he checked the emails on his iPad at 3 a.m. He was on the last night of a month-long trip to the city with his wife, when Harmers Workplace Lawyers, the firm representing Ashby, sent him the paperwork setting out the harassment claim. Slipper felt physically ill but managed to sleep, according to *Australian Financial Review* journalist Hannah Low. When he woke, he had an email from Lewis seeking an urgent comment on Ashby's claims. The following day Lewis published the lurid allegations on the front pages of the *Daily Telegraph* and *Herald Sun*.

The lawsuit was devastating for Slipper. It alleged he had had a sexual relationship with an employee in 2003, which the government knew about and didn't act on. It also accused Slipper of misusing Cabcharge vouchers issued to him for work travel. Slipper gave away blank, unsigned vouchers to a friend who drove him around, Ashby claimed. If true, Slipper might have committed fraud. The government, which was named as a defendant, was in effect being sued for not protecting Ashby from Slipper, who was portrayed as a sexual predator of young men.

Slipper quickly left New York and flew to Brisbane via Los Angeles. Someone had tipped off the media and he was met at Brisbane airport by camera crews and escorted out of the terminal by a police officer, who was there to protect him from the attention. Journalists from at least five media outlets were waiting outside his house.

An atmosphere of sleaze enveloped the government, undermining Gillard's attempts to present a calm, disciplined front. To save it some embarrassment, Slipper agreed to cease presiding over the House of Representatives. Many journalists, based on government briefings, reported that Slipper had stood aside as speaker. In reality, he kept the perks and let his deputy, Labor MP Anna Burke, run question time and the other parliamentary debates.

Believing attack is the best form of defence, the government went after Ashby. Nicola Roxon, the attorney-general, and Anthony Albanese, the head of parliamentary tactics, led the offensive.

Roxon was juggling contradictory responsibilities. As the first law officer of the Crown, she had to preserve the fairness of the legal system. As attorney-general, she was responsible for instructing the lawyers who would defend the government against Ashby's lawsuit. As a senior Labor figure, she had an obligation to defend the party's interests.

Roxon told journalists there was a conspiracy to destroy Slipper's reputation and the harassment allegations shouldn't be taken at face value. 'The Commonwealth strongly believes that this process has been one which is really for an ulterior purpose, not for the purposes of an ordinary workplace complaint,' she said. Roxon and Albanese implied that Ashby's decision to work with the *Daily Telegraph* before the lawsuit became public undermined Ashby's credibility. 'There is active involvement of at least one person from the media,' Roxon said, a reference to Lewis. Albanese, speaking in parliament, issued a warning: 'People in the media need to recognise whether they are reporters or participants, observers or activists.' Seventeen government lawyers worked on the case over a period of months.

The idea the allegations were a conspiracy between News Limited and the Liberal Party seemed to gain currency. Court documents were released that included texts from Lewis to Ashby – including the 'get him' missive – which made it look like the journalist was out to harm Slipper's reputation. The ABC reported that Ashby had had a sexual relationship with a fifteen-year-old boy in 2003 – a criminal offence in Queensland – and broadcast details of Facebook messages they sent each other. (The police investigated. Ashby was never charged.) When Lewis turned up to court for a preliminary hearing in Sydney he was followed by camera crews, an uncomfortable encounter for any journalist used to being on the other side of the news machine.

Other figures in the government piled in. Foreign minister Bob Carr said Ashby's case seemed 'more rehearsed than a [highly stylised and elaborate] kabuki actor'. Ashby's lawyer, Michael Lee, said the 33-year-old had been 'more demonised than the Exorcist'.

The truth was more nuanced. Ashby clearly wanted to inflict as much harm on Slipper as possible. But many of the messages on Ashby's phone, which government lawyers were given not long after the case was filed, showed that, on the face of it, Ashby had a credible case for harassment. Even with the political and legal might of the federal government behind him, Slipper was in deep trouble.

Putting aside Slipper's odd and explicit sexual banter, the decision to hire Ashby – a person prepared to destroy the career of his employer – highlighted his lack of judgement. Gillard's decision to handsomely reward a member of the opposition for betraying his own side had backfired on her. No-one in the Labor Party was proud of their deal with Slipper. To cut Slipper off would be to acknowledge that appointing him was a mistake. The government was locked in.

Two months after Slipper left the Coalition, Tasmanian independent Andrew Wilkie withdrew his support for the government. Gillard had reneged on a promise to place voluntary betting limits on all poker machines by 2014, a condition she accepted when Wilkie agreed to support the government after the 2010 election. 'Frankly, a deal's a deal, and I really do think our democracy is much too precious to trash with broken promises and backroom deals,' Wilkie said.

Wilkie's decision was mostly symbolic. He didn't swap his allegiance to the Coalition and the government was able to pass legislation without his support. But it was more bad publicity for a government under enormous pressure from the Slipper allegations, Labor's humiliation in Queensland and the Health Services Union affair. Gillard decided she and the government needed some distance from the scandals, which were overshadowing everything else they tried to do.

On a Saturday afternoon, 28 April, she called Craig Thomson with bad news. His membership of the Labor Party would be suspended and he would have to sit in the House of Representatives with the independents. Thomson couldn't be kicked out of Labor on the basis of unproved allegations. But the suspension effectively cut him off from all formal contact with the party. Gillard also told Slipper he wouldn't be able to immediately resume overseeing parliamentary debates as speaker. Ever the politician, Thomson claimed the suspension was reached by mutual agreement between him and Gillard. He promised to vote with Labor. Slipper stayed publicly silent, waiting for his day in court.

## I don't smoke

The week after Craig Thomson was suspended from the Labor Party the police investigation into the Health Services Union stepped up a notch. A team from the NSW Fraud and Cybercrime Squad decided to search the union's Sydney offices about 9 a.m. on 2 May 2012. The squad was using its experience of investigating complex financial fraud to pull together a picture of the money flows in and out of the union during Michael Williamson's reign. By the time the police cars got through busy morning traffic to the Pitt Street office building, something unusual was happening. Williamson, who was on paid leave from his position as HSU East secretary, had turned up a little earlier with one of his sons, Chris, placed documents in a suitcase and left the building. The police found the Williamsons loading the suitcase into a car in the building's adjacent car park.

Detective Superintendent Col Dyson, the head of the squad, appeared furious at what looked like an attempt to conceal evidence from his investigation. As his officers examined computers and removed piles of documents from the offices and placed them in a truck outside the building, Dyson threatened charges for trying to obstruct the police, although he didn't identify Williamson by name. 'I have concerns that information relevant to the case may have been tampered with,' he told reporters.

Kathy Jackson, who lived in Melbourne, arrived about 9.30 a.m. She was unable to get into the building and watched events from the footpath: the police going in and out with boxes; journalists and camera crews waiting for the next attraction, which was her. A reporter asked if she thought the raid went ahead because the police felt freer to move following Thomson's suspension. Jackson didn't buy into the conspiracy theory. She emphasised that there was corruption in the union and the police raid was part of the process of cleaning it out. 'It is a sad day for the union and a traumatic day for the organisation,' she said. The police left the building about 3 p.m.

Why did the Williamsons choose that morning to go to the union's office? Kate McClymont, the *Sydney Morning Herald* investigative journalist, reported that police were investigating whether Williamson was warned about the raid. The truth may have been more Machiavellian. Journalists were tipped off on the morning of the raid, and had gathered outside waiting for it to start. Realising what was about to happen, someone inside the building may have rung Williamson, who rushed into the city to grab some documents. This was part of the police plan, according to a person in regular contact with the investigation. Williamson was set up.

The raid ratcheted up the pressure on the government. It generated great footage for television news bulletins, which have a bigger audience than newspapers. When the *Herald* broke the corruption allegations, TV stations were forced to use file footage. This time they had live pictures, giving the story greater impact. Williamson's term as Labor Party president had ended two years earlier but he remained an important figure in the New South Wales Right.

Labor hoped to distract public attention away from the scandal. In a week's time Treasurer Wayne Swan would deliver his fifth budget, a huge undertaking that could generate some badly needed traction for the government.

The Fair Work Australia investigation into the Health Services Union was slow, expensive and frustrating. Terry Nassios, one of Fair Work Australia's top bureaucrats, had been investigating the Health Services Union since Jackson uncovered evidence of corruption in 2009. Based in Melbourne, Nassios frequently flew to Sydney to interview people who might have useful information. Nassios, who was entitled to business-class airfares, preferred to stay overnight on the trips, which allowed him to claim the public service travel allowance. For example, on 19 May 2011, he caught a 4 p.m. flight to Sydney and returned to Melbourne the next day at 3.30 p.m. He was paid $443.10 to cover his accommodation.

Basic mistakes from the beginning undermined the investigation. No-one at Fair Work Australia wrote a mission statement that defined its scope, objectives or deadline. Nassios, who had to keep up many of his other duties, didn't create a proper case-management system, which is standard in all big investigations, to keep track of the paperwork and deadlines. There was no manual to guide him as to how to conduct the complex and expensive investigation. Fair Work Australia didn't have enough qualified staff.

Confidential documents were stored on Fair Work Australia's computers and could be accessed by practically anyone in the organisation. This was a big security breach. Given the highly political circumstances of the scandal, the many former union officials working at Fair Work Australia and Jackson's partner

Michael Lawler's role as a deputy president, the files should have been locked down. Eventually the lead investigator moved the documents to her private folder on the network. Hard copies, which weren't registered on a log, were kept in her unlocked office at Fair Work Australia's Melbourne headquarters for the first two years of the investigation.

Those on the team were so uncertain about their powers they discussed whether it would be appropriate to ask credit card companies for Thomson's records. Eventually they decided the HSU should make the request on their behalf. They didn't bother to chase down electronic information that might have been useful, including emails, calendars, text messages and backups of the HSU's computer drives. Fair Work Australia had the legal power to request access to all this information. Instead, it concentrated on old-fashioned sources: interviews with the protagonists – Jackson helped a lot – and physical documents.

The very first documents placed in the public domain, Thomson's union credit card records, were the crucial evidence held by the team. Even if Thomson's spending was authorised, as he maintained it was, the expenditure on dining, entertainment and accommodation was so extreme that it couldn't be reasonably explained away. It appeared to be the smoking gun.

The investigators left it until almost the last minute to go through the credit card statements. Their analysis didn't begin until September 2011, three months before they were due to wrap up and twenty-nine months after journalist Mark Davis obtained the statements and published excerpts in the *Herald*. To speed up the analysis the investigation team could have used its external accountant to sift through the transactions. He had been a partner in an accounting firm for twenty-five years. But fifteen months earlier Fair Work Australia had decided not to renew his contract.

Nassios finished his report of the investigation in March 2012. A week later it was sent to the Commonwealth Director of Public Prosecutions, Chris Craigie, who was based in Sydney and was responsible for charging and prosecuting breaches of federal law. Craigie immediately dismissed it as useless for a criminal prosecution. As detailed as the Fair Work Australia report was, the investigators hadn't produced a document that prosecutors could use to mount a criminal case. Craigie wasn't going to touch it. The situation raised an important question: if the body that regulates unions found evidence that union officials were engaged in criminal conduct, what could it do? The answer seemed to be: very little.

There was immense political pressure on Fair Work Australia to finish the investigation and brief the world on its findings. Bernadette O'Neill, the agency's managing director, didn't want to be responsible for releasing the report, which could do huge damage to Thomson, Williamson and the government.

She had an easy way out. The Senate body that oversaw industrial relations laws, the Education, Employment and Workplace Relations committee, wanted a copy of the investigation and planned to make it public. Documents accepted as part of the committee's work were covered by parliamentary privilege, which meant the people who wrote or published them couldn't be sued for defamation. The lengthy investigation and the agency's refusal to cooperate with police had tarnished its reputation and made it a target of the Coalition. If O'Neill refused to give parliament a copy, she would be accused of a cover-up.

Thomson's lawyers were desperate to keep the investigation private. On 20 April a partner at law firm Holding Redlich, Ian Robertson, wrote to the Senate committee and essentially argued that Thomson couldn't get a fair trial if the public was allowed to read Fair Work Australia's findings.

On 7 May, the day before the federal budget, Fair Work Australia sent an electronic version of the report to the Senate committee. A few hours later, about 5.15 p.m., the 1105-page document was posted on parliament's website.

Three years and one month after Thomson was first accused in the media of abusing the HSU's finances, there was an official finding that the allegations were true. The investigation identified 181 breaches of the law. It found Thompson had committed 156 of the breaches, Ian Dick, the union's former auditor, had committed nineteen, and Williamson five. Jackson, Thomson's successor and the person partially responsible for revealing the corruption in the first place, was also the subject of an adverse finding. Nassios found she didn't lodge the union's 2007 accounts quickly enough, a civil breach of the law normally dealt with by Fair Work Australia through a polite letter.

In the history of Australian politics, the report was a rare document. It essentially catalogued how a politician bought his way into office. The gaps between the fragments published in newspapers were filled out, including the large sums Thomson spent on personal travel for himself and his wife. There was so much information that newspapers were still publishing new details days later. Surprisingly, Thomson's $5793 bill for prostitutes – the aspect of the scandal that had most captured the public's attention – was just 1.3 per cent of the $450,701 of the HSU's money he spent on himself and his political campaign.

Thomson was so cavalier about his members' money that almost no item was too small to expense. On 22 May 2006, he, or someone using his Diners Club card, charged the union for a Cherry Ripe, four bottles of Powerade and a packet of Benson & Hedges cigarettes at a Caltex service station in Forresters Beach, a town near Thomson's house. Asked about the purchases by Nassios, Thomson didn't deny they were his. He acknowledged it wasn't appropriate for a union representing health-care workers to pay for cigarettes. He said the food and drink purchases were okay. 'I don't smoke, by the way,' he said.

Thomson, who had avoided the media for years, invited journalists to a courtyard at Parliament House to hear his response. He didn't take questions. 'Well, this whole Fair Work investigation has been a joke from start to finish so we're not really expecting today to be any different in terms of that,' he said. 'I mean what clearly has been shown from Fair Work Australia is their incompetence and their inability to get things done and, you know, why should today be any different?'

Knowing the report was due, the government had a response ready. Bill Shorten called his own press conference at Parliament House. Looking grave and determined, he promised to toughen the law to make unions and employer groups, which were covered by the same legislation, disclose more about their finances. The penalties for breaking the law would be tougher and union officials would have to undergo training on how to comply with the law. If a separate inquiry into the long time it took Fair Work Australia to complete its investigation suggested changes, he promised to implement them.

Jackson felt vindicated by Fair Work Australia's findings. She was also deeply upset it had turned on her. Even though the finding against her was a minor infraction, it gave Jackson's enemies in the union movement and the Labor Party more ammunition. In an angry letter to Nassios during the investigation, Jackson had argued it would create the impression Fair Work Australia was bowing to political pressure if it took legal action against her. An adverse ruling against her would be a blow to whistleblowers everywhere, she said. Afterwards, she went even further. In comments to the author of this book, Jackson claimed the finding against her was the result of political influence, which was also the reason for the years it took Fair Work Australia to complete the investigation. 'FWA's investigation was in fact corrupted in order to deliver the delay that helped both Thomson and the ALP minority government and in order to smear me.' If Jackson or her partner Lawler – who was inside Fair Work Australia – had conclusive proof of political interference, they didn't make it public. Even Jackson's supporters thought bureaucratic inertia was more likely the cause of the long delay. O'Neill, the Fair Work Australia general manager, emphatically denied there was any 'improper influence' over the investigation and said Jackson had never produced any evidence to back her serious claim.

Bizarrely, the real power in the union and the person who had made more money from it than anyone else, Williamson, escaped with a wrist slap. Williamson told Fair Work Australia he had no involvement in the day-to-day administration of the national office. His main involvement was as national president, an honorary position that paid $10,000 to $20,000 a year, he said, a defence accepted by the investigation, which portrayed Williamson essentially as a passive bystander. 'Mr Williamson saw no role for himself and therefore failed in ensuring the rules were rigidly adhered to,' Nassios concluded. Fair Work Australia's decision to investigate the union's national office and ignore HSU East, which Williamson ran like a fiefdom, meant it had no proof of a potentially far larger fraud.

Budget day was greeted by Craig Thomson's face across the front pages of most of the nation's newspapers. The *Sydney Morning Herald* led page one with the large headline that acknowledged Mark Davis's scoop three years earlier: 'Thomson's credit card lies confirmed'.

One person following the story closely was Doug Williams. The last chief executive of the Industrial Relations Commission and the man who ordered the first official investigation into the HSU asked Fair Work Australia for a printed copy of the report. He was told it wouldn't be an appropriate use of public resources.

In 2012, as in most years, the federal budget was the government's biggest public relations exercise. About a week before, the government selectively started releasing information to media outlets on what was coming. Around lunchtime on budget day, hundreds of journalists from newspapers, radio stations, television networks, wire services and websites entered a series of large rooms in Parliament House, where they were locked up for six hours until Treasurer Wayne Swan stood up at 7.30 p.m. and began reading his budget speech.

The lock-up gave the media plenty of time to read the budget papers, which filled more than a thousand pages, before filing their reports. Government officials were on hand to explain the government's policies. Treasurer Wayne Swan worked his way around the rooms buttering up senior writers and the newspaper editors who had travelled to Canberra to oversee the coverage. So many reporters, editors and graphic artists from the *Australian*

*Financial Review* and the *Sydney Morning Herald* attended that the paper's publisher, Fairfax Media, hired a bus to take them to Canberra. Both papers, and *The Australian* and *The Age*, published large wraparound sections the next day setting out in detail the government's policy plans for the next four years.

The budget showed Labor had learnt from the electoral disasters in Queensland and New South Wales. The budget was presented as a plan to ease cost-of-living pressures on the middle class by spreading the benefits of the resources boom. Parents would get up to $820 a year for each child in high school and $410 for each child in primary school. The grants, designed to cover the cost of textbooks and other educational necessities, were already available but the requirement to fill in paperwork to get the money was lifted, which meant parents would be paid automatically, ensuring far more people received the cash. Swan cut defence spending and reduced tax concessions for sign-on bonuses and employees who lived away from their home cities, breaks that were popular with the wealthy.

The pitch to traditional Labor voters was an attempt to shore up Labor's base. The plan mirrored Kristina Keneally's campaign in the 2011 New South Wales election when she promised to respond to middle- and working-class concerns about rising prices for household costs such as electricity.

The question for the government was: was anyone listening? The dry policy detail in the budget couldn't compete with the sordid Thomson affair, which dominated the headlines, talk radio and the national conversation. In the newspapers' letters pages Australians poured out their disgust. 'And now for Gillard and Swan's next trick: replacing the superfluous Craig Thomson with a budget surplus,' wrote Michael Taplin in the *Sydney Morning Herald*. 'Well done, but who is going to fall for that one? More smoke please.'

Paul Howes, the head of the Australian Workers' Union, warned the scandal threatened the very existence of the union movement. 'We have to ensure that we never allow something like this to happen again, because if it does that could be the thing that wipes us off the map,' he told a union youth conference. Even though Howes tended towards hyperbole in speeches, he was expressing a real fear among union leaders that the Thomson fall-out would accelerate a decades-long decline in union membership.

One of the men who put Gillard into power after the 2010 election was having second thoughts. Independent MP Rob Oakeshott couldn't understand why the Labor Party hadn't checked Thomson's background more thoroughly before choosing him as a candidate. Oakeshott questioned if he should have agreed to back Gillard given Labor's power in parliament was due to someone who might be corrupt. Gillard may not 'have the legitimate numbers in the House … because it's based on people who are dodgy,' he told the *Australian Financial Review*.

Another independent MP who had backed the government, Tony Windsor, was also deeply troubled by the allegations. Like Oakeshott, Windsor's political credibility had suffered from the collateral damage of the Thomson affair. Many voters in Windsor's New England electorate, which was based around the New South Wales towns of Tamworth and Armidale, resented him for backing a government tarnished by allegations of union corruption.

A few days after the Fair Work Australia report was published Windsor went to see Thomson to hear his fellow MP's explanation. Thomson told him the allegations were false and he was the victim of a conspiracy to destroy his political career and damage the government. Thomson was trying out the lines he was about to use on a much bigger audience. Windsor wasn't convinced.

## It's a conspiracy

Craig Thomson's explanation to parliament about how he legitimately spent $450,000 of union money on prostitutes, dining, travel, cigarettes, snacks, donations and freelance political help was eagerly awaited. At noon, 21 May 2012, he stood in the House of Representatives and asked the deputy speaker, Anna Burke, for permission to talk. Thomson's fourth-row desk was in the area of the chamber assigned to independent MPs. Knowing the speech would get blanket television coverage, almost every Coalition MP was present, including Liberal leader Tony Abbott. The Labor benches to Thomson's left were mostly empty. His former colleagues didn't want to be associated with a pariah.

Thomson lacked the authoritative command of many strong orators. Speaking in a clear, slightly strained voice, he seemed controlled but highly emotional. He stood upright, looking around the chamber, gesticulating with his hands for effect.

The fifty-nine-minute speech, a mixture of broad rebuttals, counter allegations and emotional pleas, began with what may have been the most hard-hitting opening in parliamentary history. The allegations against Thomson had triggered a torrent of hate mail and abuse towards his staff, his family and him. Thomson read excerpts: 'Go cut your wrists or, better still, hang yourself. Go out the back, cut your throat – that's the only way. Have you slashed your wrists yet? You are dead. A bullet between the eyes will save taxpayers' money.'

Thomson offered a mea culpa. Even though he had done nothing wrong, Thomson said, based on his lawyers' advice, he hadn't previously given a detailed defence. He regretted this.

Thomson claimed to have tightened the union's financial controls. All budgets had to be approved by a finance committee and there was a strict limit on how much he, as national secretary, could spend without the committee's approval, he said. The union's other prominent leaders, Kathy Jackson and Michael Williamson, didn't like the tougher rules, he said. 'What are you doing?' Thomson said they asked him. 'Why don't you just collect your salary and do nothing?'

He stumbled only once: when he described how the media invaded his wife's privacy. 'What you do not expect is for Channel Seven reporters to be hovering underneath the bathroom window,' he said. Overcome with emotion, he paused to sip from a glass of water, twice. With his head bowed, on the verge of tears, he finished the sentence: '… while my pregnant wife is having a shower.'

After advancing his reformist credentials and setting himself up for sympathy, Thomson went on the attack: 'In making this statement I am very conscious that in the eyes of many of the public I have already been charged, convicted and sentenced. The public will hold these views because of the quite extraordinary media coverage which has taken place. I, like every member of this House, understand and value the importance of an independent and robust news media and the important place that it can play in our democracy. However, all of us who have regular dealings with the news media know that the news media can often get it wrong, and sometimes seriously so – particularly as today the media is dominated by self-important commentators, not reporters, and I will say a little bit more about that later.'

Thomson offered many explanations for what happened while he was national secretary of the Health Services Union from 2002 to 2007. Most of Fair Work Australia's adverse findings about him were based on an incorrect assumption that the union hadn't approved his spending, he said. When he withdrew union money from ATMs, he provided receipts. He booked hotel rooms in blocks for groups of union officials. It was reasonable for his wife to travel on some of his work trips. His driver's licence number, which appeared on brothel receipts, was accessible to most people at the union, as were his credit card numbers. Why would someone in a brothel record his driver's licence number on a receipt when all they had to do, to establish his identity, was check the photo on the licence? On some occasions sex was charged to his credit card in one city when he was in another. His mobile telephone, which was used to call brothels, may have been cloned. Fair Work Australia refused to obtain closed-circuit television footage from brothels that would have proved he didn't go to them. A Victorian official in the union, Marco Bolano, threatened to set Thomson up 'with a bunch of hookers' to end his political career.

One of the most startling aspects of the speech was Thomson's decision to turn on Williamson, his mentor. He suggested Williamson, who was fighting to save his own battered reputation, was behind the 'bunch of hookers' plot. Clearly the relationship between the men had broken down.

But it was Jackson who was the main target. Thomson brought up Jackson's pricey work car, a Volvo SUV, cited reports her childcare and gym fees were paid by the union, and referred to a big pay rise she received when she succeeded him as national secretary.

More significantly, Thomson implied that Jackson's partner, Michael Lawler, used his position at Fair Work Australia to slant the investigation. 'The main accuser's partner is second in charge,' Thomson said. 'The questions Fair Work has to answer, the questions the deputy president has to answer, are: what influence did he have in relation to the writing of the report? What relationship, if any, does he have with the Liberal Party?'

The implication that Lawler behaved improperly – perhaps corruptly – upped the stakes even higher. Lawler was roughly equivalent to a Federal Court judge. The only person more senior on the bench at Fair Work Australia was the president, Iain Ross.

Thomson ended as dramatically as he began. He declared parliament had 'completely trashed' the rule of law, looked over at Abbott, who hadn't played a big role in turning the allegations against Thomson into a national scandal, and pointed at him:

> What you have done is not just damage to an individual or their family. You have damaged democracy and you continue to damage democracy, and you should hang your head in shame for that. What it shows of the leader of the Opposition, that man, is that not only is he unfit to be a prime minister; in my view, he is unfit to be an MP.

Abbott was impassive. Booth, the speaker, thanked the MPs for listening.

The media's response to Thomson's speech was sceptical. Most commentators thought there were glaring holes in his defence and didn't believe that the bills for sex were an elaborate set up. 'If you were to believe him, Craig Thomson is the victim of the greatest conspiracy in modern Australian public life,' wrote Tony Wright, the national affairs editor of *The Age*.

To many people in the broader community, though, Thomson came across as plausible and sincere. Most people had no appreciation of the scope of allegations against him. There was a sense that even if he were guilty of misusing some of the union's money, Thomson had been hounded beyond a reasonable point. Some of Thomson's fellow MPs became concerned he might take his own life. Liberal Mal Washer, a doctor, said MPs needed to ensure Thomson wasn't placed under so much pressure he hurt himself.

However unlikely, Thomson's defence gave him and the government a little respite. His silence in the face of overwhelming evidence was no longer the issue. The allegations would now work their way slowly through the legal system. By defending himself in parliament, Thomson was able to make serious accusations against others without fear of being sued for defamation.

The speech turned the media's attention to Lawler. Out of loyalty to Jackson, the former public prosecutor had chosen to become involved. In December 2011, he had sent a letter to the New South Wales police fraud squad accusing Williamson and two other officials in the union of corruption. Lawler told police he was acting in a personal capacity.

The attacks on Lawler put the head of Fair Work Australia, Iain Ross, in an awkward position. Ross had replaced Geoffrey Giudice in the most senior job in Australian industrial relations a few months earlier – and was appointed by Bill Shorten, whose mother-in-law, Governor-General Quentin Bryce, signed the paperwork. Now Ross was caught in the middle: his boss, Shorten, was enemies with the partner of his deputy, who had been accused in parliament by an MP, a former factional colleague of Shorten's, of interfering on behalf of Jackson in a legal investigation by Fair Work Australia. Compounding the complicated relationships, the best man at Shorten's wedding, Senator David Feeney, was among Jackson's closest friends. They were Australia's most dysfunctional political family.

Ross checked out the allegations and later told a parliamentary committee he found no evidence that Lawler interfered in the inquiry. Lawler ruled on wage claims, industrial disputes and other tribunal matters and wasn't involved in the administrative arm of Fair Work Australia, which investigated the union. Ross's public comments about Lawler seemed carefully phrased. He didn't criticise his subordinate. He didn't praise him either.

Through his explanation to parliament, Thomson exposed himself to a new line of attack. The day after his speech the Coalition asked for Thomson to be investigated by parliament's powerful privileges committee to determine if he had lied. The Coalition wanted to test Thomson's elaborate explanations. Misleading parliament was a serious offence. The government, which didn't want to look like it was shielding Thomson from further scrutiny, agreed to the referral.

The privileges committee, which disciplined MPs when they broke parliament's rules, had a majority of government MPs on it, giving it some control over the process. The Coalition swapped one of its representatives, tennis great John Alexander, for Philip Ruddock, a former attorney-general who had been in parliament thirty-nine years, to give it more firepower.

At the committee's first meeting, the Labor MPs rejected a Coalition request to advertise immediately for witnesses. Instead, they decided to write to Christopher Pyne, the Liberal MP who complained that Thomson might have lied, to ask Pyne to specify which parts of Thomson's speech were untrue. It looked like Labor was trying to limit the inquiry. After the meeting, someone briefed veteran Fairfax journalist Michelle Grattan about the plan to seek more information from Pyne. Under parliament's rules the committee's proceedings are supposed to be kept secret. Some of the committee members were so outraged by the leak they began a separate investigation into how Grattan got her information. Every member of the committee and its staff of public servants were asked to sign a statutory declaration declaring they were not responsible. No-one owned up to being the source.

Adding to the sense that the drama was well past out of control, Channel Nine's *A Current Affair* located a woman who claimed to be one of Thomson's prostitutes and offered her $50,000 and a ride in one of the station's helicopters. When she declined, it upped the offer to $60,000 and added in a flight to Sydney. The woman agreed to the interview, which the network announced it had, and signed a statutory declaration that she'd had sex with Thomson at least once. Then, without explanation, Nine didn't air the interview.

Unhappy with her treatment by Nine, the woman contacted arch rival *Today Tonight* on the Seven Network, which broadcast an interview with her in a wig. Speaking with a strong New Zealand accent, the unnamed woman retracted her claim to Channel Nine. 'Why did you say that you'd slept with Craig Thomson?' she was asked by a *Today Tonight* reporter. 'I believed I had at the time,' she said. 'I used to have a lot of clients who fitted that description.'

By this stage the Thomson scandal had become so sordid a lot people gave up trying to work out whom to believe. The government and ALP, which had hoped the entire affair would go away, was deeply embarrassed. While the country followed the soap opera, Shorten and Jackson were focused on the end game: who would get control of the Health Services Union.

## Smear campaign

While Bill Shorten was manoeuvring to get the elected officials, including Kathy Jackson, removed from the Health Services Union, one of his friends, Andrew Landeryou, was destroying her reputation via the internet. The two men had known each other since they were both Young Labor members at university. Landeryou's wife, Kimberley Kitching, a Melbourne City councillor, became close friends with Shorten's first wife, Deborah Beale. Landeryou and Kitching saw the Shortens' divorce close up and found it emotionally gut-wrenching.

After a couple of failed business ventures that landed him in court and made him a regular in the pages of *The Age*, Landeryou became a political blogger. He set up a website, Vexnews, in 2008, to spread gossip and dish dirt on Victorian politics. Landeryou's site got between 100 and 2000 readers a day, depending on whom you asked. The blog, which was filled with Labor Party gossip, was well read in political and media circles and sometimes beat Melbourne's establishment media, *The Age*, *Herald Sun*, the ABC and 3AW, to interesting information and documents. Landeryou was a new breed of commentator – freelance bloggers driven by personal and political agendas who were learning how to get their message to a broader audience using the mainstream media. (The author does not suggest in any way that Bill Shorten had anything to do with the blogs or that he encouraged Andrew Landeryou to attack his political enemies.)

Charming, witty and amusing in person, Landeryou was a vicious correspondent. Jackson was his number-one target. The site was a central part of what Jackson believed was a smear campaign to destroy her reputation. In one month in early 2012 Vexnews called her 'a thief and money launderer', and a 'lunatic' who had a 'big bucks high-life hypocrisy lifestyle'. The site accused Jackson of being involved in a scam to use $22,000 in HSU money to pay for a convertible Mercedes-Benz in 2008.

On 30 April 2011, Landeryou got a scoop that was picked up by all the major media outlets. He had obtained a copy of the first officially sanctioned investigation into the Health Services Union's finances, which was written by Ian Temby, QC, a former Commonwealth Director of Public Prosecutions, and accountant Dennis Robertson. The scathing report portrayed HSU East, which Williamson ran, as a financial free-for-all lacking the most basic controls. Among the findings: the union paid more than $17 million for goods and services without tendering or seeking competitive quotes. There was no credit card policy, no budget controls, no formal purchase order system, no procurement policy and employees' job functions weren't clear. The report listed Jackson's allegations of corruption against Williamson, including the possible kick-backs from the printing firm, and said it was investigating them and would follow up with a fuller report.

On 29 May Vexnews turned its guns on Michael Lawler. 'JUDGE HANGING: What an inquiry into Michael Lawler will reveal', screamed the Vexnews headline. Lawler was described as a 'hopelessly compromised, Koolade-swilling judge' who had interfered in the internal affairs of the HSU, made false accusations to police, threatened union officials and drunkenly slagged off Jackson's rivals to journalists. Vexnews argued that Lawler had crossed the line from judge to participant and was hopelessly compromised. 'As a judicial officer, whose activities necessarily reflect on Fair Work Australia and all of his colleagues, this is highly inappropriate and warrants his removal,' the site said.

Strangely, no-one at Fair Work Australia or in the government stepped up to defend Lawler, including Shorten, who was responsible for appointments to the tribunal. The coverage did trigger a flurry of emails within Fair Work Australia as staff traded links to the articles. 'Look at Vexnews. It gets worse,' one employee wrote to another. 'Don't believe everything you read, especially on Vexnews,' another person wrote.

Shunned by her union colleagues, undermined by former allies in the Labor Party and roughed up in the press, Jackson doubled down. She became more insistent in media interviews that the HSU was corrupt and needed cleaning up. She agreed to be represented by Stuart Wood, a top industrial relations barrister. Wood was a member of the Victorian Liberal Party and friends with John Roskam, the head of the right-wing Institute of Public Affairs. Wood was involved in the H.R. Nicholls Society, a free-marketeer discussion group regarded as the anti-Christ by most trade unionists.

Wood, Ian Hanke, one of the top media advisers in the Howard government, and others were trying to lift the group's profile. They had the perfect vehicle: Jackson, who agreed to be the keynote speaker at their annual conference.

The packed H.R. Nicholls Society event was held at the Docklands Travelodge in Melbourne. Howard-era minister Peter Reith was in the audience. Several camera crews bustled in the background, including ABC's *Lateline*.

When Jackson stood up, her voice quavered as she read tentatively from a sheet of paper. She said she disagreed with the society's view that a free market provided the best outcome for labour relations. Most of the speech focused on the influence of factional leaders in the union movement and how to improve union supervision. Basic democratic processes had broken down because Labor Party factional leaders, like Shorten, wanted to preserve their political power, she said. Jackson revealed the HSU had banned candidates for internal elections from putting their photos and personal statements in election literature distributed by the Australian Electoral Commission.

'Incumbents, you see, don't need to have the photos and statements of candidates on their tickets posted out by the AEC,' she said. 'They can pay for campaigns from the large war chests that they typically have available. Bill Shorten, as minister for workplace relations, is the most obvious example of Dracula in charge of the blood bank that one can imagine. The notion of making a union more open to recapture by its own rank and file is anathema to a warlord's world view.'

Jackson said what many people, perhaps most people, working in and with unions knew already: the movement doesn't function as an effective democracy, regulatory supervision is lax, and a small elite group have disproportionate power.

Vexnews regarded the speech a case of hypocrisy run amok. It suggested Jackson's personal style was a good fit with the H.R. Nicholls Society: 'By her own pilfering, Ms Jackson, has indeed become an unusual champion of the free market. Whether it's been lavish overseas travel, childcare, household bills, luxury automobiles or whatever, it's all been "free" for her.'

If Jackson faced criminal charges over her time at the HSU, the society might regret the association, Vexnews wrote: 'Spending just one wild night with Kathy Jackson was perhaps not the good idea it had initially seemed.'

Jackson's decision to speak to the H.R. Nicholls Society probably killed any sympathy left in the labour movement for her. Her decision to pursue the allegations against Craig Thomson, and refusal to back down, badly hurt the federal Labor government and tarnished the entire union movement's reputation. Many union officials felt she was prepared to bring down Labor to satisfy her own vendetta against HSU rivals. Her $286,976 salary and union-provided Volvo station wagon grated with many union officials who were struggling financially.

Yet the intense bitterness towards Jackson seemed misplaced. As everyone agreed, the Health Services Union needed cleaning up. Who was going to do it? Fair Work Australia apparently wasn't capable of mounting a criminal prosecution. The police were wary of union investigations. The state-based corruption commissions were focused on politicians and public servants. The union movement had ignored the problems in the HSU for years. The president of the Australian Council of Trade Unions, Ged (Geraldine) Kearney, said unhappy HSU members should vote for new officials rather than complain to the media. Yet Kearney knew the record for contested union elections was abysmal. Several top union leaders had been in place for decades and were virtually impregnable, including the Australian Nursing Federation, her own union. Even if she were acting out of self-interest, the media attention created by Jackson turned a spotlight on the HSU that governments and regulators could not ignore.

Along with Landeryou, Jackson's other major internet critic was Peter Wicks. A little-known Labor Party member who stood for the party in the Liberal seat of Hawkesbury in the disastrous New

South Wales 2011 election, Wicks had his own blog and contributed to Independent Australia, a website which claimed to be for aspiring independent politicians. With headlines like 'Resist the rise of the evil psychopathic morons', its strident tone appealed to political outsiders who didn't trust the traditional media.

On the same night Jackson addressed the H.R. Nicholls Society, Wicks and his wife Felicity sorted through a pile of Health Services Union credit card statements. Wicks believed the statements showed a credit card from a Victorian division of the HSU was used at a Sydney brothel, on international travel, pay-television, clothes and alcohol; spending that had nothing to do with Craig Thomson. Separately, Wicks discovered that Kathy Jackson had hired her partner's sons in 2009 and 2010. Given the criticism of Williamson's nepotism in New South Wales – he had at least half a dozen family members and friends on the HSU payroll – Jackson's employment of Lawler's sons looked hypocritical. Wicks posted the young Lawlers' payslips online and sent links to his 1300 followers on Twitter. One of the teenagers was paid $50,226 a year. The other earned $43,680.

Wicks argued Kathy Jackson, not Craig Thomson, was the crook. He questioned why Fair Work Australia's huge report hadn't uncovered the same evidence he did. Like Thomson and Landeryou, Wicks pointed an accusatory finger at Lawler:

> It seems inconceivable to me that they [Fair Work Australia] managed to find what they did on Thomson – who has now seemingly been all but cleared – but yet missed all the Jackson documentation. This makes me question whether this was a witch-hunt – and also to question whether Michael Lawler has any influence and

involvement, behind the scenes, whether directly or indirectly, in what direction the FWA investigation took.

Apart from Thomson, no figure in the union movement, parliament or law enforcement was prepared to publicly accuse Jackson or Lawler of corruption. But their attackers on the internet were getting their allegations to a wider audience.

The ABC's online political correspondent, Simon Cullen, decided to write an article based on the Wicks documents. Appearing on the ABC website, it ran under the headline: 'Jacksons at centre of "disturbing" HSU allegations.'

Cullen quoted Kathy Jackson's denials that she had done anything wrong by hiring Lawler's sons. 'I considered that the branch was fortunate to have persons of their ability available to take that work,' she said.

The article didn't look good for Jackson.

Landeryou pushed the story on Twitter. The Australian Associated Press wrote its own version of the story, which appeared on the news.com.au website and on Fairfax websites. Jackson's critics congratulated themselves for getting the mainstream media interested. 'Well done with the article Simon :-),' Wicks tweeted.

As bloggers, Wicks and Landeryou weren't behaving like traditional journalists. They were trying to influence the political process by accumulating evidence against Jackson to push to media outlets with a wider reach.

In addition to the ABC, Wicks boasted of feeding information to Channel Nine and the *Sydney Morning Herald*. He obtained Jackson's phone records and posted information about who she had called online. He said a 'friend of a friend' connected to the union was feeding him information. Jackson thought his contact was Williamson.

One lie being spread to journalists was that Jackson expensed the cost of breast reduction surgery. Asked about the rumour, Wicks said in an email: 'I have not seen any evidence of it, but I have heard that story from many reliable sources and a tummy tuck as well I am told. However, I have no evidence so I have not run with it.'

Wicks, who didn't deny he wanted to help Thomson out, sent the embattled MP documents to help defend himself. Wicks got calls from Thomson thanking him for keeping him in the loop. 'I would hope that if I was having legal troubles and that someone else had evidence that could help, they would help me,' Wicks said later.

## Jackson versus Shorten

The Health Services Union was a national embarrassment. Hundreds of members were quitting each week. Its top officials were under police investigation. The Australian Council of Trade Unions and Unions NSW had suspended its membership.

Kathy Jackson, who had generated publicity for the scandal by going to the media, hoped to retain some of her power over the union. She faced a powerful and well-resourced opponent: Bill Shorten.

Shorten wanted the 2010 merger of the Victorian, New South Wales and ACT divisions reversed and the existing officials, including Jackson, kicked out. A break-up would give union members a chance to vote for new leaders untainted by the Craig Thomson and Michael Williamson scandals. Williamson and Jackson would lose their jobs in HSU East, although Jackson would remain national secretary and could run for office if she wanted. The break-up would, in theory, avoid a damaging power struggle between Jackson and officials in New South Wales for control of HSU East. Each side would return to their own states.

There may have been a personal agenda behind Shorten's decision. He and Jackson had detested each other since 2007, when they had allegedly become involved in a confrontation during an internal Labor election. Breaking up HSU East would reverse one of the biggest achievements of Jackson's career and kill any chance of her getting control of the union in New South Wales. Jackson believed Shorten wanted new elections to deliver the HSU in Victoria to candidates loyal to him. Shorten said he was only worried about the members' interests.

'We've done this because there are 55,000 hospital cleaners, laundry attendants, catering staff and they – we – can't continue this situation of day after day of counter-claim and allegation and counter-claim and allegation,' Shorten told the *7.30* program. 'Unions in Australia are very good and strong institutions. This particular branch is clearly in a real problem.'

Under Shorten's orders in April 2012, government lawyers asked the Federal Court to appoint an administrator to HSU East. The administrator would exercise complete control until the union could be split into the three units that existed before the merger. Elections would then be held. Other officials in the union supported the plan, including the national president, Chris Brown, who ran the Tasmanian division and wouldn't be directly affected by the break-up.[14]

Shorten's powers over HSU East, though, were questionable. The division was two legal entities: one registered federally and the other in New South Wales. Shorten was trying to exercise authority over both, even though as workplace relations minister his power didn't extend beyond federally registered organisations.

The Federal Court judge considering the case, Geoffrey Flick, was surprised by Shorten's audacity. A federal minister had not made such an application in 100 years, he said in court. The government's lawyers argued an urgent decision was needed because the union was haemorrhaging members.

Jackson, who was covering her own legal costs, knew she would struggle to defeat Shorten in court. She had a plan B. Jackson had publicly called on the New South Wales Coalition government to intervene. It was listening. On 3 May Premier Barry O'Farrell told state parliament he would introduce legislation that would override Shorten's plan to break up the union.

Shorten and O'Farrell both wanted to appoint an administrator to control the union until new leaders could be elected. Shorten's candidate was Michael Moore, a former Federal Court judge who was on the Industrial Relations Court in the 1990s. O'Farrell backed Jeffrey Phillips, a Sydney barrister who specialised in industrial relations, and was sympathetic to Jackson.

Moore was part of the industrial relations establishment. Despite their declining membership, he believed unions should have a central role in the workplace. He had a connection to Shorten, who had appointed him to a lucrative position reviewing the effectiveness of the Labor government's industrial relations laws. Phillips was more of an outsider. He was uncomfortable with the political power wielded within the ALP by union officials and believed that in some unions there were probably a majority of Liberal and National Party voters who wouldn't want their membership dues spent on donations to Labor.

The New South Wales legislation, which would allow the Coalition government to choose the HSU administrator, was rushed through the lower house on 8 May. It passed comfortably. Getting it through the upper house, where the government didn't have a majority, would be trickier.

The next day in the upper house, Labor proposed a change: the state Industrial Relations Commission would get to choose the administrator, not the government. The distinction was crucial. The government would back an administrator sympathetic to Jackson. The commission, which was staffed by appointees of the previous Labor government, was more likely to side with Shorten. The Shooters and Fishers Party, which jointly held the balance of power, agreed to support the Labor suggestion. Knowing it didn't have the numbers, the government folded. Jackson's best chance of clearing out the union and preserving her power base was dashed.

Realising she was losing the battle for control of the union, Jackson desperately wanted to explain her version of events to the public. In her telling, she was a courageous whistleblower who had risked her career and reputation to end endemic corruption while powerful union and political leaders sought to destroy her. Her HSU rivals, including Brown, thought she was exploiting the allegations against Thomson and Williamson to take over the union herself.

On 1 June Jackson sat down with a solicitor from Harmers Workplace Lawyers in Melbourne and signed off on an eighty-page affidavit. The document set out in chronological order her discovery of corruption in the HSU, how she tackled it and the professional and personal consequences for her from the scandal. It was her side of a very complicated story.

The following day, a Saturday, Jackson emailed the affidavit to the office of the judge overseeing the break-up case, Flick. Jackson wanted it placed in the court's case file, which would make it a public document. Curious journalists would be certain to get a copy. Jackson didn't ask the opposing lawyers for permission, a serious breach of protocol. The government was entitled to oppose the affidavit becoming part of the evidence. Flick was extremely annoyed and ticked off Jackson two days later. Chastened, she withdrew the affidavit.

The last day of the court case, a Friday, was a disaster for Jackson. When the hearing began, Jackson's barrister, Brett Shields, stood up and told the court he would no longer be representing Jackson and it was possible another barrister, David Rofe, would replace him.

Rofe was in court. He opened by apologising for not wearing his silk barrister's robes, which were being cleaned. He asked for a short break to talk to Jackson. Flick gave him a few minutes. Rofe asked for a few more minutes and got a fifteen-minute break. He then asked for the case to be delayed one to two weeks. Flick, who had already decided there was enough evidence to appoint an administrator, asked why he should adjourn the case. Rofe, who knew little, if anything, about the evidence, gave up and sat down.[15]

Jackson then decided to represent herself. She quickly got to the nub. She didn't want control of the union to be handed to Moore, she wanted Flick to remove himself from the case because of bias, and she wanted her full affidavit read in court.

Jackson complained Moore was too close to Shorten. She said the union's members were disgusted with the Labor Party's handling of the Craig Thomson affair. Letting Moore run the union would disenfranchise them further. 'We need an independent administrator,' she said.

Jackson's rant reinforced Flick's determination to appoint an administrator. He chose Moore. Four days later at 4 p.m. Moore suspended Jackson, Williamson and six other HSU East branch officials from their posts, without pay. Jackson remained national secretary. Moore gave them twenty-four hours to return any union property, including credit cards and computers. He later fired them all.

Shorten, who never set foot in the courtroom, had triumphed. Jackson couldn't hide her disappointment. Outside the court she urged reporters not to conflate the merger with the corruption in the New South Wales division. Later, she would express bitterness towards Flick, who she felt didn't grant her a fair hearing. 'I was the victim of an appalling injustice,' she said. (Flick declined to respond to Jackson's claim for this book.) In a farewell email to members, Williamson said he was proud their interests were always placed first and that he would not seek re-election. He was bowing out. He took one last shot at Jackson. 'The union doesn't deserve what has occurred and I think we all know where the dysfunctionality exists,' he wrote. Jackson had lost, badly, but wasn't giving up.

## Shooting the messenger

The plain Australia Post padded envelope didn't have a return address or a label to identify its origin. Inside was the explosive affidavit Kathy Jackson had tried to place into the Federal Court file. Someone had sent it to an editor on the *Australian Financial Review*.[16]

Eighty pages long and signed in front of a lawyer, the document was her side of the HSU East story. It was the only written account of how Jackson concluded Michael Williamson was corrupt, her efforts against him and the campaign that followed to destroy her reputation.

One of the most sensational sections of the affidavit didn't directly relate to the Health Services Union. It was about Bill Shorten.

Jackson described a confrontation with Shorten shortly before he became an MP. The incident took place in 2007 at a Labor Party ballot to select a candidate for the seat of Corangamite, which takes in part of Geelong. Jackson, who controlled four votes, supported trade union official Darren Cheeseman from the Left faction. Shorten, who was secretary of the Australian Workers' Union, backed Peter McMullin, the son of Ian McMullin, the founder of Spotless catering group and one of Victoria's richer men.

About 350 people had crammed into a room at the Labor Party's head office in West Melbourne. Shorten desperately wanted McMullin to win the ballot and the seat, giving him another supporter among Labor's federal MPs.

Jackson left the building to have a cigarette and was leaning against a wall when Shorten approached her, according to the affidavit. He asked why she wouldn't vote for McMullin, according to the document.

'Because he is part of Spotless,' Jackson said she replied. 'Spotless have been screwing our outsourced members. I cannot vote for someone who is associated with a business that is screwing our members.'

'Oh look. That doesn't matter. Peter will make a fine candidate.'

'No, Bill, you don't get it. I am not going to vote for him.'

'But we need your votes or he won't get up.'

'Find another candidate that I can vote for.'

'I require you to cast your votes as I say.'

'No, Bill.'

Jackson claimed Shorten then pushed her.

'The veins were standing out on his forehead,' the affidavit said. 'He was red in the face. He said words loudly to the effect: "You will fucking well vote for the candidate that I tell you to vote for. If you defy me, you will never be welcome in my home again and you will never have our support when you fucking well need it."

'Several little gobs of spittle hit my face as he said this. I hit his arm and pushed him away shouting back words at him to the effect: "You can go fuck yourself, Bill. I am not going to be intimidated by the likes of you. How dare you? How dare you demand that I vote for a candidate that has been screwing my members? Put yourself in the position I am in. That is like me asking you to vote for the son of the mine manager at Beaconsfield [the site of a Tasmanian goldmine collapse that killed one of Shorten's union members and trapped another two for fourteen days]."'

Thanks to Jackson's support, Cheeseman won by two or three votes out of about 180. He was selected as the Labor candidate and won the seat from the Liberal Party at the 2007 election by 771 votes, making Corangamite the most marginal Labor seat in the country.

Jackson's allegation had the potential to damage Shorten politically. Compounding the seriousness of the situation, her partner, Michael Lawler's, position at Fair Work Australia placed him in Shorten's ministerial portfolio.

The claim left the *Financial Review* with a tough choice. Should it publish inflammatory allegations against a cabinet minister by a union leader whose integrity was under question? Although he had a sharp tongue, Shorten didn't have a history of physical aggression.

The paper rang one of Shorten's press secretaries, Sam Casey, to let him know it was considering publishing Jackson's allegation. Casey was courteous but didn't offer any immediate comment. A journalist then set about trying to corroborate the story. He rang Cheeseman, who was in question time in parliament. Cheeseman rang back a few minutes after question time finished. 'I haven't heard that before,' he said, when told about the allegation. 'Do you believe it?' the journalist asked. 'If it's coming from Kathy Jackson, no,' he said. Cheeseman said he didn't want to be quoted in the article.

Asked if he would ever support Shorten to become party leader, Cheeseman laughed and said: 'I'm a member of the Left.'

Cheeseman rang back about an hour later. He had changed his mind. I'm happy for you to quote me, he said. 'No such incident happened and this is just a part of Kathy Jackson's vendetta against the government,' he said. 'These allegations would have been reported five years ago if there was any truth to them.'

Behind the scenes, Shorten was doing everything he could to kill the story. One of his advisers rang the *Financial Review*'s editor, Paul Bailey, and tried to talk him out of publishing anything about Shorten from the affidavit. He suggested the paper would be punished if it did not toe the line.

Shorten then called editor-in-chief Michael Stutchbury, who was weighing up whether to publish the article. The government's lawyers on the Health Services Union case, Corrs Chambers Westgarth, rang the *Financial Review*'s in-house lawyer, Richard Coleman, to brief him on why the Federal Court didn't want to accept Jackson's affidavit as evidence, a step that would have made it public and legally protected.

Even though the affidavit wasn't part of the court record, Coleman believed the paper was legally allowed to publish the allegations as long as the journalist writing the article believed they were true. Stutchbury then got a call from Gail Hambly, the group general counsel and company secretary of Fairfax Media, the *Financial Review*'s parent company. Shorten had called Fairfax chief executive Greg Hywood to ask him to intervene. Hambly wanted to know what the fuss was about. Shorten was threatening to sue if the article went ahead. Corrs Chambers Westgarth had emailed the paper and said the article 'would cause irreparable damage to Minister Shorten's reputation and would hinder Minister Shorten from being in a position to properly perform his duties as a senior minister in the federal government'.

Corrs identified paragraphs in the affidavit that the government didn't want published. All except one were about the alleged confrontation. The other cited Shorten's friendship with Andrew Landeryou, the blogger who Jackson believed was running a smear campaign against her. Corrs said Shorten unequivocally denied the allegations, but didn't want the paper to publish his denial. His advisers repeatedly emphasised that Shorten would not respond to the allegations, even to deny them.

McMullin's family background would have made him an unusual Labor candidate. (After his failed tilt at federal politics he was elected president of the Victorian Employers' Chamber of Commerce and Industry.) The *Australian Financial Review* reached McMullin on his mobile phone about 5.30 p.m. and asked if there had been a confrontation between Shorten and Jackson at the vote. 'I have heard rumours of that but I didn't see anything and no-one mentioned it on the night,' he said. 'She was clearly angry about something and it wasn't clear what she was angry about.' McMullin said he didn't believe Shorten assaulted Jackson. The paper rang Jackson to let her know an article was being written. She didn't return the call.

The *Australian Financial Review* decided to publish the story on the front page with the headline: 'Shorten abused and threatened me, says Jackson'. Under the word 'Exclusive' in red letters, it began: 'Employment and Industrial Relations Minister Bill Shorten was involved in a physical confrontation with union leader Kathy Jackson and threatened to cut her off politically and personally when she refused to back his ally in an internal Labor election, the national secretary of the Health Services Union has claimed.'

The most sensational allegation – that Shorten made some kind of physical motion towards Jackson in anger – was left out. Almost every other detail of the alleged encounter was included. The article included Cheeseman's view that the confrontation never happened.

About 1.15 a.m., shortly after the article appeared on the *Financial Review*'s website, Hywood was woken by a call on his mobile. It was Shorten again, furious about the story. He spoke so loudly Hywood held the phone away from his ear. Hywood, who was in the middle of a serious restructuring of the company's operations that involved cutting almost 2000 staff, refused to intervene and went back to sleep.

The next morning Shorten and his lawyers tried to stop the story spreading. The *Business Spectator* website and smh.com.au published reports based on the *Financial Review* article. Corrs threatened to sue if they weren't taken down. Both complied.

Coincidentally, Jackson appeared in court that day for a final decision on control of HSU East. Geoffrey Flick ruled that Michael Moore, the former judge he had temporarily put in charge of the union, would run HSU East until it could be broken up into its three original divisions and new elections held. In a sign of how Jackson had become the story, most articles about the case focused on her $120,000 pay cut and didn't mention that Williamson had in effect been fired. Flick accepted that Jackson genuinely believed she was seeking to expose corruption and there might be 'considerable factual merit in her position'. But he said she was at least partly responsible for the union's collective dysfunction.

Outside the hearing Jackson was asked by reporters about her sensational claims against Shorten. 'I stand by everything in the affidavit,' she said.

Even though no other newspapers published Jackson's allegations the next day, Shorten was determined to punish the *Financial Review*. Two days after the article appeared, *The Australian* published its own scoop. Shorten, who had kept the financial services portfolio when he was given industrial relations, told the paper he planned to allow accountants to give advice to people investing in managed funds and other common investment products. The decision was a victory for the accounting industry and a story the *Financial Review* would have loved to break. When the paper's superannuation reporter rang Shorten's office to ask why the story was leaked to its competitor, she was referred to the front-page Jackson article.

Wednesday, 27 June, six days after the article was published, was the highlight of the Canberra social calendar. The press gallery mid-winter ball, held in parliament's great hall, was attended by 640 people from the political world: ministers and MPs from all parties, business leaders, lobbyists, media executives and journalists. Prime Minister Julia Gillard presented *Sydney Morning Herald* political correspondent Phillip Coorey with an award. Gillard expressed sympathy for journalists at Fairfax Media and News Limited, which were both preparing for job cuts, and joked she 'didn't know what it would be like to wake up every morning not knowing if I had a job'.

The night was awkward for Shorten. As a flourishing cabinet minister working on high-profile policy with a glamorous wife, Chloe Bryce, on his arm, he should have revelled in the adulation of fawning admirers. Instead, he chose to snub his host for the night, Fairfax Media, which had invited him to attend the dinner before Jackson's allegations were published. The Shortens sat on a different table.

The government's lawyers, Corrs, threatened to sue unless the *Financial Review* published, within seven days, a correction on page one or page three. The paper declined. Shorten then hired Leon Zwier, a partner at Arnold Bloch Leibler with a reputation as one of the most ferocious litigators in Melbourne. Zwier made a few attempts to extract an apology and eventually gave up.

## Daggers in men's smiles

From almost the moment Julia Gillard defeated Kevin Rudd in the February leadership challenge she didn't face one opponent. She faced two. In parallel with Tony Abbott's open campaign for the Lodge, Rudd ran a guerilla campaign to return as leader. He travelled the country almost constantly for public appearances and speeches. He helped backbenchers raise money for their campaigns. He had more followers on Twitter than Gillard. He sparred with her for media attention. When the prime minister promised to increase education spending in response to a review of schools policy led by Sydney businessman David Gonski, Rudd posted photos of himself with schoolkids.

The decision to replace Rudd with Gillard, which was carried out so quickly that almost no-one saw it coming, was now hurting the party like a festering wound. The almost constant focus by the media on the leadership, fanned by backbenchers likely to lose their seats under Gillard, undermined the government's legitimacy. The party's poll numbers were appalling. Labor's two-party support hit 41 per cent versus 59 per cent for the Coalition over the weekend of 28-29 April 2012, according to Newspoll. The government was facing a New South Wales-magnitude wipeout. Steven Conroy and others involved started privately playing down their role in the leadership swap.

Some MPs and union leaders were convinced Gillard would be gone by Christmas. The initial euphoria over Australia's first female prime minister masked doubts among many conservative Labor voters about her unconventional background. 'They don't like Gillard,' said one backbencher from New South Wales Labor's Right. 'They don't like the way she speaks, they don't like the colour of her hair, they don't like the fact that she's a woman, they don't like that she's unmarried and they don't like that she lives with her boyfriend in the Lodge.'

Other MPs thought Rudd's popularity would quickly dissipate if he returned as leader and his personal flaws once again became clear. Several ministers, including Attorney-General Nicola Roxon and Treasurer Wayne Swan, disliked Rudd so much they said they wouldn't serve in another Rudd government.

Rudd had about thirty votes of the 103 Labor MPs. Even if he could convince an extra twenty-five MPs to support him, the personal resentment among the losers would be so great it would make it almost impossible for Rudd to unify the party, his opponents argued. Others countered that Rudd would call an immediate election if he were made leader, making the internal dissent largely irrelevant.

Rudd's nice-guy media persona belied an indifference to the havoc he was creating. In late 2011 he attended a conference held by Rainbow Labor, a group of Labor activists who advocate for lesbian, gay, bisexual, transgender and intersex rights. Rudd suggested his opposition to same-sex marriage was wavering, a shift that delighted the group. The following September, when a law to legalise gay marriage was put to parliament, he helped defeat it. (So did Gillard.) On 12 September Rudd was interviewed on the ABC's *7.30* program. Gillard, whose father had just died, was on bereavement leave. Asked by interviewer Leigh Sales if Labor could win the election under Gillard, Rudd had to be prompted four times before he said yes. Some MPs and union leaders, including Paul Howes, the head of the Australian Workers' Union, thought Rudd's timing tasteless.

The biggest obstacle to changing leader was, of course, Gillard. The disastrous fallout from Rudd's removal had demonstrated that the success of any leadership change hinged on the smoothness of the transition. If Gillard were going to be replaced, it would have to be her decision. She would need to be convinced the party was heading towards a disaster. Her departure would have to be voluntary, gracious and without the duelling press conferences of Rudd's defeat by Gillard. She would have to be psyched out of the job.

As the popularity contest between Gillard and Rudd consumed the parliamentary party, others were looking at a third option: Bill Shorten. Support for the government hit its nadir around April 2012.

Some MPs privately urged Shorten to consider challenging Gillard. They argued he could bring the Rudd and Gillard supporters together, energise the party and outshine Abbott.

Gillard's office, which seemed to fear Shorten, was worried about a leadership challenge at the end of the year. For reasons not entirely clear, Labor often swaps leaders in December. MPs seemed to want to resolve festering political tension before the summer holidays, perhaps to give them more certainty about the future when they return to their electorates to recuperate from the busy year. Gough Whitlam, Bob Hawke, Simon Crean and Kim Beazley were all replaced in December.

Shorten enjoyed the attention. He assiduously worked his network with the backbench. MPs reported he made time in his ministerial workload to send text messages and emails. The messages were friendly, sometimes charming. There was no overt plea for support. Some backbenchers played the game back. They would praise Shorten for a cutting or funny line he had deployed in parliament or to the media. Shorten, who was proud of his debating skills, loved the approval.

Rudd's supporters were wary of Shorten's popularity. Privately they argued he needed to be patient. 'He doesn't need to get there so quickly,' one Rudd adviser said. 'You've got a lot of time in politics.'

Publicly and privately Shorten continued to back Gillard, making him the major obstacle to a Rudd comeback. Through his control of the Victorian Labor Party, along with Stephen Conroy, David Feeney and Kim Carr, Shorten influenced a big chunk of Labor MPs. Not only did Rudd need Shorten not to run, he wanted his active support.

Yet eight months in cabinet had shown up some of Shorten's weaknesses. In a government on the defensive, Shorten's aggression was a powerful weapon against the Coalition. Yet his confidence – which sometimes bordered on arrogance – could backfire. In April he chided Abbott for not knowing the date of the Reserve Bank of Australia's monthly board meeting. 'We all make mistakes but when you want to be the alternative prime minister of Australia, interest rates is just such an important issue and the Reserve Bank board has been meeting on the second Tuesday of the month since 1960, according to the RBA archive,' he told ABC Radio. But Shorten, who had been assistant treasurer, was wrong too. The central bank board meets, and always has, on the first Tuesday of the month.

Within the government it was regarded as a stupid error that illustrated the soft treatment Shorten often received in the press. The gaffe would have triggered an avalanche of criticism if made by Gillard or Treasurer Wayne Swan, some ministers thought. A senior government adviser described Shorten's behaviour as 'temperamental' and said he had scheduled public events and abruptly pulled out.

A few days later Shorten got into trouble again. When asked a question he didn't want to answer, Shorten's standard tactic was aggression or sarcasm. In an interview on Sky News, presenter David Speers asked if Peter Slipper should remain speaker of the House of Representatives. The issue was extremely sensitive for the government. Slipper had just been accused of sexual harassment and Shorten didn't want to get involved. 'I understand that the prime minister has addressed this at a press conference in Turkey in the last few hours,' Shorten told Speers. 'I haven't seen what she's said, but let me say I support what it is that she's said.'

'Hang on, you haven't seen what she's said,' Speers replied, incredulous.

'But I support what my prime minister's said.'

'Well, what's your view?

'My view is what the prime minister's view is.'

The interview became a minor internet sensation, and Shorten was mocked for mindless loyalty. Even Britain's *The Guardian* wrote about it, under the headline: 'Is Bill Shorten the world's most loyal politician?'

Behind the scenes, Shorten's staff created a sense of patient certainty about his leadership prospects. 'There's some degree of inevitability about him taking it, so why force it to occur?' Shorten's press secretary, Tom Cameron, told a journalist in early 2012. Shorten's main rival, Greg Combet, lacked charisma, Cameron said, and his leadership prospects were dependent on the success of his signature policy, the carbon tax, which at that point was dragging the government down in the polls.

There were good reasons for Shorten to wait until after the election. Around June, when Gillard's leadership was at its weakest, Shorten had clocked up less than two years as a minister and only seven months in cabinet. He'd had four-and-a-half years in parliament. Rudd became prime minister after nine years in parliament and six years on the frontbench. He had held senior jobs in the Queensland government before becoming a politician. Paul Keating, whose advice Shorten sought around this time, was treasurer eight years before he became leader. Shorten's limited experience would make it harder for him to get the government to run smoothly and dominate parliament, which is vital for any prime minister's authority.

His lifelong goal so close, Shorten couldn't bring himself to grab it. As one of the plotters who made Gillard leader, he knew he would look doubly traitorous if he tore down another democratically elected prime minister. The trauma to the party would be immense.

Eager to make history, Shorten didn't want to be a victim of it. He may have been wary of the lesson of Shakespeare's great villain, Macbeth, who killed his patron to become king. Haunted by the murder, Macbeth became a tyrant feared by those around him and unloved by his people.

## Haunted by history

In the meantime Julia Gillard had other problems. An unhappy piece of her history would not go away: an ex-boyfriend, Bruce Wilson. In 1991 Wilson was a charming young union leader on the way up. By the time Gillard reached the pinnacle of political life, Wilson was a down-and-out cook at an RSL club at Fingal Bay in New South Wales.

Gillard dated Wilson for four years, from 1991 to 1995. Like Gillard, Wilson lived in Melbourne, where he was Victorian secretary of the Australian Workers' Union from 1992 to 1995.

The relationship became the obsession of a group of political outsiders. They worked behind the scenes to convince anyone who would listen, including the media and Coalition politicians, that Gillard was involved in a fraud committed by Wilson at the AWU. Among them was John Pasquarelli, a figure in the far-right One Nation political party in the 1990s. Pasquarelli had urged a disgruntled AWU official, Bob Kernohan, to make a statutory declaration that accused Wilson of fraud. Pasquarelli offered the document around, including to radio host Alan Jones, who declined to get involved. There was also an obscure Melbourne lawyer, Harry Nowicki, who spent hours sifting through court files looking for Slater & Gordon records and evidence against Gillard and Wilson. He told journalists he was writing a book about the history of the AWU between 1985 and 1997.

The story he was digging into was way juicier than that. Wilson was kicked out of the union in 1995 after extorting hundreds of thousands of dollars from construction and engineering companies that employed AWU members, according to Kernohan and Wilson's former sidekick, Ralph Blewitt. Gillard did the legal work to establish the non-profit association used for the scam. Gillard's connection to the fund emerged in 1995 when her managers at Slater & Gordon found out and considered terminating her employment. Gillard had always maintained she was duped by Wilson and didn't know the money would be misused. Gillard's detractors argued it wasn't credible for such a smart operator not to have realised her partner was a crook.

The few commentators who initially broached the allegations publicly paid a high price. Radio broadcaster Michael Smith tried to air an interview with Kernohan on Sydney station 2UE in September 2011. The pre-recorded interview discussed Gillard's connection to the AWU slush fund. When the station refused to broadcast the interview, Smith's position became untenable and he left the station. (The radio station is owned by Fairfax Media, which said the interview was not broadcast for legal reasons. Smith asserts he resigned on principle. Fairfax sources indicated he was fired.) The same day the interview was due to run, former Channel Seven journalist Glenn Milne wrote in *The Australian* that Wilson bought a house with the money from the slush fund (which was true). Milne also claimed Gillard shared the house (which wasn't). Gillard was so furious she rang the head of the paper's publisher, News Limited chief executive John Hartigan, at 8 a.m. on the morning it appeared and demanded an apology. She also sought a promise the allegation never be repeated in any News Limited publication – a prohibition that would have covered two-thirds of Australian newspapers. Gillard got the apology but not a promise that the allegations would be off-limits for future articles.

Gillard had never lived in Wilson's house, although she stayed there from time to time. Milne, who looked like a conspiracy theorist loose with the facts, was dumped from his column with *The Australian* and a regular slot on the ABC's *Insiders* program.

After Smith and Milne lost their jobs the story went quiet. It took a disgruntled former minister to get the media interested again.

Gillard replaced Robert McClelland as attorney-general, a job he loved, in December, 2011, with one of her cabinet allies, Nicola Roxon. It took McClelland, now a backbencher, six months to take his revenge. On 21 June he gave a speech in parliament calling for tougher penalties for union corruption and the legal right for union members to trigger investigations if they suspected corrupt behaviour. Given the high profile of the Health Services Union scandal, McClelland's suggestion would have otherwise been unexceptional. Except he didn't cite the HSU as an example. He went back in time much further, to the 1990s and the AWU fraud case.

Amazingly, McClelland was directly involved. As a partner at Sydney law firm Turner Freeman he had worked with the AWU joint national secretary, Ian Cambridge, to try to get the money repaid. McClelland pointed out in his speech that union governance laws in the mid-1990s did not cover union officials who had retired. That meant Wilson could not be pursued under industrial relations laws because he left the union soon after the allegations were made, a loophole that almost created an incentive for corrupt behaviour.

As McClelland explained his concerns about the lack of safeguards against union corruption, he made reference to Gillard. 'Indeed, I know the prime minister is quite familiar with this area of the law, as lawyers in the mid-1990s [we] were involved in a matter representing opposing clients,' he said.

It sounded innocuous. But for those following the case McClelland's reference to Gillard's professional relationship with Wilson and the AWU slush fund was extraordinary. Why would a former Labor attorney-general bring up a scandal from Gillard's past that had the potential to do so much damage to her reputation?

He seemed to be sending a coded message that the media should start taking the allegations against Gillard more seriously. McClelland later insisted privately he wasn't driven by animosity towards Gillard and was speaking to clarify his own role in trying to fight corruption in the AWU as a lawyer because he could see the issue was gaining currency in the press. Gillard supporters didn't buy the explanation.

*The Australian*'s national chief correspondent, Hedley Thomas, decided to start digging deeper. He went back to Gillard's fellow partners at Slater & Gordon and the others looking into the events at the law firm. He obtained a transcript of the September 1995 interview between Gillard and Slater & Gordon's chairman, Peter Gordon, to discuss her AWU work. The transcript proved Gillard knew Wilson's fund wasn't set up to train members of the union or improve safety, which was the reason stated on the incorporation documents she filed. Gillard admitted in the interview it was, in her words, a 'slush fund' to finance candidates in union elections. She hadn't told other officials in the AWU, which was her client, she had set up a separate association using the AWU name for her boyfriend. She hadn't opened a file at Slater & Gordon for the work, which made it invisible to the other partners.

On 18 August 2012 Thomas published the first of a series of articles that propelled the seventeen-year-old scandal back onto the front pages. The article began: 'Julia Gillard left her job as a partner with law firm Slater & Gordon as a direct result of a secret internal probe in 1995 into controversial work she had done for her then boyfriend, a union boss accused of corruption.'

The timing was appalling for the government. Gillard had been starting to gain political momentum. Now, she was being personally linked to union corruption. The AWU connection reminded many voters of the Health Services Union scandal. It reinforced the perception the Labor Party was compromised by its relationship with the union movement.

Gillard ignored the story, hoping interest would peter out. But the voice of a future prime minister echoing back through the decades was too compelling for the media to ignore. Gillard's tone in the 1995 transcript was similar to her approach as a leader under fire: a hint of anger underlying the calm, logical delivery. In this case, though, she was in a position of weakness, a proud woman being forced to justify her conduct to sceptical employers.

All major media outlets followed up *The Australian*'s story.

After five days the pressure became too great. Parliament was about to resume after a break and the Coalition was preparing an assault on Gillard's integrity. Gillard decided to call a snap press conference in Canberra to give her side of the story. Reporters had little time to prepare detailed questions or review the evidence. Thomas, the journalist who knew most about the issue, lived in Brisbane and wasn't present. Editors at *The Australian* frantically emailed suggested questions to their political reporter, Sid Maher, who was sitting in the front row. Maher was reluctant to check his phone during the press conference lest it look like his questions were being orchestrated from head office, according to his fellow reporter, David Crowe.

'For a number of months now, there has been a smear campaign circulating on the internet relating to events seventeen years ago,' Gillard told the journalists. 'Much of the material in circulation is highly sexist. I've taken the view over time that I will not dignify this campaign with a response either. However, this morning something changed on that.'

What had changed? 'A false and highly defamatory claim about my conduct' in *The Australian*, Gillard said. Gillard wasn't referring to the front-page exposé by Thomas. She was talking about a minor article that day, written by a different reporter, which misidentified the AWU slush fund as a 'trust fund', a legal distinction that had no relevance to the substantive issues of the affair. Gillard used the trust fund mistake to portray herself as a victim of a media hate campaign.

Gillard took questions for about an hour, an unusually long time for a prime minister. She said she wasn't involved in the operation of Wilson's slush fund – an allegation that had never been made – and none of the money was used on her home. She voluntarily left Slater & Gordon. 'I did that in circumstances where there had been growing tension and friction amongst the partnership,' she said. 'I think these are matters of public record.'

The case raised questions about where the line fell between legitimate political reporting and muck-raking. Some reporters were worried about the professional backlash from pursuing links between union corruption and a prime minister. Aware of the high price paid by two of the journalists who had previously pushed the story forwards, Michael Smith and Glenn Milne, Thomas felt reporters had allowed themselves to be intimidated out of delving into events that challenged Gillard's integrity and professionalism. Thomas criticised what he perceived as a pro-Labor bias among some political journalists and their employers. 'Disclosures in the past week highlight that many journalists have not done their job properly on matters of great public interest and significance, in my opinion,' Thomas wrote in a letter to the ABC's *Media Watch* on 25 August. 'I include myself in that category.'

Others thought *The Australian*, owned by Rupert Murdoch's News Corporation, was trying to tear down Gillard over minor indiscretions decades old and help put the Coalition into power.[17] *Sydney Morning Herald* commentator Peter Hartcher wrote that the newspaper was pursuing the 'destruction of the Labor government' aided by Labor MPs who were her enemies. Mark Latham, who was developing a career as a political commentator, said *The Australian*'s focus on the story had ended a long-established convention of not judging politicians by their lives before they were elected to parliament. Latham argued no politician had a pristine background and it was unfair to judge any by common imperfections. 'The Murdoch flagship has raised the bar on personal behaviour in public life,' Latham wrote on 27 September in the *Financial Review*. '*The Australian* is now operating as a stand-over merchant for the Abbott campaign, directly threatening the prime minister with personal and political reprisals.'

Latham and others, including Melbourne ABC Radio presenter Jon Faine, argued there was no substance to the story. The media was allowing itself to act as the weapon of a shadowy group of conspiracy-obsessed outsiders who wanted to bring the prime minister down, critics said.

Momentum was building, slowly, for the believers. Under relentless reporting by *The Australian*, much of it incremental and difficult for outsiders to follow, other journalists and editors started to wonder exactly how much Gillard knew about Wilson's slush fund.

To the government's horror, the scandal started to gain traction. One of the remarkable aspects of the coverage was the importance of journalistic-like sources outside the mainstream media. After months of pushing by Michael Smith and his co-conspirators, no major media outlet felt they could ignore the story.

Some Coalition politicians who had been given the files made half-hearted attempts to spread the information. Eric Abetz, Nick Minchin, Barnaby Joyce and George Brandis all had copies of an AWU dossier, according to journalist Peter Hartcher. But none of them pursued the allegations publicly until the mainstream media started referring to it as the 'AWU scandal'. The political fringe succeeded where the political establishment had, initially, been too cautious to tread.

## Turning the tide

The government was desperate for James Ashby's sexual harassment suit against Peter Slipper to go away. Lawyers from the attorney-general's department had made two confidential settlement offers, which were rejected. Then, in late September, Ashby got a deal he could live with. He would be paid compensation of $50,000.

Each side would cover their own legal costs. As part of the deal, the government agreed to provide training for MPs about sexual harassment. Ashby was free to continue suing Slipper, who had to cover his own legal expenses.

In October, a hearing was held at the Federal Court offices in Sydney. A pack of journalists, photographers and camera crews waited outside for Slipper and Ashby. Ashby, who hadn't been seen in months, walked in wearing a blue suit and blue tie, his short hair fashionably ruffled. The attorney-general, Nicola Roxon, who had an office in the Macquarie Street building, helped Slipper avoid the media throng by allowing him to drive straight into the building's underground car park. The judge hearing the case, Steven Rares, complained that Roxon had cut Slipper a favour. Roxon and Slipper apologised.

In court, Ashby's lawyer read out a few of the text messages traded between the men when they were working together. Katie Walsh, a reporter from the *Australian Financial Review* who was present, was surprised by what she heard. Slipper had written about going to a 'fish shop' to 'buy the bottle of shell-less mussels', the reference to female genitalia. As the texts were read, Slipper, who represented himself, stood up and complained. Rares let Ashby's lawyer admit the text messages into evidence, a decision that gave the press open slather to publish them. The next day Walsh reported Slipper had used 'vulgar language to describe women's sexual organs in messages to his former press secretary, James Ashby'.

A few days later the floodgates opened. Ashby's publicist gave 200 pages of text messages from Ashby's mobile phone to selected journalists. Rares, the judge, then told Federal Court staff to place the messages, which had been admitted as evidence, on the court's website. The main evidence of harassment was available for anyone to assess. The press was awash with Slipper's crude language, which most people saw as bizarre and sexist. Any moral authority Slipper had left over parliament was shot.

The Coalition, which had been waiting for a chance to punish Slipper for his defection, seized its chance. Tony Abbott and his closest aides decided that morning to call for a vote in the House of Representatives to sack Slipper as speaker – even though there was no proof he had broken any laws or behaved corruptly. If successful the vote would be an incredible demonstration of Abbott's power in parliament. Gillard's authority would be undermined, perhaps fatally, and perceptions of the balance of power in Canberra would flip.

About an hour before question time was due to start, one of the independents who held the balance of power, Tony Windsor, sought out Slipper. He gently suggested Slipper resign before he was removed. Slipper wanted to hang on. He had enjoyed the speaker's perks for eleven months. But he had only spent nineteen days overseeing proceedings in the House of Representatives. Being removed after such a short time would reinforce the ignominy of his downfall.[18]

At 2.01 p.m., Abbott stood in parliament and asked if Gillard still supported Slipper. Gillard said Slipper's texts were offensive. She didn't say if she supported Slipper or not. Abbott then called for a vote to remove Slipper as speaker, a two-stage process required by parliament's rules of procedure. He compared Slipper to Craig Thomson and said Gillard had run a 'protection racket' to look after both men. 'This whole sorry Slipper saga illustrates the ethical bankruptcy of this government,' he said.

Slipper was in his office a few metres from the entrance to the chamber. His television was tuned to the proceedings to unseat him. The government was for him. The opposition was determined to take him down. The outcome would depend on the independents. As Abbott worked through his twenty-four-minute speech, Windsor and another independent, Rob Oakeshott, ducked out and walked to Slipper's office.

The two men told Slipper they were going to vote against the motion to remove him. But Slipper, who was emotionally distraught at the public humiliation, would have to resign that day. Windsor and Oakeshott offered Slipper a little time to call his elderly parents and his wife. Shortly after 3.10 p.m. Anthony Albanese, the government's lead parliamentary tactician, left the chamber to find out what was happening in Slipper's office.

In parliament, Abbott pinned Slipper's behaviour on Gillard. She'd made him speaker and should take responsibility for his behaviour, he said. 'Every day the prime minister stands in this parliament to defend this speaker will be another day of shame for this parliament and another day of shame for a government which should have already died of shame,' he said. The comment triggered gasps from the chamber. It seemed to be a deliberate repeat of a widely criticised comment by radio presenter Alan Jones a few weeks earlier that Gillard's father, John, 'died of shame' over the behaviour of her government.

Julie Bishop, Abbott's deputy, seconded the motion and spoke for sixteen minutes. Gillard then stood and turned on Abbott:

> I rise to oppose the motion moved by the leader of the opposition, and in so doing I say to the leader of the

opposition: I will not be lectured about sexism and misogyny by this man. I will not. The government will not be lectured about sexism and misogyny by this man – not now, not ever. The leader of the opposition says that people who hold sexist views and who are misogynists are not appropriate for high office. Well, I hope the leader of the opposition has a piece of paper and he is writing out his resignation, because if he wants to know what misogyny looks like in modern Australia he does not need a motion in the House of Representatives; he needs a mirror.

Everyone in the chamber, including the press gallery, watched in fascination. Gillard argued that Abbott had a history of sexist comments, had been a friend of Slipper's, and no-one in the opposition had taken responsibility for Jones's comments about the death of her father: 'I indicate to the leader of the opposition that the government is not dying of shame – and my father did not die of shame. What the leader of the opposition should be ashamed of is his performance in this parliament and the sexism he brings with it.'

It may have been the speech of her career. Gillard, who had gone out of her way to avoid gender politics since she became prime minister, spoke forcefully on an issue that so many of her female colleagues stayed silent about: sexism. Some commentators were dismissive of the speech and saw it as a bravura attempt to distract attention from the question of the day, which was Slipper's character. But Gillard had homed in on one of Abbott's main weaknesses: he was less popular with women than men.

A YouTube clip of the speech became a minor sensation. The story was picked up by the international media, including London's *Daily*

*Telegraph* and *The New Yorker*, where a young Australian production editor, Amelia Lester, wrote in a blog that Barack Obama could learn a lesson from Gillard in how to call out an opponent 'for his own personal prejudice, hypocrisy, and aversion to facts'.

The vote to oust Slipper failed sixty-nine votes to seventy. Oakeshott, Windsor and Greens MP Adam Bandt sided with the government. Bob Katter abstained. The independents saved the government from another political crisis and denied Abbott a huge parliamentary victory.

Slipper walked into the House of Representatives, wearing his speaker's gown, at 7.19 p.m. The chamber was silent. The press gallery was empty. He stood up from the heavy, green speaker's chair and announced that he had formally resigned to Governor-General Quentin Bryce.

Anthony Albanese, speaking to the media, claimed Slipper's decision was his own. He didn't mention the independents' ultimatum. The unremarkable Victorian who had filled in for Slipper, Anna Burke, got his job.

A wave of relief swept through the government. Slipper's move to the backbench would take him out of the headlines. He was no longer the Labor Party's biggest embarrassment. There was other good news too. Labor's poll numbers were improving. Gillard was more popular than Abbott. The political tide finally seemed to be turning.

## Pin down the leader

In early August 2012, Julia Gillard decided to cauterise one of the Labor government's biggest policy failures: the thousands of wretched people making their way to Christmas Island in rickety boats to claim asylum under the Universal Declaration of Human Rights. Between October 2009 and August 2012, 21,175 asylum seekers reached Australia by sea. At least 604 died on the voyage. To staunch the flow, Gillard reintroduced one of the Howard government policies most hated by the Left, the so-called Pacific Solution of making asylum seekers wait in camps before they got a shot at settling in Australia.

On the morning of 14 August, Gillard and immigration minister Chris Bowen briefed Labor MPs in Canberra on the plan. Parliament House buzzed at the audacity of Gillard's U-turn. The army and immigration officials would set up camps on Nauru and Manus Island, which is part of Papua New Guinea. At an annual cost of about $1 billion, the asylum seekers would be forced to wait, possibly for years, on the two hot, remote islands for their claims to be processed. The number of refugees admitted each year would be increased to 20,000 from 13,750.

Despite the jump in refugee places, human rights advocates were aghast. Amnesty International complained the asylum seekers would be held indefinitely in overly harsh conditions. That was the point, of course. An unpleasant stay in Nauru or Papua New Guinea was designed as a deterrent to the Sri Lankans, Iranians, Afghans and other people fleeing their homelands.

The plan, which had been Liberal Party policy for two and a half years, was well received in marginal seats. Many immigrant families resented the new arrivals, who they felt were circumventing the rules. A voluntary poll on *The Age* and the *Sydney Morning Herald* websites found 86 per cent of people favoured Gillard's decision.

Labor's other big headache, the carbon tax, was receding. Tony

Abbott's relentless criticism of the tax, from the middle of 2011 to its introduction on 1 July 2012, drove the Coalition's poll numbers up. After the tax began and prices barely increased, the Coalition attack lost momentum. Big compensation payments helped. Everyone earning less than $80,000 got a tax cut. Anyone on a pension or receiving government financial assistance got extra money.

The government had other successes. It won a seat on the United Nations Security Council for the first time since 1986. It published a long strategy paper, *Australia in the Asian Century*, which proposed driving up living standards by improving economic links to Asia. Although the paper was mostly aspirational, it was hard for even Labor's opponents to argue that getting closer to Asia was a bad idea.

Gillard had demonstrated her great strengths as leader: a pragmatic willingness to dump unpopular policies and take her opponent's, and a steely resilience to attacks on a policy she thought would prove popular in the long run. Voters liked it. Labor starting clawing back some of the support lost in the first half of 2012, although still trailed the Coalition. On a two-party preferred basis, which allocates preferences based on previous elections, Labor's support rose to 49 per cent from 47 per cent, according to Newspoll. Gillard's personal popularity rating rose to 46 per cent in November from 39 per cent in August. Abbott's rating fell to 32 per cent from 38 per cent over the same period.

There were signs of preparations for the election too, which was due before the end of November 2013. Gillard's senior political strategist, John McTernan, accompanied her on a trip to the U.S., where he met the lead pollster for Barack Obama's presidential campaign, Joel Benenson. Labor hoped to borrow some of the sophisticated campaign techniques used in the U.S., where huge databases were used to identify individual voters' concerns and target them with letters and emails.

Faced with a surge in Labor support and a relatively popular prime minister, the Coalition decided to go after Gillard personally. Reports about her involvement in an Australian Workers' Union slush fund had been published in fits and starts for more than a year. In August 2012, Julie Bishop, the Liberal deputy leader and shadow foreign affairs minister, started boning up on the case. She decided to pursue Gillard in parliament over her relationship with Bruce Wilson and the AWU scandal.

Appointing Bishop chief inquisitor looked like a smart tactic by the Coalition. Before entering politics she was managing partner of law firm Clayton Utz's Perth office, which gave her the credibility to challenge Gillard over her actions as a lawyer. Gillard's misogyny attack on Abbott had resonated with many women. Questions from Abbott about a distant boyfriend of Gillard's could reinforce negative perceptions of him.

By October Bishop started asking Gillard about the AWU in question time, questions that appeared to deeply annoy Gillard. Bishop's pursuit of the scandal changed the coverage of the affair in an important way. Previously, the main way for media outlets to advance the story was to uncover long-forgotten documents from the 1990s that provided new information, or to track down people directly involved. Both options were time-consuming and difficult. Other outlets struggled to catch up to *The Australian*, which had assigned investigative reporter Hedley Thomas full time to the story. Bishop's intervention gave the rest of the media a straightforward way to cover the story by reporting her questions and assertions.

On 14 November *The Australian* reported that in 1995 Wilson had ordered another union official to deposit $5000 in Gillard's bank account. The article didn't explain the source of the money or what it was for. But the implications were serious: a possibly corrupt union official handed over a big wad of money to his girlfriend, a lawyer who had helped him set up a union slush fund.

Gillard, on a visit to a Brisbane building site, was asked if the article was true. She complained there was a smear campaign against her. 'This matter has been trawled over for the best part of twenty years, and at the end of it … there is not one finding of wrongdoing by me,' she said. 'I'm not going to dignify it by becoming involved in it.'

A few hours later Bishop went through the events of the early 1990s in detail in a lengthy interview on Sky News. Bishop had clearly taken many hours to understand the intricacies of the complicated case. The opposition had thick folders of documents, including a chronology. Bishop argued that Gillard's decision in 1992 not to open a file on the AWU re-election fund was professionally negligent. 'In fact I would have sacked her on the spot if she had given those explanations to me,' Bishop said. 'It goes not just to her professional standards at the time, it now goes to her honesty, her integrity and her ethics today as she seeks to, and I'll say this, as she seeks to mislead journalists.'

The government took four days to counter-attack Bishop. An article appeared in the *Sunday Telegraph* – Australia's top-selling newspaper – on 18 November raising questions about Bishop's role as a lawyer defending the building-materials company CSR from compensation claims over its deadly asbestos mine in Western Australia the 1960s. The article reported an allegation that Bishop fought to deny victims speedy trials because they were dying. Small business minister Brendan O'Connor then appeared on the ABC's *Insiders* program and said Bishop 'allegedly [used] procedural tactics to deny victims of asbestosis their day in court'. The message coming from the government was clear: if Bishop were going to pursue Gillard over the AWU fund, it would rake over her past too. Bishop denied acting unethically and said she was following the instructions of her clients.

The primary source of the allegations about the AWU slush fund came from a shady former union official, Ralph Blewitt. A Vietnam veteran who lived in Malaysia, Blewitt had told Smith and others that he was Wilson's 'bag man' and chief lieutenant. Blewitt had promised to return to Australia and tell police all if authorities promised not to prosecute him. The ex-union lawyer Nowicki came forward and offered to pay Blewitt's expenses.

Blewitt arrived in Melbourne in late November and gave a statement to the Victoria police, who declined to give him immunity. After the interview, the police said it was 'reviewing' a union, without identifying the AWU. Blewitt met with Julie Bishop for about ten minutes in Melbourne.

The man at the heart of the scandal broke cover on 25 November. After being pursued by journalists for more than a year, Bruce Wilson granted an interview to Steve Lewis, the journalist who first reported the Peter Slipper harassment allegations. In Lewis's article, which was published on the front pages of the *Sunday Telegraph* and *Sunday Herald Sun*, Wilson said Gillard knew nothing about the real purpose of the slush fund and questioned Blewitt's honesty. 'Relying on Ralph to be your star witness is a very, very risky strategy,' Wilson told Lewis.

The next day, Gillard called a press conference in Canberra. Gillard defiantly challenged the press gallery to make a choice – between her credibility and that of her accusers. 'Mr Blewitt, according to people who know him, has been described as a complete imbecile, an idiot, a stooge, a sexist pig, a liar, and his sister has said he's a crook and rotten to the core,' Gillard said. 'His word against mine. Make your mind up.'

Gillard even referred to former *Sunday Age* journalist Jason Koutsoukis, who mocked attempts to drag up the scandal in a 2007 article.

It was another intrepid performance by Gillard. By speaking to the press first, she turned a planned attack by the opposition in question time later that day into a non-event. But the fact she felt compelled to make a direct distinction between herself and a con man like Blewitt illustrated how the scandal was spiralling out of control. Not perhaps since Paul Keating was accused in 1999 of ripping off his business partner had a prime minister, past or present, been forced to defend their integrity under such attack. By then, Keating had left politics. Gillard was still trying to govern.

Adding to the atmosphere of drama, Wilson gave his first broadcast interview to the ABC's *7.30* program the next day. Speaking calmly and clearly in a blue flannel shirt, Wilson said two people involved were entirely innocent: he and Gillard. He again blamed Blewitt, who he said had buried bundles of cash from the slush fund in a backyard, where the money was partially destroyed by moisture.

Blewitt appeared on Sky News a few minutes after Wilson's appearance on the ABC. In a rambling appearance he accused Gillard of 'consorting with lesbians' before he was cut off.

Was Gillard's and Wilson's defence coordinated? It was impossible to know. But Blewitt's statement to police must have deeply concerned the down-and-out Wilson, whose cooking job undoubtedly didn't generate the cash needed for good criminal lawyers. After seventeen years the chances of prosecution over the slush fund had stepped up a notch.

Wilson's defence added to the confusion about the case. The *Australian Financial Review* summed up Wilson's appearance: 'The comments, made on the ABC's *7.30* program, further complicate the highly contested details about Ms Gillard's work as a lawyer at Melbourne firm Slater & Gordon.'

In parliament the next day Gillard seemed confident, almost cocky. She mocked Abbott, who had suddenly dropped his profile, for asking only one question in question time – which was about foreign policy, Bishop's portfolio. She ripped into Bishop, who had to backtrack after appearing to accuse Gillard of knowingly committing fraud.

'The deputy leader of the opposition wanted to spend this week as a starring character in an investigative drama,' Gillard said. 'She's ended up as the winning candidate on Red Faces.'

Gillard pursued Bishop over her admission she wasn't sure if she'd spoken with Blewitt on the phone the previous week. Bishop had admitted she got a call from Michael Smith, the former 2UE presenter, who passed the phone to someone else who may have been Blewitt. After a few words the phone dropped out and Smith didn't call back, according to Bishop. Given Blewitt's notoriety, direct contact didn't help the credibility of her arguments.

'Who was she expecting?' Gillard asked in parliament. 'Humphrey B. Bear? Oh no, he can't talk. Tom Cruise? He's not in Australia. Who on earth was she expecting on the phone, and why didn't she tell the truth about it yesterday?'

Nick Styant-Browne, the former Slater & Gordon partner, was following developments closely. He decided to turn up the heat on Gillard and rang three of the journalists covering the story – Hedley Thomas, *The Age*'s Mark Baker and Mark Skulley of the *Financial Review* – and offered a scoop.

Gillard had sent a letter to authorities vouching for the association that housed the slush fund. When challenged by a West Australian government department about the purpose of the fund in 1992, Gillard cut-and-pasted the rules from a political group she had helped set up, Socialist Forum, into a letter and sent it back. She had always said she thought the purpose of the fund was to help candidates get up in union elections. Yet she told authorities in Western Australia it was to improve safety in the workplace, and sent them the extra information to back it up. The *Australian Financial Review* and *The Age* ran the story on their front pages the next day.

That morning Abbott appeared on Nine's *Today Show*. He said the new information demonstrated Gillard misled the West Australian Corporate Affairs Commission, which was responsible for registering the association housing Wilson's fund. 'That is obviously a very serious matter,' he said. 'That would certainly be in breach of the law.'

Prime ministers cop a lot of criticism. But their opposition counterparts rarely accuse them of criminal activity. Dennis Atkins, a political commentator for *The Courier-Mail*, hadn't heard it happen in thirty-one years of covering politics. Abbott was alleging a serious breach too, one carrying a jail term of up to eighteen months, according to Atkins.

It was the last day of parliament for 2012. Question time, the main daily battleground between the parties, would be politically and symbolically crucial to both leaders. How would Gillard respond to this incredible challenge to her integrity – and her fitness even to be a member of parliament – from a man she clearly held in contempt? Could Abbott support his case that Gillard may have behaved like a criminal? Had he gone too far? Unless there was a major development after parliament ended, the day's events would help establish the narrative likely to persist over the summer.

Under attack, Gillard was often at her best. As question time was about to begin, she stood up and proposed a change to parliamentary procedure. Abbott would get fifteen minutes to substantiate his claim she had broken the law. If he refused to debate he would have to 'unreservedly apologise'. Gillard would get a fifteen-minute right of reply. Abbott had often tried to disrupt question time by triggering a side debate about the political issue of the day. The government always used its numbers in the House to shut him down. Now, without notice, it offered to place his issue, the AWU scandal, at the centre of the parliamentary day. Gillard had confronted her accuser head on.

Abbott accepted the challenge. In an unemotional speech he gave an overview of the main allegations and said it was obvious Gillard was involved in unethical and 'possibly' unlawful behaviour. A judicial inquiry was necessary, he said, to settle what had happened all those years ago. 'This is not about gender,' he said. 'This is about character and, Prime Minister, you have failed the character test.' Abbott drew a link between the AWU scandal and the Health Services Union:

But this is not just about an old scandal: corruption that dogged one union a long time ago. It is also about the ability of this government and this prime minister to stamp out union corruption wherever it occurs. We know that there is a very long echo of the AWU corruption scandal in the Health Services Union scandal, which is taking place to this very day.

Gillard's delivery was intense, controlled and brimming with anger. She said Abbott's claim she had broken the law raised doubts about his judgement. She warned Abbott he was risking his leadership by making claims he couldn't back up.

In the Senate the debate was nastier. Shadow attorney-general George Brandis, a barrister from Queensland, called out to the Labor side: 'You are the ones with a criminal in the Lodge.' He withdrew the remark but not the accusation. 'Let me make it perfectly clear that I am not withdrawing an allegation that the prime minister has committed a breach of the criminal law because I make that allegation,' he said.

Once the press would have been excited by such high-stakes rhetorical combat. Now, like the rest of the country, it seemed exhausted by the bitterness that had enveloped politics.

The main commentators split. Michelle Grattan and the *Australian Financial Review*'s Laura Tingle came down for Gillard. 'It has not always been pretty or smart but in the tradition of *Fantastic Mr Fox* and the wolf, we raise a silent paw to the prime minister in homage to her sheer resilience,' Tingle wrote.

One surprising response came from Paul Kelly, the editor-at-large of *The Australian*. Kelly, from the paper that had done the most to damage Gillard, wrote that the prime minister was more psychologically complex than Abbott, high praise from an intellectual leader of the Australian media. 'The final parliamentary week of 2012 was dominated by the stunning political persona of Julia Gillard – fierce, feminist and unrestrained – whose will-to-survival is Labor's last, best but highly dangerous hope,' he wrote.

Writers who had followed every twist in the scandal saw holes in Gillard's defence. Skulley, the *Financial Review*'s veteran industrial relations reporter, said Gillard's office was being too cute when it said she couldn't be expected to remember a twenty-year-old letter vouching for her partner's re-election fund. Skulley, who knew Gillard personally and once lived in the same Melbourne street, didn't have an axe to grind. Gillard's aggressive director of communications, John McTernan, spent twenty minutes on the phone to him the next day complaining about the article.

In a sign of the pressure they were under, Gillard's staff had become hypersensitive to press criticism. Gillard sent a letter to Fairfax Media chief executive Greg Hywood, which was released publicly, complaining *The Age* reported that her office declined to comment when asked about her letter vouching for the slush fund. Her media staff hadn't exactly declined to comment. They had sent the journalist an aggressive email criticising the paper for planning to publish 'allegations you can't substantiate'.

Amid the endless and confusing argument about Gillard's AWU work at Slater & Gordon, there was a serious internal snub to her authority. Gillard had decided Australia would vote against Palestine being admitted to the United Nations as an observer non-member state, the same status as the Vatican. The decision was a sign of Gillard's determination to stick close to U.S. President Barack

Obama's administration. She had formed an unusually friendly relationship with Obama, who had a reputation for businesslike dealings with most international leaders.

Palestinians saw the vote as an important step towards statehood. Many Labor MPs, including the foreign minister, Bob Carr, agreed. On Tuesday, 27 November, a meeting of Labor MPs opposed Gillard's decision. She caved. The government directed its mission at the United Nations to join the forty other member states that abstained. Amid jubilation in the General Assembly and on the West Bank, the resolution was passed by 138 votes in favour to nine against, led by Israel and the U.S. As someone who started her political career as a self-described socialist, Gillard's support for the U.S. position on the Israeli-Palestinian conflict was remarkable. Even more surprising was that she didn't realise her own party wouldn't follow her on such a contentious issue.

Parliament finally ended for the year on 29 November. A blistering heatwave, the first in what was one of the hottest summers in history, settled across the south-east of the continent. Most MPs flew out of Canberra the next day. There remained no definitive answer to the question preoccupying the media and politics for months: could Gillard have known Wilson was possibly corrupt when she gave him legal advice in 1992?

The Coalition would have loved to uncover compelling evidence that Gillard broke the law or behaved unethically. But it never expected to. Its objective was to use the media to drive awareness of the AWU slush funds and Gillard's relationship with Wilson.

Gillard was more popular than Abbott. By reminding voters of her connection to union corruption through a boyfriend who was a union leader, Gillard would be seen as the latest in a long line of compromised Labor politicians. The Coalition didn't want voters to think of the AWU slush fund as an anomaly. It wanted it to be seen as the normal way of doing of business in the labour movement, which included the antics of Craig Thomson, Michael Williamson and the Health Services Union, Eddie Obeid in New South Wales, smears against Campbell Newman in the Queensland election, and the plotting against Kevin Rudd. Abbott, Bishop and their Liberal Party colleagues were trying to define a new narrative for the ALP: not the party of the working classes and Ben Chifley, Gough Whitlam and Bob Hawke, but the party of a corrupt elite that had seized power for its own ends. Politics had become a struggle over the identity of modern Labor.

# 9

The biggest show in town – ICAC – Eddie Obeid's amazing networks – Craig Thomson's challenge – Follow the leader – What went wrong and what Labor can do about it

On 6 November 2012, Eric Roozendaal hastily left a hearing of the New South Wales Independent Commission Against Corruption in central Sydney. Thirteen months earlier he was the state's treasurer and one of the most powerful politicians in New South Wales. A man everyone wanted to know. A man to envy.

Now camera crews pursued him like the common criminals seen leaving court on evening news broadcasts. Silent, Roozendaal stared straight ahead, a slightly pained look on his face. A day earlier his soon-to-be estranged wife, Amanda, ran the same gauntlet. The Roozendaals' appearances as witnesses at ICAC were front-page news. Both denied doing anything wrong. But the questions and evidence put to them by the commission's barrister, Geoffrey

Watson, publicly and directly raised a disturbing question that had troubled everyone who closely followed the state's politics for years: was Roozendaal part of a corrupt cabal of politicians who controlled the government for more than a decade?

Watson, one of Australia's top lawyers, thought so. 'If it is corruption then it is corruption on a scale probably unexceeded since the days of the Rum Corps,' he told the commission.

The new Labor leadership wasn't waiting for a conclusive answer. It had already decided to suspend Roozendaal's membership of the party he once ran from Labor's headquarters on Sussex Street.

Over the next five months former ministers, ministerial advisers, unionists and business leaders made the same walk of shame along Castlereagh Street into the office building used by ICAC. In the hearing room on the seventh floor the commission's prosecutors portrayed Eddie Obeid, the former resources minister and faction leader, as the heart of an enterprise that had used the Labor government as a giant money-making machine.[19]

The sums involved stunned Sydney, a city not unused to political corruption. Watson estimated Obeid and his family stood to gain roughly $100 million out of the coal licence covering their farm in the Bylong Valley and related property transactions. Obeid's son Moses told the commission the figure was more likely $75 million. He agreed that if the licence was converted to a mining lease the family's wealth could increase by a further $100 million.

The link between Obeid and the crucial coal licences was Ian Macdonald, according to the commission's investigators. Macdonald and Obeid, who served together as MPs in the upper house, were political soul mates. They spoke constantly, dined together and plotted.

As a minister, Macdonald had responsibility for overseeing mining licences in New South Wales from 2005 to 2010, with the exception of a short period in 2009 when Premier Nathan Rees fired him.

When investigators searched the office of one of Macdonald's closest friends, businessman Greg Jones, they found a handwritten note. It said: 'Cascade Coal Mt Penny 5 per cent … $4m approved by 6 June 2010.' The sentence suggested Macdonald's cut for approving the exploration licence over the Obeid's farm was $4 million, according to Watson.

Apart from the money, the investigation provided an almost unique insight into how Labor politics really operates. Mostly through sheer persistence, Obeid gradually extended his power through the party. His diaries, which were submitted as evidence in the investigation, revealed an endless stream of meetings with political and business contacts. His regulars included Sam Dastyari, the young administrative head of the state party; his predecessor, Matt Thistlethwaite, who became a senator; Kristina Keneally, who became premier thanks to Obeid's patronage; Eric Roozendaal; Michael Costa, another former treasurer; and Tony Kelly, the planning minister who tried to cover up a property purchase in the dying days of the government. Obeid's favourite meeting places included a Darlinghurst coffee shop, Latteria; a cafe at Sydney Hospital, which is adjacent to State Parliament; and Leichhardt's Tuscany Ristorante, where Macdonald picked out a pretty Asian prostitute over dinner in 2009. Obeid loaned out his ski lodge at Perisher Valley to political contacts so often he forgot their names. Those who stayed at the lodge included Stephen Conroy, the federal communications minister; Tony Burke, the federal environment minister; Mark Arbib, the former Right faction leader; and John Robertson, who was head of Unions NSW at the time and became state Labor leader after the 2011 election wipeout.

When Obeid retired from parliament two months after Labor lost power, Robertson thanked him for his contribution to the state. When the corruption hearings that began in November 2012 unleashed a torrent of embarrassing publicity, Robertson asked head office to suspend the party membership of Obeid and Macdonald. 'I, like most people, can't believe the magnitude and the seriousness of these allegations,' he said. The move didn't help the party much. A poll taken by the *Daily Telegraph* on the second anniversary of Labor's defeat showed its support was even lower than its abysmal election vote.

Only a few Labor figures emerged from the hearings with their reputations enhanced. One of the Left faction's leaders in New South Wales, Luke Foley, described how he tried to get Macdonald dumped as an MP as early as 2006. Over Chinese at a Sydney restaurant Foley argued Macdonald's behaviour as a minister was inappropriate and that the party needed to withdraw its support for him before the 2007 state election. The head of the Australian Manufacturing Workers' Union, Doug Cameron, who was present, vetoed the idea. Macdonald had a long career in politics and deserved 'to go out with some dignity', he said. The *Daily Telegraph* later reported that Cameron's daughter, Fiona, worked in Macdonald's office for seven years, mainly as a policy adviser. Cameron became a senator at the 2007 federal election.

One of the people who stood up to another Macdonald ally, John Maitland, was his successor as head of the miners' union, Tony Maher. Maitland asked Maher to help convince the New South Wales government to approve what he described as a 'training mine' near the rich Doyles Creek coal deposit. Maher told the commission he refused to get involved because he thought the plan, which was really about getting Macdonald to approve a coalmine, would end in scandal. 'If it looks like a duck and walks like a duck, it's corruption,' he said.

Many prominent figures in Labor politics and Newcastle society had backed Maitland, who watched Macdonald sign the Doyles Creek licence over a magnum of pinot noir at Catalina Restaurant on Sydney Harbour on 15 December 2008. The dinner of seafood, duck and suckling pig was described to the commission by Macdonald's then chief of staff, Jamie Gibson, who later turned on his former boss. The indulgent meal – one of countless enjoyed by Macdonald and his cronies in government – emerged as a coda for the entire scandal-ridden clique that will surely sully the Labor Party's reputation in New South Wales for a generation.

Obeid, Macdonald, Roozendaal, Maitland and everyone else accused of wrongdoing at the anti-corruption commission staunchly proclaimed their innocence. Commissioner David Ipp will recommend to authorities if criminal offences should be pursued. It will then be up to the Director of Public Prosecutions, or perhaps a specially appointed prosecutor, to file any charges and conduct what would certainly be an expensive and complicated court process that could take years to resolve.

Civil action over the coal leases could go on a long time too. On Christmas Eve 2012, two wealthy Sydney businessmen, Neville Crichton and Denis O'Neil, sued Obeid and others linked to one of the coal deals. They had invested $13 million in Cascade Coal, the company planning to develop a coalmine based on one of the leases issued by Macdonald's department. The lawsuit alleged the money was diverted to someone or something else. Who exactly, they couldn't determine. They want their money back with interest.

The commission's report is due to be given to parliament, which will make it public, in July 2013. The timing guarantees it will cause even more damage to Labor before the federal election campaign officially begins on 12 August. The government doesn't need more headaches. Earlier in the year, investigations into the scandals that have plagued Julia Gillard's leadership began to make their way through the justice system and into courtrooms.

On 15 October 2012, Craig Thomson, the federal MP and former Health Services Union national secretary, was charged with sixty-two civil counts by Fair Work Australia. The charges were for a mixture of breaking the union's rules and breaching the duties required of all union officials. Thomson quickly hired an aggressive lawyer and former industrial relations commissioner, Chris McArdle, who threatened to sue any journalists who reported that Thomson spent union money on prostitutes. In December Fair Work Australia obtained subpoenas for closed-circuit television footage, credit card receipts and other potential evidence from some of the escort services Thomson was accused of using. It also sought information from the Labor Party about his campaign to win the seat of Dobell between 2005 and 2007. A trial is possible towards the end of 2013.

On 30 January 2013 Thomson was arrested by New South Wales police and charged with 154 counts of fraud. He was fingerprinted, strip-searched and ordered to face a magistrate in Victoria. A few days later, at the Melbourne Magistrates' Court, after sitting through several driving, domestic violence and other small-time criminal cases, Thomson's charges were heard and he was granted bail. The federal government said it would invoke an obscure law to make sure he didn't have to attend court and miss important votes in parliament.

Thomson vigorously maintains his innocence. He is trying, under difficult circumstances, to carry out the normal functions of an MP. He remains an independent and asks ministers questions in question time. The Labor Party will run a different candidate in his electorate at the 2013 election.

After it became clear former Health Services Union leader Michael Williamson would be charged, his daughter, Alexandra, resigned as a media officer on Gillard's staff. Alexandra had been organising a big farewell party for her father but it was cancelled in July 2012. On 4 October Williamson was charged with twenty counts, including fabricating documents, destroying evidence and hindering police investigations. On 31 October he was charged with an extra twenty-seven counts of defrauding the union of $620,000 and one count of dealing with the proceeds of crime.

John and Carron Gilleland, the Sydney printers accused of paying kickbacks to Williamson and Thomson, were cooperating with police, their lawyer told the *Sydney Morning Herald*. Ron Mah-Chut, Williamson's architect, died in 2012 aged seventy-six.

Kathy Jackson, the HSU whistleblower, left Victoria and moved to the coast south of Sydney in late 2012 with her partner, Michael Lawler. They plan to marry. She didn't stand in elections for the union's new New South Wales and Victoria divisions, and took long-term sick leave from her job as national secretary over the stress caused by the HSU scandal.

A candidate aligned with Jackson missed out on winning control of the New South Wales division by 306 votes out of the 7777 cast. She was heavily outspent by a group backed by the Right faction of the Labor Party. The new secretary, Gerard Hayes, will be paid $140,000 a year, 65 per cent less than Williamson got for the same job. 'The Williamson-Jackson era is over,' Hayes told *The Australian*. 'There is no more self-indulgence.' Hayes' brother is federal MP Chris Hayes. In Victoria, the biggest HSU division was captured by Labor Party members aligned with Bill Shorten and Stephen Conroy. The union's new executive hired a Labor activist and lawyer, Kimberley Kitching, to run the union on a day-to-day basis. Kitching's husband is Andrew Landeryou, the political blogger who waged a campaign against Jackson and Lawler through his website, Vexnews.

Some Liberal Party MPs privately said they would like a royal commission into union corruption. They didn't expect Liberal leader Tony Abbott to promise one before the election because it would trigger even bigger political donations from unions to the Labor Party.

In January the Fair Work Commission, which had changed its name from Fair Work Australia at Bill Shorten's direction, began legal action against the Health Services Union's national office. The commission said the union, under Kathy Jackson, didn't prepare its 2006–07 financial accounts as soon as practical. When it did file the accounts, they weren't signed or dated. The accounts were the responsibility of Jackson to file and covered the end of Thomson's period at the union.

In March, Shorten appointed two vice-presidents to the Fair Work Commission, a step that demoted Lawler from number two at the tribunal to the forth-ranked slot. Shorten ignored pleas from the legal profession not to interfere with the seniority of the tribunal's members, who are meant to have the same protections from government meddling as High Court judges. Val Gostencnik, a lawyer at Corrs Chambers Westgarth who represented Shorten in the HSU case, was made a deputy president.

To the government's relief, coverage of Gillard's involvement in the Australian Workers' Union affair petered out at the end of 2012. The damaging effects on those involved persisted. Michael Smith, the former 2UE presenter, maintained his obsession with Gillard's work for the AWU on his personal website. Robert McClelland, the former attorney-general who called for tighter regulation of unions and indirectly criticised Gillard over her 1992 involvement, told associates he was professionally threatened after speaking out.

There was good and bad news for the government out of the Slipper affair. In December 2012, Federal Court judge Steven Rares dismissed the sexual harassment case against Peter Slipper. The lawsuit was an abuse of process, Rares said, because it was designed to damage Slipper's reputation and political career. Rares criticised the Liberal Party's Mal Brough, who plans to run for Slipper's seat at the federal election. Slipper is seeking payment of his legal costs from his accuser, James Ashby, who said he would appeal.

In February Slipper was charged over the use of government Cabcharge vouchers. The three criminal charges, which carry a maximum sentence of five years' jail each, allege he toured vineyards north of Canberra at a cost of $1074. If found guilty Slipper won't be allowed to remain in parliament, although a trial is unlikely before the election. The former Liberal and Nationals MP has mostly voted with Labor since he resigned as speaker.

Without displaying any sense of irony, Rudd gave a speech in his electorate on 15 January 2013 that praised ordinary people who shunned the limelight. He said seeing the work of volunteers was more important to him than meeting global leaders. 'When I've been addressing the United Nations General Assembly, when I've been in the Oval Office with the president of the United States and with Thérèse and I having a cup of tea with the Queen, you know something?' he said. 'What we honour today … are those silent, solid contributors not out there doing flashy stuff for the newspapers, not out there strutting their stuff for the nightly news.'

The speech by Rudd, a man who so obviously delighted in the power of high office, didn't get much attention. It was part of an undeclared campaign to portray himself as a viable alternative to Prime Minister Gillard. Shortly afterwards, he argued that Western nations might need to provide military support to the rebellion in Syria, a position at odds with the government's policy of seeking a diplomatic solution. He criticised the United Nations Security Council, which Australia had just won a seat on, over its failure to end the war. He argued for an increase in unemployment benefits. Having being removed by the new leaders of the Right, his comments seemed to be appealing to those in Labor's Left who were disillusioned with Gillard.

When the Federal Police closed the investigation into who posted his foul-mouthed rant on YouTube without charging anyone, Rudd demanded they continue hunting. They did.

The leadership tensions climaxed again in March. Stephen Conroy, the communications minister, proposed regulating newspaper content for the first time outside of wartime and an end to a rule that made it difficult for television networks to merge. Even though the changes had been in the works for two years, Conroy badly misjudged the industry's mood. The plan triggered opposition so vociferous from media companies that it looked like the party could turn on Gillard and Conroy and remove them from office. Behind the scenes Labor

MPs desperate to remove Gillard told journalists the government was heading towards a catastrophic loss at the election unless she was replaced. Joel Fitzgibbon, who was embarrassingly forced to resign as defence minister in 2009, emerged as Rudd's chief public advocate and tried to build momentum for a change of leader.

But Rudd knew any credibility he had left would be shot if he broke his promise after the 2012 leadership ballot not to challenge again. Gillard had no reason to give him a free shot at her job. The government was paralysed. The whole country knew it.

It took the one person who stood up to Gillard the night she removed Rudd in 2010 to end the crisis. At a hastily called press conference in Canberra, regional development minister Simon Crean, himself removed as leader in 2003, said he would stand as deputy leader against Wayne Swan. Even though Rudd didn't want Crean as his deputy, the move was designed to provide an opening for Rudd by triggering a spill of the leader's position too. Gillard, her toughest when under threat, sacked Crean from cabinet and agreed to a vote the next day.

The result was a debacle. Rudd, finally realising he didn't have the majority support of Labor MPs, didn't even stand and renounced his leadership ambitions permanently. Other Rudd supporters, including Fitzgibbon, Martin Ferguson and Kim Carr, were forced to resign their government posts. Crean, who had shown great bravery, was humiliated. The Labor Party elite looked incompetent: it had allowed the party to go to the brink and lose three cabinet ministers for zero benefit to anyone apart from Gillard and her backers, including Conroy.

For reasons few people outside her inner circle understood, Gillard had already decided, in January, to hold the election on 14

September. The embarrassing leadership spill in March made victory even more likely for the Coalition. 'Julia Gillard still can't win the next election,' pollster and former Labor senator John Black wrote in the *Australian Financial Review* after the aborted vote. 'Kevin Rudd would still have a chance and Tony Abbott is so unpopular Julia Gillard is the only Labor PM he could beat.'

The great leadership experiment had failed. The decision by Bill Shorten, Stephen Conroy, Mark Arbib, Don Farrell, David Feeney and Kim Carr to remove a democratically elected prime minister in his first term of office was one of the great political miscalculations of the modern era. It split the party for almost three years, created deep personal bitterness within the government's top ranks, and exposed voters to the ugly amorality of factional politics. Labor's downfall was almost complete.

## Hope

Let's not mince words. The Australian Labor Party is in a ruinous state. The once proud party has been wracked by scandals at state and federal levels. The membership is demoralised and disengaged. The party's biggest supporter, some would say its effective owner, the union movement, is in decline and disgrace. The great hope for the rebirth of the party fostered by Kevin Rudd in 2007 is a distant, bitter memory.

Federally, the Coalition is on the cusp of returning to power. Labor has lost government in New South Wales, Victoria, Queensland, Western Australia and the Northern Territory. In Tasmania and the Australian Capital Territory minority Labor governments cling to power. South Australia's Labor government bought peace with its own unions through a big budget deficit. The party that created many of the core elements of the modern state, including universal health care, social security, labour protection, multiculturalism, superannuation, low tariffs and a floating currency, barely qualifies for party status in one of its birthplaces, Queensland.

Academics, politicians and journalists have offered up many explanations for Labor's malaise. They include: society's growing affluence and the decline of class identity; a lack of a clear philosophy and reform agenda; the rise of a professional political class; limited internal democracy; union influence in a de-unionising economy; the popularity of the Australian Greens and the environmental movement; the lack of charismatic leaders like Bob Hawke, Paul Keating and Gough Whitlam; the inability of governments to shield voters from global economic turmoil; unpopular policies.

There is probably truth in all of them. Here are some simpler explanations: allowing people who may be criminals to wield significant political power; attacking whistleblowers and internal dissidents; trashing the reputations of external opponents; unethical behaviour by party leaders before they became politicians; corruption.

Too harsh? In October 2009, reporters Tracy Ong and Angus Grigg published an article in the *Australian Financial Review* entitled 'Labor Powerbroker Hits A Rich Seam'. They revealed that Eddie Obeid, the state Labor MP and former resources minister, had purchased a farm in the Bylong Valley that covered part of a valuable and newly issued coal lease. For a down payment of $1.02 million, the Obeids netted a profit of $13.35 million. Obeid, an astute business operator, said he didn't know about the coal licence in advance and just bought the picturesque farm because he loved it. 'You mean to say a minister for mining for four years would know where all the minerals are? That's a joke,' he told Grigg. In late 2012 the Independent Commission Against Corruption heard that the Obeids' Bylong Valley land deals were structured to net the family as much as $100 million.

While acknowledging that Obeid and his family are entitled to the presumption of innocence, it is known that many of his fellow Labor MPs had suspected him of corruption for years.

At least two other Labor ministers had questionable dealings with Obeid. Ian Macdonald, the resources minister, was politically intimate with the MP. Eric Roozendaal, the roads minister who became treasurer, relied on his political patronage. It took the Labor Party more than three years after the Ong/Grigg article appeared to suspend Obeid's membership of the party. Obeid had already retired from parliament, which meant the suspension had little practical effect.

It may take years for a court to decide if Obeid is corrupt. Obeid and other family members deny breaking the law and have the financial firepower to mount a vigorous defence. He may never be charged. The reality is he was one of the most powerful half-dozen political figures in New South Wales for at least a decade. He was at the apex of power in the biggest state, owned substantial unexplained wealth, and was accused by a reputable newspaper of involvement in what appeared to be, at the very least, dubious behaviour. The question of Obeid's and Macdonald's possible corruption was a subject of public debate. After Obeid bought the coal-rich Cherrydale Park farm, a Greens MP in the state upper house, Lee Rhiannon, asked Macdonald in parliament if he had talked to Obeid about the possibility of a coalmine on the property. Macdonald didn't answer the question.

It is not surprising Macdonald didn't feel accountable to parliament. He was barely accountable to his own party. Macdonald was an MP because one union, the Australian Manufacturing Workers' Union, was prepared to support him every eight years in preselection votes. Three ballots were enough for a parliamentary career spanning three decades.

Who inside Labor challenged Macdonald's right to be an MP? Who questioned Obeid's fitness to be a lord of Labor? Who in power supported an investigation into Thomson's use of Health Services Union funds? Who in authority stood up and said: why do we allow these sleazy figures to represent this political party and the people of New South Wales?

Labor prime ministers Kevin Rudd and Julia Gillard didn't. The secretaries and presidents of the New South Wales division of the ALP didn't. There is no evidence that any of the national or state union leaders, who are so influential in selecting Labor's parliamentary representation, tried to remove Obeid, Macdonald or Thomson from parliament. The national president of the party, a position with the platform, some might even say the responsibility, to protect the party's interests, took no action against Obeid. That too may not be surprising. The person holding the position when Ong and Grigg's article appeared, Michael Williamson, was charged in 2012 with forty-seven criminal counts over the Health Services Union scandal.

One politician did challenge Obeid, albeit indirectly. After he became premier in 2008, Nathan Rees obtained the power to choose his own cabinet – a right his Coalition rivals always had – and used it to remove two of Obeid's proxies: Macdonald and Joe Tripodi. Soon after, Rees was replaced by Obeid's candidate, Kristina Keneally. Her first act was to reinstate Macdonald as resources minister.[20]

Ultimately it took elements of the media and the anti-corruption commission to pursue the allegations of corruption in New South Wales. The public didn't wait for them. In March 2011 the state Labor government was swept from office in a landslide. In a 13 per cent swing against Labor, 75 per cent of voters chose another party. The Coalition could be in power for a generation.

Years after his removal, Rees is disappointed the Labor Party hasn't begun the painful process of reforming itself. 'What I, and others, find so frustrating is that there is zero recognition of a need for cultural change,' he says.

The lesson? In politics, ethics count. Voters hate corruption. And they don't like the other behaviour that has become common in politics too: special treatment for political allies and family members, lying, misrepresentation of opponents and the removal of democratically elected leaders because they have upset factional chiefs.

If the Labor Party leadership wants to rebuild its trust with the electorate and its members, it needs to give voters what they most want: clean government. The party can't wait for the legal system to judge allegations of wrongdoing. That's too slow for the democratic process. It needs to weed out the individuals who are tarnishing the party's reputation as the rot occurs, not years after the electoral damage has been inflicted.

Some in the party already understand this. In New South Wales, which has had the highest-profile problems, the awareness seems to be most acute. Former ministers and current shadow ministers know voters threw Labor from office because they believed the government lacked integrity. The experience, which was personally painful for all decent Labor members, is still reverberating through the party's collective consciousness.

'In New South Wales there is a crisis,' says Luke Foley, a state MP and shadow minister who was an internal critic of Macdonald's. 'People woke up to the fact some seriously bad, unethical characters, or worse, hijacked the government for their own ends. When you combine it with them and the HSU, Labor has got a real problem. It is seen as rotten in the way it conducts its affairs.

'The Labor Party has to address that before it can grapple with the question of how to implement good public policy or develop a program for the next ten years. We need to get rid of the shonks and seedy characters who seem to have found a home inside the Labor apparatus.

'Following the capitulation of the ETS [emissions trading scheme] in April 2010, the no-carbon-tax promise and the revolving door of leaders, people think the controlling powers of the day don't believe in anything but staying in power. That's a national problem for the Labor Party.'

John Faulkner, the New South Wales senator, wants an end to the requirement for MPs to vote in line with what their factions decide, the practice that is the foundation of factional control. He wants internal party disputes – which are usually about the spoils of power – settled by eminent, ethical people rather than the factional leaders who control the party's annual conference and administrative bodies. Faulkner's suggestions are sensible, practical reforms. Yet he and Foley are from the Left, which is a perpetual minority in New South Wales. They can change little.

Paul Howes, the national secretary of the Australian Workers' Union and a member of the Right, supports minor changes to how the party operates. Two options he would like to see are trials of primaries for selecting candidates, which would open voting to a much larger group, and a direct election by party members of some delegates to the national conference. Howes, who seems to be one of the faces of Labor's future, believes Labor's problem isn't primarily structural. He thinks it is a failure to stand for specific policies:

> The real problem is the way we prepared our party for government. In 2007 we got elected without a clear agenda. That was the problem. Not the party structure. From 2007 to 2010 it was very hard, apart from the response to the global financial crisis, to know exactly what we did in a proactive way. Howard came to power with a clear plan. Hawke and Keating had an agenda. In 2007 it was clear what we were opposed to, not what we wanted to do.

A lot of the debate about Labor's problems focuses on its structure. Trade unions get 50 per cent of the votes at the party's national conference, the top decision-making body. On a day-to-day basis, progress through the party is almost impossible without the patronage of the factions, which are themselves controlled by an alliance of unions and parliamentary leaders. Senator Stephen Conroy, for example, comes from the Transport Workers' Union. Senator David Feeney was supported by the Health Services Union. Bill Shorten's power base remains the Australian Workers' Union, even though he resigned as national secretary in 2007.

Some reformists advocate separating the party from the union movement. Despite the undoubted good they have done for society in the past, unions are irrelevant to most Australians. (Membership had declined to 13 per cent of the private sector workforce and

43 per cent of public servants by August 2011.) The unions' huge political power is part historical anomaly and part financial reality.

Splitting unions and the Labor Party is not realistic, at least not in the short term. Their leaderships are personally and financially entwined. A separation would be so disruptive that neither side would allow it to happen.

Unions spend millions to get Labor politicians elected. Modern elections aren't cheap. Getting a new candidate known in a federal electorate can cost $200,000 in letter and leaflet drops. Where is that money going to come from if the unions walk away? Labor would have to turn more to business, which would demand its own favours. Anyone fancy a Labor Party beholden to property developers, banks or mining companies?

An easier option would be to make the party more democratic. By giving individual members a bigger say, the theory goes, Labor MPs will come from more diverse backgrounds, the party will be more responsive to the concerns of the community, and the membership will grow and be more engaged. Bruce Hawker, a chief of staff to Bob Carr when he was New South Wales premier, professional Labor election campaigner and confidant of Kevin Rudd's, thinks the main problem is that the party rewards loyalty more than initiative:

> We don't choose people who think for themselves. These people are conditioned into following even when they stand to lose. There has been every indication they are prepared to walk like lemmings over the cliff even though it runs against every basic instinct of political survival that they have.

Understandably, a lot of attention is paid to the selection of party candidates, the process that is the basic instrument of power in Labor. Rodney Cavalier, a minister in the Wran and Unsworth governments in New South Wales, believes part of the problem is a new political class has captured the party. Cavalier argues that Ben Chifley, who was prime minister from shortly after John Curtin's death in 1945 to the election of Robert Menzies in 1949, wouldn't be chosen as a Labor candidate today. Before being elected to politics Chifley was a railway man in Bathurst, a dirty, tiring job that didn't give him access to a telephone. Today, most Labor candidates are union officials, advisers to ministers or backbenchers, or party employees. Some work in law firms specialising in industrial relations. Only these people have the time and connections required to get themselves selected by factional leaders to stand for the Labor Party, Cavalier argued in *Coming to the Party*:

> Once upon a time Labor could draw from all the factories in Australia and all the mines, the railways and ships and trucks, the waterfront, the gangs working in the open air. It could supplement that gene pool with a growing army of adherents in the liberal arts, teaching, the law and other professions, essentially anyone we might have characterised as progressive in a whole range of social issues, foreign policy, nationalism, civil liberties. Either directly or through the ranks of union officials, Labor could draw on the best out there for renewal. Each such source of supply has dried up.

Many Australians love the idea of a railway worker becoming prime minister. It reinforces our faith in the ability of talent and hard work to triumph over privilege.

Is it realistic in today's world for a tradesman to reach the highest political office? Probably not. Twenty-five per cent of Australians aged between seventeen and nineteen were in tertiary education in 2010, and the numbers are rising rapidly. Most university fees are subsidised and deferred. Anyone smart and driven enough to become prime minister today doesn't have to slog it out on a factory production line in an outer-city suburb while they build support within their local branch. They can get a job straight out of university advising a cabinet minister.

Labor MPs who emerged from the big ideological debates at university in the 1970s, including former finance minister Lindsay Tanner, complain the party is 'swamped by careerism'. It's true. Like consulting, accounting and the law, politics has become a career and a profession. Professionals require skills and networks. There are rules and procedures. Politics is no longer class warfare. It's advanced people and media management.

The 'political class' that Cavalier and others complain about isn't going to go away. It's likely to get stronger. Sam Dastyari, the secretary of the New South Wales Labor Party, who hasn't had a career outside politics, thinks altering the way Labor candidates are chosen won't have much of an impact on who gets picked. That's because he thinks – and he's probably right – the sharpest political operators will always work their way through the selection system, whether it is a vote by branch members or 'five guys sitting around a table at a Chinese restaurant', as he once put it.

The most important task of the Labor MPs who survive the next federal election will likely be a personnel decision: choosing their new leader. If Labor loses the election and goes into opposition, which seems likely, the party's leadership could shift a generation.

Labor needs honest, brave leadership. This isn't naive. It is a political necessity. The electoral wipeouts in New South Wales and Queensland were painful lessons of what happens to governments when they lose the electorate's trust. Federal Labor's new leadership team will have to spend years repairing the damage to the party's reputation from the scandals described in this book. The cases will grind through the court system, creating ugly headlines for Labor for years.

There is hope. Labor at its best is visionary, progressive and brave. One of its best ideas is the National Disability Insurance Scheme, a plan to share the cost of caring for the disabled among all Australians. The scheme should improve the quality of care, lower costs, give the disabled more control over their lives and reduce the incredible stress on their parents, partners or carers. Pilot programs begin operating in 2013 in South Australia, Tasmania, the ACT, the Hunter Valley in New South Wales and the greater Geelong region of Victoria. They will cover 20,000 people. If successful, all 410,000 disabled Australians could be covered by 2018. Every Australian will be certain that if someone in their family becomes significantly disabled, they will have access to comprehensive support.

Disability insurance helps the most disadvantaged, promotes fairness and will make government more efficient. The scheme is so sensible Liberal Party leader Tony Abbott has enthusiastically embraced it. It demonstrates the potentially virtuous relationship between personal ambition and good governance – the opposite of the unethical behaviour that has caused Labor so much damage.

Bill Shorten deserves a lot of credit. When he was made parliamentary secretary for disability services – a backwater of public policy – Shorten did what he does best: get attention. He used his public relations and advocacy skills to convince the public and his fellow politicians that disabled people weren't getting the fair-go treatment of Australian lore.

He gave speeches, did interviews and held events. With Thérèse Rein, Kevin Rudd's wife, he hosted a meeting in 2009 at the prime minister's Sydney residence, Kirribilli House, to discuss how to design houses and apartments that are easier for the disabled, elderly and injured to live in.

The meeting and other events helped shift the political climate. By 2012 disabled policy was a big enough issue that Julia Gillard was able to convince a Liberal-led government, New South Wales, to jointly fund a pilot disability insurance scheme. 'Bill Shorten was critical to stamping disability on the mainstream consciousness,' says Fiona Anderson, the mother of a teenager with cerebral palsy and the Queensland state coordinator for Every Australian Counts, a campaign to build support for the insurance scheme.

Shorten's main internal rival for the leadership of the Labor Party, Greg Combet, has clocked up his own achievements. In 2011 Combet negotiated a carbon tax with several independent MPs and the Australian Greens. The tax will reshape the economy. Coal-fired power generation will fall by 70 per cent over the next thirty-seven years, aluminium production will fall 62 per cent and iron and steel production 21 per cent, according to forecasts by the federal

Treasury Department. Six thousand five hundred million tonnes of carbon dioxide that would have been released, won't be.

Other potential leaders have their own strengths. Yet none carries the sense of expectation surrounding Shorten, whose ambition and capacity for self-promotion, it seems, is limitless. Howes, the object of much leadership speculation, waits on the sidelines in the union movement.

If Labor loses the election, Gillard will most likely step down as leader. Her successor will have a tough job. He or she will have to do more than defeat the Liberal Party and Nationals. They will have to overcome the vested interests in their own party who support the status quo.

Could Shorten win government for the Labor Party? Almost certainly. He is a great communicator, the public likes him, and he has an instinctive understanding of Australians' fears and desires. Since he took over Young Labor in his early twenties, Shorten has proved himself a capable campaigner and a comfortable leader.

Can he fix the Labor Party? That's a tougher question. Shorten is a pillar of the power structures that did little to stop – many would say tolerated – the unethical behaviour described in these pages. He has been a pragmatic minister and a ruthless faction ruler. As the ALP's leader, consensus would probably be more important to him than reform. Factional power would be embraced rather than challenged. Internal criticism wouldn't be encouraged.

That's not to say Shorten couldn't become a good prime minister. Just as Paul Keating grew from a Labor numbers counter into a policy pioneer, Shorten may emerge a visionary leader. The choice is his.

# Acknowledgements

Many good people in the Australian Labor Party, union movement and business generously gave up their time for this book. Given the controversial subject matter, I won't name them. They have my profound gratitude for being prepared to talk frankly about their experiences, the party's problems and their views on how Labor can learn from its mistakes.

This book wouldn't have been possible without the work of the reporters who cover politics, industrial relations and the legal system. Their reporting shows that newspapers, for all their problems, are essential for a healthy civic life. I acknowledge the work of the following journalists who helped shape my understanding of many of the events described in this book. Some are friends. Many I have never met. All do fantastic work: Kate McClymont, Hedley Thomas, Angus Grigg, Phillip Coorey, Lisa Murray, Sally Neighbour, Tony Walker, Jennifer Hewett, Peter Hartcher, Ian Kirkwood, Linton Besser, Mark Ludlow, Mark Simkin, Mark Skulley, Brad Norington, Belinda Hawkins, Andrew Clennell, Shaun Carney, Hannah Low, Laura Tingle, Mathew Dunckley, James Massola, Sally Patten, Geoff Kitney, John Kerin, Sophie Morris, Fleur Anderson, Gemma Daley, Marcus Priest, Katie Walsh, John Kehoe, Tracy Ong, Neil Chenoweth, Jamie Freed, Pamela Williams, Michaela Whitbourn, John van Tiggelen, Alison Caldwell, Adam Shand, Philip Dorling, Richard Baker, Nick McKenzie, Samantha Maiden, Michelle Grattan, Laurie Oakes, Lenore Taylor, Dennis Shanahan, Phillip Hudson, Sid Maher, Susannah Moran, Chris Uhlmann, Barrie Cassidy, Lisa Davies, Steve Lewis, Simon Benson, Niki Savva, Imre Salusinszky, Leo Shanahan, Sam McKeith, Vanda Carson, Dylan Welch, Louise Hall, David

Marr, Andrew Bolt, Andrew Cook, Troy Bramston, Tony Wright, David Speers, Dennis Atkins, Ewin Hannan, Andrew Fowler, Bridie Jabour, Rick Wallace, Andrew Rule, Ross Brundrett, Paul Barry, Matthew Schulz, Peter Lloyd, Geesche Jacobsen, Amy Dale, Linda Silmalis, Jason Koutsoukis, Sean Parnell and Sean Nicholls.

I would also like to acknowledge the media executives and editors who work, or did work, at the outlets that published their articles. They take the heat when things go wrong. They also make sure journalists like me get paid. Thank you to Brett Clegg, Greg Hywood, Gail Hambly and Brad Hatch at Fairfax Media. I am particularly grateful to those generous people who made invaluable suggestions about the manuscript: Angus Grigg, Mark Ludlow, Hannah Low, Kate McClymont, Hedley Thomas, Tom Skotnicki and Matthew Sheehan. Nicole Thomas at the NSW Independent Commission Against Corruption answered every one of my questions with good grace. Any mistakes are mine.

I owe an enormous debt to Michael Stutchbury, the *Australian Financial Review* editor-in-chief, who gave me permission to write this book and indulged my reporting while I was doing my day and night job. Thank you to *Financial Review* editor Paul Bailey for your personal and professional support and to Richard Coleman, the paper's lawyer, just for listening. My ever patient, calm and wise publisher, Amruta Slee, deserves credit for making this a far better book. Cindy MacDonald was a superb editor. Thank you to Sarah Haines for publicity. My deepest gratitude goes to Shona Martyn, HarperCollins Australia's publishing director, who instantly saw the potential in the idea. Most of all I want to thank my wife, Kate Bain, for her patience, support, encouragement and advice. As with all other worthwhile things in my life, it would have been impossible to do this without you.

# Author's note

The press closely covered most of the events in this book. Newspaper reports were an important source of information about public events. In all cases I attempted to verify the information independently. Where I couldn't, I have sought to acknowledge my media colleagues in the text or endnotes. Whenever I used a single published source for a quote or fact, I endeavoured to give credit.

To re-create conversations and events I relied on first-hand witnesses, public information, trusted sources and official investigations. In a few cases where the recollection of those involved differed, I relied on the account of the disinterested witness. References to MPs refer to upper and lower house members of parliament.

Most of the information about the Obeid family's political and business activities was obtained from hearings at the New South Wales Independent Commission Against Corruption. I believe that the targets of civil and criminal investigations are entitled to the presumption of innocence and have not concluded that any person named in this book broke the law.

The first chapter is based in part on two of my articles: 'Getting To Know Bill', published in the *Australian Financial Review Magazine* on 24 September 2010, and 'How Shorten Learnt About Inside Running', published in the *Australian Financial Review* on 15 June 2012. I was a Labor Party member from age sixteen to twenty-one and a member of Bill Shorten's Young Labor group.

# Endnotes

1. 'Bill Shorten: the son also rises', Andrew Rule, *The Age*, 26 September 2009.
2. Gattellari pleaded guilty to being an accessory before the murder in July 2012. Ron Medich, Christopher Estephan and Haissam Safetli pleaded not guilty to murder. In May 2013 Gattellari was sentenced to ten years jail with a minimum period of seven and a half years.
3. The investigation by the Independent Commission Against Corruption found Michael McGurk's claims the recording could bring down the government were 'nonsense' and there 'is not a scrap of evidence that Mr Haddad' was corrupt. The Commission said *The Herald* accurately reported what it had been told by McGurk.
4. This account is based on testimony to the New South Wales Independent Commission Against Corruption by Gardner Brook and Arlo Selby, a commodities trader with links to the Obeids. Moses Obeid told the commission the purpose of the meeting was to discuss the Obeids' Streetscape Enterprises business and Gardner Brook raised the issue of Monaro Mining first. Obeid said the list was read to him by Macdonald over the phone and they were merely names of mining companies investing in New South Wales which he passed onto Brook to chase up as business leads. He said the only information Macdonald gave him was that exploration licences would 'open up' around the area where the Obeids owned land and then referred him to the Department of Primary Industries.
5. The sale never went through.
6. Eddie Obeid denied lobbying Roozendaal about the Circular Quay cafes.
7. Craig Thomson later denied using union funds to pay for prostitutes. The expenses detailed in this chapter are based on investigations by Fair Work Australia and Ian Temby, QC, and accountant Dennis Robertson.
8. A source close to Kim Carr later denied the meeting took place in his office. This assertion was disputed by several other people with direct knowledge of the meeting.
9. The new nominal rate was 30 per cent. An automatic reduction cut it to 22.5 per cent.

10  Kathy Jackson later said she opposed the pay increases and was overruled by Michael Williamson's supporters.
11  Kathy Jackson's account of this meeting is taken from an affidavit she signed on 1 June 2012.
12  The payments to contractors and other information about the union's finances and administration were set out in an investigation by Ian Temby, QC, and accountant Dennis Robertson.
13  The bill was defeated 98 votes to 42 in the House of Representatives the following September.
14  Responsibility for the court application to appoint an administrator to run HSU East was ultimately taken over by Chris Brown and other state secretaries with the support of the federal government.
15  The description of the court hearing is based on a report in the *Sydney Morning Herald* on 9 June 2012 by Lisa Davies, 'HSU boss sacks her lawyers and tells judge to stand down'.
16  The editor and author of the article about Bill Shorten described in this chapter was Aaron Patrick.
17  This book is published by HarperCollins*Publishers* Australia, a unit of News Corporation. HarperCollins publishes ABC Books under licence from the Australian Broadcasting Corporation.
18  Tony Windsor and Rob Oakeshott's conversations with Peter Slipper were revealed by Fleur Anderson and Laura Tingle in 'How Independents told Slipper to go' in the *Australian Financial Review* on 11 November 2012.
19  Geoffrey Watson, counsel to the New South Wales Independent Commission Against Corruption, told the commission in a memo the Obeid family was implicated in the corrupt sale of a car to Eric Roozendaal although 'no submissions are made that a finding of corrupt conduct be made against Eddie Obeid' over the car sale. The statement was made public at the request of Obeid's lawyer, Stuart Littlemore. Roozendaal resigned from Parliament in May 2013, six years before his term was due to end.
20  Kristina Keneally fired Ian Macdonald six months after she appointed him when he was accused of accepting free airline upgrades.

# Index

Abbott, Tony, 191, 213, 233, 236, 259, 262, 263, 274–7, 279, 280, 284–90, 298, 302, 312
Abetz, Eric, 272
Abood, John, 70
Access Focus, 176
Albanese, Anthony, 138, 219, 220, 275, 277
Alexander, John, 238
Alexander, Paul, 115, 118–19
Amalgamated Metal Workers' Union, 38
Arbib, Mark, 75, 93, 95, 96, 102, 106, 124, 125, 129, 133–5, 138, 139, 141, 145, 157, 174, 189, 206, 293, 302
Ashby, James, 215–21, 272–3, 299
Asylum seekers, 97, 130–1, 132, 149, 277–8
Atkins, Dennis, 285, 286
Atkinson, John, 62
*The Australian* AWU story, 266–72, 280–1
Australian Council of Trade Unions, 47, 107, 247
*Australian Financial Review*, 192, 231, 252–9, 284
Australian Labor Party (ALP)
   control over leadership, 10
   factions *see* Factions
   future of, 302–14
   Gillard government, 4
   history, 10
   members accused at ICAC, 3, 291–6, 303–5
   national conference, 10
   national executive, 174
   ruinous state of, 4, 302
   strong Labor Party, need for, 5
   structure, 10
   2007 election, 32–5, 96, 104, 121, 302
   2010 election, 149–58
   unions and, 11–12, 27, 308–9
Australian Manufacturing Workers' Union, 94, 305
Australian Theatrical & Amusements Employees' Association, 16–20
Australian Workers' Union, 12, 21–7, 140, 175, 232, 253, 265–72, 307
   Gillard, 22–6, 265–72, 280, 299
   Shorten, 21–2, 26–35, 124, 308
   Wilson scandal, 22–5, 27, 265–72, 280–90, 299
Australian Workers' Union Workplace Reform Association Inc, 22

Bailey, Paul, 255
Baillieu, Ted, 158
Baker, Mark, 285
Bandt, Adam, 277
Barnett, Stuart, 48
Barr, Clayton, 87
Barrett, Chris, 158
Batchelor, Peter, 13
Beale, Deborah, 29, 30, 156, 240
Beale, Julian, 29
Beattie, Peter, 194, 196, 206
Beazley, Kim, 28, 93–5, 97, 114, 262
Benenson, Joel, 279
Besser, Linton, 70
BHP Billiton, 45, 127, 129, 147
'Big Australia' strategy, 151
Birmingham, John, 195
Bishop, Julie, 275, 280–2, 290
Bitar, Karl, 102, 125
Bjelke-Petersen, John, 208
Black, John, 302
Blewitt, Ralph, 22–4, 266, 282–4
Bligh, Anna, 174, 193–9, 204–12
Bligh, Bill, 194
Bligh, William, 193
Bolano, Marco, 235
Borger, David, 86
Borowick, Michael, 13, 14, 16, 18
Bowen, Chris, 191, 278
Bracks, Steve, 32, 190
Bradbury, David, 149
Brandis, George, 180, 272, 287
Brennan, Frank, 157
Brook, Gardner, 60, 61
Brough, Mal, 215, 217, 218
Brown, Chris, 174, 176, 248, 250

Brown, Matt, 73
Brown, Norman, 112
Brumby, John, 25, 81, 158
Bryce, Chloe, 156, 259
Bryce, Quentin, 150, 156–7, 237, 277
Budget 2012, 230–3
Buffier, Mick, 48
Burke, Anna, 219, 233, 277
Burke, Matthew, 102, 103, 106
Burke, Tony, 138, 293
Burrow, Sharan, 47
Butler, Casey, 68

Cain, John, 13, 21
Calwell, Arthur, 151
Cambridge, Ian, 23, 267
Cameron, Doug, 294
Cameron, Fiona, 294
Cameron, Tom, 264
Campbell, David, 85
Campbell, George, 38
Carbon tax, 159–60, 166, 216, 278–9, 313
Carnell, Ian, 117
Carr, Bob, 39–43, 71, 72, 114, 220, 289, 309
Carr, Kim, 20, 93–4, 132, 138, 145, 146, 189, 206, 262, 301, 302
Carson, Andrea, 30
Carson, Vanda, 55
Cascade Coal, 62–4, 293, 295
Casey, Sam, 255
Cassidy, Barrie, 143, 154
Catholic Church, 11, 12, 188
Cavalier, Rodney, 310–11
Chalmers, Jim, 125
Cheeseman, Darren, 253, 254, 255, 257
Cherry, John, 57
Cherrydale Park, 57–60, 304
Chesher, Matthew, 86
Chifley, Ben, 154, 290, 310
Chisholm, Anthony, 196, 197, 204, 208
Circular Quay cafes, 58, 70
Clague, Grace, 117
Claven, Jim, 32
Clayton Utz, 50, 90, 91, 166, 280
Clennell, Andrew, 89
Climate change, 122, 126, 159–60
Coal licences *see* Mining licences
Coastal Voice, 103, 104

Coggan Creek, 57, 59
Coghlan, Matthew, 158
Coleman, Richard, 255, 256
Collins, Jacinta, 138, 139
Collins, Matt, 196
Combet, Greg, 47, 119, 120, 182, 189, 264, 313
Communigraphix, 176, 180, 184
Conroy, Stephen, 14, 31, 32, 93, 101, 124, 132–5, 138–45, 206, 260, 262, 293, 298, 300, 301, 302, 308
Construction, Forestry, Mining and Energy Union, 44
Coombs, Robert, 48
Coorey, Phillip, 133, 258
Corcoran, Ann, 34
Corrs Chambers Westgarth, 255, 256, 257, 259, 299
Costa, Michael, 41, 60, 293
Costello, Robert, 162
Country Energy, 50–2
Coutts, Alan, 47, 62
Cragg, David, 27
Craigie, Chris, 226
Crean, Simon, 34, 93, 94, 130, 132, 139–40, 145, 146, 201, 262, 301
Crichton, Neville, 295
Cridland, Christina, 10
Crime and Misconduct Commission (Qld), 208, 209
Crowe, David, 270
Cullen, Simon, 246
Currawong purchase, 161–3, 167

Dads in Education, 103
Daley, Michael, 163
D'Amore, Angela, 86
Dastyari, Sam, 86, 87, 111, 164, 165, 185, 186, 293, 311
Davidson, Kenneth, 159
Davis, Ben, 28
Davis, Mark, 109, 110, 182, 225
Della Bosca, John, 40, 73, 74
Dick, Ian, 227
Doyles Creek mine, 46–50, 79, 84–5, 89, 294–5
Dreyfus, Mark, 34
Duncan, Travers, 62, 63
Dyson, Col, 222

Eagles, Mick, 27
Electrical Trades Union, 32, 45
Emerson, Craig, 206
Emissions trading scheme, 126, 307
Emmett, Belinda, 95
Equine influenza outbreak, 44
Estephan, Christopher, 54
Evans, Gareth, 13, 14, 18, 19

Factions, 11–16, 122
    Centre Unity (NSW), 11, 40, 43, 76, 98, 223, 260
    gay marriage debate, 187–8
    Hawke government, 12–13
    HSU, 106–7
    importance of joining, 11
    Labor Unity, 11
    Left, 11, 13, 15, 37, 188
    MPs not belonging to, 11
    NSW Labor Party, 40, 43, 45, 76, 78
    Right, 11, 12–16, 40, 94, 122, 188, 206
    Rudd government, 122
    Socialist Left, 11, 13, 135, 139
    2007 election, 32–5, 96
    unethical conduct of, 5
    unions and, 11–12, 308–9
    Young Labour, 13–16, 31
Fahey, John, 39
Faine, Jon, 271
Fair Work Australia, 108, 173, 224–30, 298
    Education, Employment and Workplace Relations committee, 226
    HSU investigation, 111, 181–3, 224–30, 235–8, 244, 298
    Lawler, 173, 225, 235–8, 241–2, 245–6, 254, 298
Fair Work Commission, 298
Fairfax Media, 110, 171–3, 181–3, 231, 256, 259, 266, 288
Falk, James, 165
Faris, Peter, 156
Farrell, Don, 124, 133, 134, 135, 138, 145, 157, 188, 206, 302
Faulkner, John, 66, 75, 119, 125, 137, 145, 188, 307
Federated Clerks Union, 17
Federation of Industrial, Manufacturing and Engineering Employees, 23, 26

Feeney, David, 15, 29, 31, 32, 96, 106, 124, 133–5, 138, 145, 157, 173, 181, 185, 186, 206, 238, 262, 302, 308
Fenn, Stephen, 162
Ferguson, Laurie, 139
Ferguson, Martin, 301
Financial Services Council, 192
Firth, Verity, 86, 163
Fitzgibbon, Eric, 113
Fitzgibbon, Joel, 112–20, 301
Fitzgibbon, Mark, 114, 115, 117, 118, 119
Fitzhenry, Peter, 66, 67, 69
Flannery, Brian, 47, 62, 63
Flick, Geoffrey, 249, 251, 252, 257
Foley, Luke, 75, 76, 165, 294, 307
Forrest, Andrew, 127, 128, 129, 130, 131, 147
Fortescue Metals Group, 127, 128, 129, 131, 147
Fraser, Andrew, 196, 210, 211
Fraser, Malcolm, 97
Frewen, Bill, 50, 51

Gageler, Stephen, 157
Gallacher, Mike, 180
'Gang of four', 144, 153
Garrett, Peter, 11
Gattellari, Fortunato, 52, 53
Gay, Duncan, 89, 90
Gay marriage, 12, 187–8, 261
Gibson, Jamie, 49, 84, 295
Gillard, Julia, 15, 22–6, 94, 108, 123, 125, 126, 130–59, 174, 187–204, 213, 221–2, 231–2, 258–90, 296, 300–2, 305, 313
    Abbott and, 274–7, 279, 280, 284–90, 302
    AWU scandal, 22–7, 265–72, 280–90
    carbon tax, 159–60, 278–9
    first election, 149–58
    mining tax, 147–8
    Rudd and, 123, 125, 130–4, 150–3, 199, 201–4, 259–61, 300–2
    Rudd's overthrow, 130–48, 155
    Shorten and, 261–5
    Slater & Gordon, 22–5, 27, 265, 266, 268–70, 284, 288
    Slipper affair, 274–7, 299
    Socialist Left, 135, 139

2012 leadership challenge, 205–6, 259–60
Gilleland, Carron, 180, 184, 297
Gilleland, Ian, 180
Gilleland, John, 180, 184, 297
Giudice, Geoffrey, 187, 237
Glen, Carol, 186–7
Gonski, David, 259
Goodman, Keith, 67
Gordon, Peter, 24, 25, 268
Goss, Wayne, 196
Gostencnik, Val, 298
Grattan, Michelle, 152, 153, 239, 287
Gray, Gary, 139
Green, Antony, 164
Greiner, Nick, 38, 39
Griffiths, Terry, 39
Grigg, Angus, 303, 304, 305

Haddad, Sam, 54, 55
Haines, Stacey, 49
Hambly, Gail, 256
Hanke, Ian, 242
Harris, Lachlan, 125, 135, 136
Harrison, Steve, 26
Hartcher, Chris, 166, 167
Hartcher, Peter, 133, 152, 271, 272
Hartigan, John, 266
Hatzistergos, John, 56
Hawke, Bob, 12, 13, 14, 21, 97, 104, 142, 154, 203, 262, 290, 308
Hawker, Bruce, 142, 309
Hawkes, Graham, 49
Hayes, Chris, 298
Hayes, Gerard, 176, 177, 298
Health Services Union, 97–112, 141, 171–87, 221–53, 290, 297–8
   corruption, 107–12, 178–85, 192, 222–39, 244, 286–7
   HSU East, 174–5, 222, 241, 247–8, 252, 257
   Jackson, 106, 171–87, 192, 223–5, 227, 229, 234, 235, 240–58, 297
   Shorten and, 237, 239, 240, 247–53, 298
   Thomson, 98–104, 110, 172–85, 222, 225–39, 244, 250, 296
   Williamson, 98–102, 107, 109, 141, 172–87, 192, 222–3, 227, 229–30, 234, 235, 237, 241, 245, 250, 252

Henry, Ken, 126
Hickey, Kerry, 48, 86
Holding, Tim, 14, 20, 31
Houston, Angus, 143
Howard, John, 25, 93, 95, 96, 97, 121, 155, 308
Howes, Paul, 140, 141, 175, 232, 261, 307–8
H.R. Nicholls Society, 242, 243, 244
Hubbard, Ben, 108
Hudson, Phillip, 154
Hurley, Annette, 125
Hutchins, Steve, 102
Hywood, Greg, 256, 257, 288

Iemma, Morris, 40, 45, 71, 72, 80, 194
Independent Australia, 245
Independent Commission Against Corruption (ICAC), 1–3, 38–9
   D'Amore, 86
   Greiner and, 38, 39
   Kelly, 162, 167
   Macdonald, 38, 39, 63, 166, 167, 292–5
   McGurk–Medich case, 55–6
   Maitland, 294–5
   MPs accused at, 3
   Obeid, 1–3, 63, 71, 166, 169, 292–5, 304
   O'Farrell increasing budget, 166
   opposition to, 39
   Rees increasing powers, 56
   Roozendaal, 3, 291–2, 295
Ipp, David, 1, 3, 56, 167, 295
Irvine, Monique, 178

Jackson, Kathy, 29, 105, 109, 110, 171–87, 192, 223, 227, 229, 234, 235, 237, 238, 240–59, 297
Jackson, Rex, 38, 240
Jenkins, Harry, 213
Jennett, Greg, 137
Johnston, David, 118, 119, 120
Jones, Alan, 265, 275
Jones, Barry, 35, 174
Jones, Greg, 293
Jordan, Alister, 119, 125, 133, 135, 140, 141, 143
Joyce, Barnaby, 272

Kaidbay, Andrew, 63
Katter, Bob, 155, 210, 277
Kearney, Geraldine (Ged), 244
Keating, Paul, 25, 203, 264, 283, 308, 314
Kelly, Paul, 287
Kelly, Tony, 161–3, 167, 293
Kelty, Bill, 21
Keneally, Ben, 79, 87, 164
Keneally, Kristina, 55, 78–89, 159–66, 194, 211, 231, 293, 305
   NSW Premier, 78–89, 159–66
   Rudd and, 81–2
   2011 election, 159–66, 211
   Terrigals, 78, 80
Kennedy, Gary, 48
Kennett, Jeff, 20, 124
Kernohan, Bob, 265, 266
Kerr, John, 156
Kinghorn, John, 62, 63
Kirner, Joan, 13
Kitching, Kimberley, 240, 298
Koutsoukis, Jason, 283

Landeryou, Andrew, 240, 241, 244, 246, 256, 298
Landeryou, Bill, 15
Lang, Jack, 164
Langbroek, John-Paul, 195
Latham, Mark, 93, 122, 271
Lawler, Michael, 173, 177, 178, 186–7, 225, 235–8, 241–2, 245–6, 254, 297, 298
Lawler, Sir Peter, 173
Lawrence, Carmen, 174
Lawrence, Neil, 80
Lee, Michael, 220
Lehman Brothers, 60, 61
Leigh, Andrew, 11
Leo, Frank, 27
Lester, Amelia, 277
L'Estrange, Michael, 143
Lewis, Justin, 57
Lewis, Steve, 218, 220, 282
Linz, Allen, 161
Littlemore, Stuart, 1
Liu, Helen, 113, 114, 116
Low, Hannah, 218
Ludlow, Mark, 210

Ludwig, Bill, 26, 31, 140
Lyons, John, 143

Macarthur Coal, 44
McArdle, Chris, 296
McArdle, Mark, 217
McClelland, Robert, 145, 189, 267–8, 299
McClymont, Kate, 55, 70, 178, 179, 183, 184, 223
Macdonald, Anita, 83
Macdonald, Ian, 2, 3, 37–53, 60–5, 74, 76–9, 83–5, 90, 91, 166, 292–5, 304–5, 307
   background, 37
   fired by Rees, 76, 77, 84
   ICAC, 2, 3, 38, 39, 63, 166, 167, 292–5
   Maitland and, 44–50, 63, 295
   mining licences, 2, 44–50, 60–5, 74, 90, 91, 166, 292–5, 304
   overseas travel bills, 74, 83–4
   prostitutes, 52–3, 293
   reinstated by Keneally, 79
   resignation, 84
   Terrigals, 40–5, 76, 77
McGrath, Ann, 8
McGuigan, John, 62
McGurk, Kimberley, 54
McGurk, Luc, 54
McGurk, Michael, 53–5
McKew, Maxine, 97, 143, 155
McLeay, Leo, 88
McLeay, Paul, 85, 88–90
McLeod, John, 169
McManus, Rove, 95
McMillan, Cheryl, 178, 179
McMullan, Bob, 131
McMullin, Ian, 253
McMullin, Peter, 253, 256, 257
McTernan, John, 279, 288
Mah-Chut Architects, 175, 179
Mah-Chut, Ron, 179, 297
Maher, Sid, 270
Maher, Tony, 294–5
Maitland, John, 44–50, 79, 84–5, 90, 91, 166, 294–5
Majella Global Technologies, 196, 198
Mamouzelos, Nicholas, 178, 184
Mannix, Daniel, 29

Marles, Richard, 34
Marsh, Cliff, 48
Maurice Blackburn, 21, 22, 26, 173
Meagher, Reba, 41
Medich, Ron, 51–5
Mehan, David, 111
Melbourne University, 15
Melhem, Cesar, 27
Metherell, Terry, 39
Milne, Glenn, 266, 267, 271
Minchin, Nick, 272
Mineral Resources Rent Tax, 147–8
Mining licences, 2, 44–50, 59–65, 74, 89–91, 166, 292–5, 303–4
   Doyles Creek, 46–50, 79, 84–5, 89, 294–5
   Mount Penny, 59, 61–5
   Yarrawa, 64
Mining tax, 126–30, 143, 147–8
Moio, Frank, 51
Monaro Mining, 60–2, 64
Monsour, Frank, 196–7, 207
Monsour, Seb, 198, 207
Moore, Michael, 249, 251, 252, 257
Moore, Steve, 17, 18
Morris, Barry, 39
Mount Penny exploration licence, 59, 61–5
Mullard, Brad, 46, 47, 62
Murdoch, Rupert, 218, 271
Murphy, Bernard, 25, 26
Murray, Craig, 50–2
Muscat, Terry, 27

Nassios, Terry, 111, 112, 224, 226, 227, 228, 229
National Disability Insurance Scheme, 312
National Union of Workers, 31, 32, 34
Neho, Richard, 68
Neighbour, Sally, 33
Network, 13–20, 31
New South Wales Labor Party
   Carr, 39–43, 71, 72
   Currawong purchase, 161–3, 167
   factions, 40, 43, 45, 76, 78
   Iemma, 40, 45, 71, 72, 80
   Keneally, 78–89
   leader-centric approach, 71–2
   Left, 37, 45, 76
   1988 election, 38
   Rees, 45, 49, 50, 55, 56, 71–9, 80
   Right (Centre Unity), 11, 40, 43, 76, 98, 223, 260
   salaries, 43
   scandals, 73, 85–6, 88
   Terrigals, 40–5, 66, 72–8, 80
Newman, Campbell, 98, 193, 195–200, 205, 207–11, 290
Newman, Jocelyn, 196
Newman, Kevin, 196
Newman, Lisa, 196–8, 207
News Limited, 218, 220, 259, 266, 267
NIB, 114, 115, 117, 118
Nowicki, Harry, 265, 282
NuCoal Resources, 63, 79, 84–5, 91
Nugan Hand Bank, 38
Nuttall, Gordon, 198

Oakes, Laurie, 146, 151, 152
Oakeshott, Rob, 155, 156, 232, 275, 277
Obama, Barack, 277, 279, 288–9
Obeid, Damien, 58
Obeid, Eddie, 1–3, 5, 40–5, 57–66, 69–71, 77–9, 166, 168–9, 290, 292–5, 303–5
   bribery allegations, 41
   Cherrydale Park, 57–60, 304
   family businesses, 58, 70, 168
   ICAC, 1–3, 63, 71, 166, 169, 292–5, 304
   mining licences, 1–3, 60–5, 166, 292–3, 303
   Terrigals, 40–5, 66, 73, 77, 78
   wealth, 64–5
Obeid, Gerard, 58, 59
Obeid, Judith, 64
Obeid, Moses, 58, 60, 61, 65–71, 168, 169, 292
Obeid, Paul, 58, 59, 70
O'Connor, Brendan, 138, 145, 282
O'Connor, Gavan, 34
O'Connor Marsden, 90, 91
O'Connor, Rory, 91
O'Farrell, Barry, 75, 159, 160, 166, 249
O'Neil, Denis, 295
O'Neill, Bernadette, 226, 229
Ong, Tracy, 303, 304, 305
Online porn scandal, 88–9

**325**

O'Reilly, Brendan, 83, 162, 163
Owen, Michael, 203

Packer, James, 210
Packer, Kerry, 57
Pakula, Martin, 14, 20, 31, 34, 158
Palaszczuk, Annastacia, 212
Palaszczuk, Henry, 212
Palestine's admission to UN, 288–9
Paluzzano, Karyn, 85
Parental leave scheme, 151–2
Park, Ryan, 87
Parker, Jamie, 165
Pasquarelli, John, 265
Phillips, Jeffrey, 249
Plibersek, Tanya, 189
Pooley, Tony, 161
Pope, Neil, 13, 14, 19
Port Macquarie development, 58, 70
Pratt, Jeanne, 29
Pratt, Richard, 29
Pyne, Christopher, 238

Queensland Labor Party, 140, 155, 193–212
  2012 election, 199–212

Rainbow Labor, 261
Rampe, Mart, 61
Rares, Steven, 273, 299
Ray, Robert, 13, 14
Re, Nata, 67, 68
Rees, Nathan, 45, 49, 50, 55, 56, 71–80, 84, 293, 305, 306
  ICAC, supporting, 56
  NSW Labor Party leader, 71–9
  public service restructure, 73–4
  sacking Tripodi and Macdonald, 76–7, 84, 293
Rein, Thérèse, 141, 300, 313
Reith, Peter, 242
Resources Super Profits Tax, 126–30
Rhiannon, Lee, 304
Richardson, Graham, 40, 41, 54, 182
Rio Tinto, 45, 59, 127, 129, 147
Riordan, Bernie, 45, 72
Ripoll, Bernie, 139
Rivercorp, 51
Robertson, Dennis, 241
Robertson, Ian, 227

Robertson, John, 294
Robertson, Struan, 178
Rofe, David, 251
Roozendaal, Amanda, 65–8
Roozendaal, Eric, 3, 41, 65–70, 73, 95, 291–3, 304
  car purchase, 65–8
  ICAC, 3, 291–2, 295
  NSW Labor Party secretary, 65–6
  Obeid family and, 65–71
  treasurer, 73
Roskam, John, 242
Ross, Iain, 236, 237, 238
Rothbury coalmine, 112–13
Roxon, Nicola, 189, 219, 220, 260, 267, 273
Rudd, Jessica, 141
Rudd, Kevin, 5, 33, 76, 81, 82, 94–7, 104, 121–55, 174, 199, 214, 259–61, 299–302, 305, 309
  after overthrow, 146–55
  apology to Stolen Generations, 122, 146
  Big Australia strategy, 151
  climate change policy, 122, 126, 160
  election victory 2007, 96–7, 104, 121, 302
  Fitzgibbon and, 114, 117, 119, 120
  foreign minister, 157, 199, 201–2
  Gillard and, 123, 125, 130–4, 146–55, 199, 201–4, 259–61, 300–2
  leaks during 2010 election, 151–3, 157, 202
  mining tax, 126–30, 143
  overthrow in 2010, 5, 7, 131–48, 290, 302
  reasons for removal, 142–6
  resignation as foreign minister, 201–2
  2012 leadership challenge, 205–6, 259–60
  unpopularity in Party, 122–5, 143, 201, 204, 260
  YouTube clip, 199, 201, 300
Ruddock, Philip, 238
Rumore, Chris, 60
Russell, David, 217

Sackett, Penny, 160
Safetli, Haissam, 54
Sales, Leigh, 261

Sanger, Liberty, 29, 173
Sartor, Frank, 78
Sassine, Sid, 169
Saunders, Nicholas, 48
Scipione, Andrew, 180, 183
Scully, Carl, 40
Scurrah, Nicole, 196
Secord, Walt, 83, 84, 86–9, 91, 164, 165
Seeney, Jeff, 198
Sercombe, Bob, 32–4
Sexism, 176
Shaw, Geoff, 24
Sheikh Mohammed bin Rashid Al Maktoum, 83
Sherry, Nick, 137, 139
Shields, Brett, 251
Shipley, Kim, 51, 52
Shop, Distributive and Allied Employees' Association, 12, 188
Short-Con alliance, 31–4
Shorten, Bill, 5–10, 13–35, 93, 96, 101, 105, 124, 132–9, 145, 155–8, 173, 189–92, 206, 237, 239–43, 247–52, 261–5, 298, 302, 308, 313, 314
   ATAEA takeover attempt, 16–20
   AWU, 21–2, 26–35, 124, 308
   background, 7–10, 28
   challenge to Gillard, 261–5
   epitomising modern Labor, 5, 6, 314
   Gillard government, 155, 156, 189–92, 206
   HSU and, 237, 239, 240, 247–53
   Jackson and, 247–59
   Maribyrnong candidate, 32–5
   National Disability Insurance Scheme, 313
   overthrow of Rudd, 7, 132–5, 138, 139, 145, 155, 302
   Right faction, 13, 15
   Rudd government, 96, 124
   Young Labor, 13–20, 158
Shorten, Robert, 8
Shorten, William Robert, 8, 9, 10
Shultz, David, 117
Simkin, Mark, 135–7, 146
Singleton, John, 80
Skulley, Mark, 285, 288
Slater & Gordon, 22–5, 107, 265, 266, 268–70, 284, 288

Slipper, Inge, 215
Slipper, Peter, 3, 213–22, 263, 272–7, 282, 299
Smith, Bob, 23, 26
Smith, Michael, 266, 267, 271, 272, 282, 284, 299
Snowdon, Warren, 115, 139
Speers, David, 263
'Stability Pact', 132
Stevens, Criselee, 102, 103, 106
Stevens, Glenn, 106
Stevens, Joshua, 102
Stranger, Russell, 118
Streetscape Enterprises, 69, 168
Strike Force Carnarvon, 185
Stutchbury, Michael, 255, 256
Styant-Browne, Nick, 25, 285
Swan, Wayne, 125, 127–30, 141, 144, 147, 153, 156, 158, 206, 224, 230, 231, 260, 263, 301
Sword, Greg, 31, 32

Tanner, Lindsay, 17, 144–5, 153, 311
Taplin, Michael, 232
Temby, Ian, 241
Terrigals, 40–5, 66, 72–8, 80
Thistlethwaite, Matt, 75, 76, 293
Thomas, Hedley, 268, 269, 270, 280, 285
Thomson, Christa, 182
Thomson, Craig, 3, 5, 97–112, 171–85, 221–39, 244, 247, 274, 290, 305
   abuse of HSU funds, 100–12, 171–85, 227–39, 250
   charges against, 296–7
   Dobell campaign, 102–5, 109, 296
   explanation to parliament, 233–9
   lawsuits, 110, 171–2, 181–2
   maiden speech, 105–6
   suspension, 221–3
Ticehurst, Ken, 102
Tiffanie, 52–3
Tingle, Laura, 287
Tinker, Nathan, 44
Trad, Jackie, 196, 212
Tripodi, Joe, 41, 60, 75–8, 87, 305
Triulcio, Rocco, 68, 69, 168
'Trogs', 40
Turnbull, Malcolm, 110, 119

Tuscany Ristorante, 50–1, 293
Twitter, 246, 259

Uhlmann, Chris, 135, 136
Unions, 11–12, 27, 308–9
    ATAEA takeover attempt, 16–20
    AWU *see* Australian Workers' Union
    factions and, 11–12, 308
    HSU *see* Health Services Union
    leaders, influence of, 27
    registration of membership, 12
University of Newcastle, 48, 49
Unsworth, Barrie, 38
Usher, Philip, 207

Vexnews, 240–3, 298
Victoria Labor Party
    Labor Unity, 11
    2007 election, 32–5
    2010 election, 158
    Young Labor, 13–20
Vrana, Gemma, 168

Walker, Frank, 37
Walsh, Katie, 273
Washer, Mal, 237
Watkins, Warwick, 161–3, 167
Watson, Chris, 10
Watson, Geoffrey, 1–3, 292, 293
Watson, Peter, 200–1
Wedderburn, Graeme, 75, 77
Welch, Dylan, 183
Wensley, Penelope, 199
West, Graham, 85
Whan, Steve, 89
White Energy, 63
Whitlam, Gough, 156, 262, 290
Wicks, Felicity, 245
Wicks, Peter, 244–7
Wilkie, Andrew, 155, 221

Williams, Doug, 107, 108, 111, 112, 230
Williamson, Alexandra, 174, 179, 297
Williamson, Chris, 178, 179, 180, 185, 222
Williamson, Darren, 178
Williamson, Elizabeth, 179
Williamson, Julieanne, 179
Williamson, Madeline, 179
Williamson, Michael, 3, 5, 98–102, 107, 109, 141, 172–87, 192, 222–30, 234, 235, 237, 241, 245, 247, 250, 252, 257, 290, 305
    abuse of HSU funds, 176–87, 227, 229–30, 237, 241, 250
    charges against, 297, 305
    suspension, 252, 257
Williamson, Nicholas, 179
Wilson, Bruce, 22–5, 27, 265–7, 280–4
Windsor, Tony, 155, 156, 232, 233, 274, 275, 277
Withers, Greg, 212
Wood, Stuart, 242
WorkChoices, 95, 96, 104, 108
Wran, Neville, 38
Wright, Tony, 236

Xstrata Coal, 48, 129, 147

Young Labour, 13–16, 240
    ATAEA takeover attempt, 16–20
    factions, 13–16, 31
    national conference 1990, 15
    Network, 13–16, 31
    Shorten, 13–20
YouTube
    Gillard on Abbott, 276
    Rudd swearing, 199, 201, 300

Zangari, Guy, 87
Zwier, Leon, 259